BLACK SHEEP

'The achievements of those who work in the theatre are no more than writing on the sand. There may well be a vivid and important message for all to see, for a while, but by and by the tide comes in, and when it next goes out, that writing has disappeared.'

Sir Trevor Nunn

'You always felt that he was searching for something more alive, daring and emotionally revealing than the average actor.'

Roland Jaquarello

'All great artists have damaged childhoods but when you have a damaged childhood it breeds imagination. What would have happened if it hadn't turned out like this?'

Tom Kempinski

'Dad had many flaws, but he owned most of them rather well.'

Luke Williamson

'No one would ever persuade me that there was ever a more powerful actor than he.'

Patrick Phillips QC

'Other actors, including, for all his brilliance, George C. Scott, were earth-bound by comparison with Nicol. Nicol displayed magic all the way through, not just in the final performance but also in rehearsals.'

Tony Walton

'He had an allergy to offices. He refused to see even the most grand of movie moguls in their offices, no matter how powerful they were, or what was at stake.'

Leslie Megahey

'A dream to some, a nightmare to others ...'

As Merlin in *Excalibur*

BLACK SHEEP

THE AUTHORISED BIOGRAPHY OF
NICOL WILLIAMSON

GABRIEL HERSHMAN

The
History
Press

For my mother, Jose, my father, Nathan, my wife, Dessi, and
children, David and Natalie.

First published 2018

The History Press
The Mill, Brimscombe Port
Stroud, Gloucestershire, GL5 2QG
www.thehistorypress.co.uk

British Library Cataloguing in Publication Data.
A catalogue record for this book is available from the British Library.

ISBN 978 0 7509 8345 7

Typesetting and origination by The History Press
Printed and bound in Great Britain by TJ International Ltd

CONTENTS

FOREWORD

BY LUKE WILLIAMSON

Consulting on this book has been a bittersweet experience for me. So many memories of a man who meant the world to me, without whom my life would have been so much greyer and so very different. A man whose absence I feel on a daily basis.

How can I possibly convey the feeling and essence of a person through words to others who have never met him? No matter what I say, it's impossible to encompass Dad and distill him into a few paragraphs, I will always fall short.

He was funny and kind and brilliant and sad and angry, and the vagaries of existence swirled around him visibly like universal ingredients. He was magnetic and creative, he altered the dynamic of everything he was near.

Being close to Nicol was like being in the front seat of an exhilarating, terrifying rollercoaster. It could be more than you could bear, but you always came back for another ride.

There will be compliments given and axes ground, but in the end Dad lived his life exactly as he wished, and stood up for the principles he believed in. I will always be proud of him, and I will always miss him.

ACKNOWLEDGEMENTS

Writing a biography – and this is my third – is like a detective chasing a trail. Occasionally the trail runs cold. Sometimes a sliver of information becomes a major anecdote and triggers vivid memories. Interviewees sometimes claimed they had little to offer, and then proved painstakingly detailed in their recollections. It is clearly a lesson that all 'leads' are worth pursuing.

I am very grateful to the following who took time to comment on Nicol Williamson's extraordinary life and career: Sally Alexander, Robert Bierman, Kate Binchy, Brian Blessed, Ingrid Boulting, Bruce Boxleitner, Rand Bridges, Elaine Bromka, Laura Cella, Brian Cox, Tony Croft, Sam Dastor, Ro Diamond, Sally Dietzler, Ray Dooley, Ron Fassler, Edward Fox, Tony Garnett, Peter Gill, John Goldstone, Sally Greene, Vivienne Griffiths, Daria Halprin, Anthony Heald, Lady Pamela Hicks, Tara Hugo (a particularly fastidious contributor), Luciano Iogna, Glenda Jackson, Roland Jaquarello (whose recollections of the great moments in Nicol's stage performances were truly impressive), Tom Kempinski, Ted Kotcheff, Lionel Larner, Stephen Lyons, Leslie Megahey (who deserves my special thanks for his extremely generous contributions), Nicholas Meyer (who also kindly sent me *The Baker Street Journal*, a veritable mine of 'Sherlockian' information), Trevor Nunn (whose detailed recollections were especially invaluable regarding Nicol's work on *Coriolanus* and *Macbeth*), Tony Osoba, David Parry, Julie Peasgood, Louise Penn, Michael Pennington, Natasha Pyne, David Rabe, Bob Rafelson, Keith Reddin, Shane Rimmer, Laila Robins, Tony Rowlands, Jeanne Ruskin, George Segal, Carolyn Seymour, Janet Suzman, Clive Swift, Philippa Urquhart, Marianne Velmans, Tony Walton, Dreya Weber and Saskia Wickham.

Special mention must go to Nicol's first wife, Jill Townsend-Sorel, and Nicol's son, Luke, without whose help this book would not have been possible. They both understood, and supported, my vision – the need to present a truthful, balanced portrait of a complex man, neither coffee-table saccharine nor a hatchet job.

I would also like to send my love and appreciation to my wife, Dessi, and children, David and Natalie, for their understanding and patience. You are my world!

And that's *my* nickel's worth …

INTRODUCTION

'The terrible-tempered tiger of the English stage, smiter of David Merrick, scourge of critics, accused assassin of Hamlet, carouser, brooder, pub-crawler and brawler.'

New York Times on Nicol Williamson

Nicol Williamson was the finest British stage actor of his generation. Yet today he's semi-forgotten. If he *is* remembered at all, it's rather for his temper and eccentricity. The press greeted his passing with prim, perfunctory obituaries but not really the respect such an outstanding actor deserved.

This was the man who had performed a one-man show at the White House, whose Hamlet was acclaimed as the finest since Gielgud's, whom John Osborne had hailed as the greatest actor since Marlon Brando, whom Samuel Beckett had said was 'touched by genius', who had bested George C. Scott in *Uncle Vanya*, who had given what theatre director Roland Jaquarello had described as 'the greatest ever performance in a modern play' in *Inadmissible Evidence*.

Why did a few incidents of unprofessional (shall we say 'inadmissible'?) conduct feature so prominently in Nicol's obituaries? Biographers find that accounts of alleged bad behaviour are endlessly and wearisomely rehashed, copied and pasted from one (dubious) source. It becomes rather like a game of Chinese whispers until the details subtly change. Suddenly, a dressing room altercation becomes something more – 'he threw David Merrick into the Hudson river, hands and feet bound …' etc. and totally, completely false.

Such outbursts in Nicol's professional life, although not necessarily excusable, were comparatively rare. His physical 'skirmishes' probably constituted, cumulatively, a mere sixty seconds in a remarkable forty-year career. Yet they gained more coverage than his many achievements. I am not Nicol's defence lawyer, but probably many of us would be embarrassed if examples of our occasional misbehaviour were endlessly dredged up. Perhaps it was understandable, therefore, that Nicol resented the press, rarely granted interviews and shunned publicity.

I prefer to remember Nicol not for his waywardness, but for his riveting performances. If there's one role irrevocably associated with Nicol it was as Bill Maitland in *Inadmissible Evidence*. It was the first film I ever saw of his, one I found deeply affecting. Nicol repeated his portrayal on stage several times, becoming so much *the* definitive incarnation of Maitland that the first comments on any revival of *Inadmissible Evidence* usually lament his absence!

Nicol pioneered a new form of acting, power-driven, never pandering to the audience, offering total truthfulness and full exposure. He bore the burden of titanic stage roles, not just Macbeth, Hamlet, Coriolanus and Lear, but other tour-de-force parts in which he really was the whole show. His Maitland in *Inadmissible Evidence* was in every scene for almost three hours, likewise his Henry VIII in *Rex*; his Poprishchin in *Diary of a Madman* ran for almost two hours. As the *Los Angeles Times* wrote in 1969, Nicol seemed drawn to roles that presented 'a marathon challenge to his ability to portray the darker human emotions'.

Sadly, Nicol never seemed professionally satisfied, possibly secretly resenting that true film stardom eluded him. Ultimately, he always went his own way. A character actor who disliked playing bad guys, a hellraiser who refused to be everyone's favourite hellraiser – in the Ollie Reed manner. He would turn right if you told him he simply *must* turn left. He was not a team player. *Inadmissible Evidence* was virtually a one-man show; *Jack* was, of course, just that. In *The Hobbit*, his wonderful recording of the Tolkien classic, he played every part. He was like a lighthouse, compelling attention, drawing all towards him.

Theatrical biographies should, I believe, discuss acting in depth. As such, I have quoted extensively from a variety of critics. Also, as with other biographies, I have spent longer analysing Nicol's most notable performances and less time on smaller parts. The internet has made it easier to access certain facts than before. My purpose here has not been to provide a mere factual résumé of Nicol's life. Some of that information is available elsewhere, albeit not always reliable. Where I have uncovered inaccuracies I have, of course, noted them. But a biographer's principal task, especially where the subject is as arresting as Nicol, is to analyse why his performances were so powerful. Hence, if there is an element of cutting to the chase, then *mea culpa*. Yet this, ironically, was Nicol's style in acting too, rolling through routine dialogue and lingering over key moments.

I hope I have succeeded in illuminating the talent of this sadly neglected performer.

PROLOGUE

'To thine own self be true, And it must follow, as the night the day, Thou canst not then be false to any man ...'

London, May 1994

Luke Williamson, then 21, was dining with his father at the exclusive Ivy restaurant in Covent Garden on the third night of Nicol's one-man show *Jack: A Night on the Town with John Barrymore*. Also at the same table was producer Sally Greene and the director of *Jack*, Leslie Megahey. Nicol enjoyed dining out and always had a hearty appetite. But his appetite for being accosted by fellow diners varied. Such interruptions are, of course, an occupational hazard of the famous. Mere mortals feel somehow compelled to sashay over, compliment the celebrity and pick up an autographed wine bottle or, failing that, a serviette with an indecipherable scrawl.

Most stars are usually polite. The most acerbic responses I have traced are from Lee Marvin who greeted the inevitable opening salvo of 'I do hate to interrupt you' with 'But you will'. Or Yootha Joyce who would reply, 'So why do you do it, then?'

The celebrity to celebrity encounter is, on the other hand, usually a guaranteed shoo-in, ushering in mutual backslapping and that strange kinship that bonds the famous. Nobody, after all, *wants* anything.

Dining two tables away from Nicol in the Ivy that night were Mick Jagger and Jerry Hall.

'I hope they don't come over,' Nicol told his son. He had never cared much for Jagger or his singing. Nicol was being admirably consistent. Many years earlier, while dining at a restaurant in Rhodes, also with his son, Luke, Nicol had found himself sitting near Jagger. On that occasion Nicol had studiously avoided eye contact. And now Nicol was doing just the same in the Ivy. Luke says that, personally, he loves the

Rolling Stones but could just about gauge where his dad was coming from. 'Jagger's voice was perfect for the Stones but he's no Freddie Mercury.'

According to Luke, Nicol was starting to enjoy his dinner when an outstretched palm suddenly blocked the route between utensil and mouth.

The palm in question, of course, belonged to Jagger. A long standoff ensues. Nicol does not look up. He just stares at the hand being proffered by the rock superstar. No words are spoken. Perhaps 'superstar' assumed that Nicol had already seen him? Or that he would recognise his hand? After some thirty seconds, Jagger decides to speak. 'I heard you're doing this play and that it's going well. Congratulations!' Nicol still says nothing and doesn't look up.

Jagger, rather thrown, tries again. 'Hi, I'm Mick.' Long pause. 'Mick Jagger.'

Another long pause. No response. So Jagger shuffles off, arm in arm with Hall.

Luke reflects, 'You could say I almost met Mick Jagger. Twice.'

Nicol simply refused to play the game of celebrities.

1

LITTLE HILLS

'I was always an outsider on the edge of the group.'

Nicol Williamson

It was an unlikely beginning for someone whom Laurence Olivier apparently viewed as his 'closest challenger' for the accolade of Britain's greatest actor. Hamilton, 12 miles south-east of Glasgow, was hardly brimming with culture. John Calder, Scottish publisher and friend of Nicol's, later wrote that 'it is difficult to imagine him [Nicol] as a boy in that quiet little town where the main cultural event of the year is the Salvation Army's Christmas carol concert'. People made their own entertainment in a place where, in the thirties, a rousing singsong in a pub was the nearest to organised entertainment.

The only other theatrical 'name' to come from Hamilton, born eighteen months before Nicol, was the hard-drinking actor Mark McManus, best known as Taggart – 'the Clint of the Clyde' – whose impassive, granite-like, yet slightly mournful expression seemed quintessentially Glaswegian.

It was often noted that Nicol had a touch of the Viking about him, a word frequently used to describe his Nordic air and appearance. The Williamsons were Clan Gunn, an old Highland clan associated with lands in north-eastern Scotland. They probably originated from Norway – original Norse seafarers – but they were avowedly proud Scots.[1] Some of the clan had moved to America in the late nineteenth century and, according to Nicol's first wife, Jill Townsend, President Woodrow Wilson[2] was a distant relative. But all of the traceable relatives of Nicol's father had lived in Scotland.

Nicol's father, Hugh, was born on 30 June 1913. Hugh was later described by John McGrath (who became an important collaborator of Nicol's) as 'an imposing man, strong and gentle and very Scottish'. Jill Townsend remembered him similarly,

'He was a giant of a man; he just had that power, a big heart, and respect for people.'
He was also a huge man physically with very broad shoulders and large hands,
something Nicol inherited. He could always stem one of Nicol's moods with a
mild reproach.

Nicol's mother, Mary Brown Hill (née Storrie), was born on 6 March 1914. Her
father had been in a Scottish regiment during the First World War but was killed
three weeks before the war ended. Jill speaks of her glowingly, as does Nicol's son
Luke, although his recollections are, inevitably, more second-hand because she
died prematurely in 1975. Nicol credited Mary for his lifelong interest in music.
'My mother had a wonderful singing voice, which has been a great influence on
me,' he once revealed.

Jill recalls Mary's 'dignified and very loving nature' as well as her beautiful voice.
When she visited Nicol's parents they would all sing together in the car, especially
songs by American star Ruth Etting.[3] Mary was also artistic, occupying herself
during the war by making little paintings on ceramics and delicate hand-painted
plates and cups. Jill describes Hugh and Mary as 'the best parents and grandparents
in the world' and everyone agrees that Nicol adored them both.

Hugh and Mary's wedding early in 1936 was hardly glittering. 'When they got
married, they came out of the registry office with half a crown in their pockets,'
Nicol later recalled. 'That was in the morning. Dad went back to work, in the local
aluminium plant in the afternoon.' Despite their straightened circumstances their
marriage was very happy; Nicol described them as 'lovebirds'.

Nicol was born Thomas Nicol Williamson, on 14 September 1936[4] at Beckford
Lodge maternity hospital. Tradition had it that, in the Williamson family, boys were
either called Hugh or Thomas Nicol. It appears that Nicol was the first in the
family to use his middle name.

At the time of his birth registration his parents lived at 192 Quarry Street,
Hamilton. When Nicol was 18 months old the family moved to Birmingham – to
Hansons Bridge Road, Erdington – where Hugh worked as a labourer in a foundry.

A childhood friend of Nicol, and later an accomplished producer, Tony Garnett,
who later collaborated with Nicol on *The Resistible Rise of Arturo Ui*, describes the
atmosphere in his autobiography:

In the centre of England was Birmingham, restless and insecure beneath its sang
froid; the city of a thousand trades and the centre of the twentieth century's
dominant technology, the internal combustion engine. Small workshops were
everywhere, handed down from father to son, often since the late eighteenth
century. In the suburbs and the surrounding small towns were the immense
factories of the twentieth century, busy with anything the world market would

buy, from motor cars in Longbridge to motorbikes in Small Heath, to chocolates in Bournville.[5]

Life in Birmingham was dull for Nicol. 'I had the usual boring suburban childhood. I kept saying to myself. I've got to get out of here or I'll die.' Nicol compensated by reading a lot. 'By the time I was five I knew all about the Macedonian phalanx and things like that. But when I was 12 or 13 I stopped reading – or at least I stopped amassing useless knowledge.'

The outbreak of war brought a momentous wrench. Birmingham was susceptible to bombing and so Nicol was sent back to Hamilton to live with his grandparents. It wasn't until after the war, when Nicol returned to Birmingham, that he discovered he had a sister, Senga.

Luke Williamson recalls what his father told him about that period:

My grandfather and his brother worked at the Spitfire factory, building planes and bombers for the war. The house was only a couple of miles from the plant and also one of the air bases. They were constantly worried that they were going to be bombed by the Germans. Nicol was sent back to Scotland. But Senga, born at around the time Nicol went to stay with his grandparents, was too young to be away from her parents, so she stayed in Birmingham. Dad looked at that and believed that, for whatever reason, they loved Senga more and that's very much something that as a child you can convince yourself of. And, of course, there's no doubt that Senga was very much loved. Boys are generally told to 'pick themselves up, dust themselves down' – that sort of thing. His grandmother was ok but his grandfather was not fond of Nicol and gave him a very hard time. Nicol didn't think anything less of Senga. Indeed he was protective and loving and supported her for some time.

Yet Nicol nursed a grudge about the period away. Jill Townsend believes that this was a traumatic event:

What happened to Nicol during the war had an awful effect on him … the sense of being 'thrown away' when he was sent back to Scotland to his grandmother and aunties and the realisation after the war ended that his mother had given birth to a girl but *she* hadn't been sent back to Scotland. The rage and unfairness of the world loomed over everything now.

Nicol also referred to the separation in a 1986 interview. 'All that splitting up is ghastly. The good, solid family is the most solvent institution we have. If it splits up, the trauma stays with you forever. When a child asks, "Do you love me?" that's a mask for a sense of rejection."[6]

Nicol's relationship with his parents was *not* troubled. Numerous accounts – from close friends and Jill, his first wife – attest to how close Nicol was to them both. Perhaps it was precisely because Nicol *was* so close to his parents that he always resented the separation. It's like the child despatched to boarding school. If he gets on well with his parents, then he resents it even more. Nicol was very young when he was sent back to Scotland, probably too young to realise what was happening at the time; but retrospective bitterness can also count for a lot.

Nicol returned to Birmingham after the war. He later said that, by the age of 7, he had already decided to be an actor after listening to radio dramas:

> I can never remember a time when I wanted to do anything else but be involved in the richness of language. And I was always around music. When I was 4, I hung around a piano player named Jimmy Duncan who played a wonderful version of *In the Mood*. 'Play it again, Jimmy,' I'd say. I could listen to it forever. All the family were singers. No one watched TV. On Saturday nights people would get together and sing. The memory of it recalls summer and autumn nights, the sound of a lawn mower in the distance, people making their own entertainment, telling jokes and stories. I'd be sent to my room, but I'd creep to the top of the stairs to listen. I'm a great lover of life and energy.

Nicol attended Birmingham's Central Grammar School between 1947 and 1953, after passing the eleven-plus, which (for the uninitiated) is a kind of intelligence and general knowledge exam. One of Nicol's school friends – and indeed lifelong friend – Tony Croft, reckons that about 5 per cent of children would have passed it.

Nicol did not enjoy school. Neither did Tony Garnett who later wrote, 'Central Grammar was a rough school with, anomalously, a baronet for a head. Sir Rodney M.S. Pasley, Bart[7], MA, tried – unsuccessfully – to run it on the lines of his own public school. There was rugby and prefects and caning. I hated it.'

Memories are always subjective. Another pupil in Nicol's year remembers the staff differently and, writing on a noticeboard about Birmingham, adds an ironic postscript:

> Having spent five happy years at Central Grammar School (1948–1953), I would like to add a few memories of my own to the above comments. Sir Rodney Pasley was the perfect headmaster, supported by an excellent staff, including Mr Merryman (Music), Mr Paddock (Maths), Mr Dixon (German), Mr 'Caggy' Carter (French), Mr 'Pippy' May (French), Mr Greatrex (Art), Mr Evans (History),

Mr Heslop (Maths), Mr Weightman (PE), Mr Faulkner (English) and Mr Reader (English). In my form was Nicholas (later Nicol) Williamson who, despite an unpleasant demeanour, became a well-known film star playing mostly 'baddies' in a variety of films.[8]

Tony Croft was damning about the school's facilities:

> You would not be able to imagine the state of our post war school. It was 1913 vintage, bomb and shrapnel scarred, had no gym, library, canteen or any other facility considered normal in a school today. The only available playing field was several miles and two bus rides away. Boys were gathered from all corners of Birmingham so there was no common area factor, which actually wasn't a bad thing as it meant each boy was confronted with others from diverse economic backgrounds.

Pupils sometimes have an inspirational adult figure, a teacher cum mentor. In Nicol's case – who, despite an impressive physique, took little interest in sports – it was his English teacher, aptly named Tom Reader, who predicted success for Nicol as a classical actor. Reader remained a lifelong friend. Nicol dedicated his book, *Ming's Kingdom*, to him. Tony Croft recalled, 'Tom Reader was a fine teacher and Nicol would credit him for the encouragement which led him to be serious about an acting career … He saw no reason why he couldn't aspire to become a great actor and so he proved to be.'[9]

Tony Garnett also remembers Reader fondly:

> He was the only teacher in that crap school I responded to. He simplified my writing style, cut out too many adjectives and made me express myself parsimoniously. I owe him a debt. Growing up in a home without a single book, indeed where books were thought of as a waste of time, he legitimised my love of them.

Garnett is less flattering about the other teachers:

> Apart from Tom Reader, the staff were lazy. They made boring subjects unbearable and interesting subjects boring. After a couple of years, I decided to ignore them.

Nicol always kept in touch with Tom Reader:

> One rainy day in 1963, when I was feeling miserable because of a bird, I got on

a train and went to see him at his home in Staffs. We went out to a pub, but he insisted on buying the drinks, which meant beer when I was dying for vodka.

Reader made such an impact that three of his former pupils, Trevor Philips, Rob Woodford and Luke Prodromou, set up valued annual reunions. They call themselves 'the chums' after Reader's nickname for his prodigies.

By the time Nicol was in his teens it was clear he had a budding thespian talent. School friend David Parry recalled Nicol's earliest performances, 'He played Marlowe's *Dr Faustus* with mesmeric power when only 15. In a very unsympathetic school-hall setting, he captivated a sparse opening-night audience. So riveting was his performance that word went round and the three following performances were packed, with some unable to get in.'

The following review of *Faustus*, dated June 1952, was written by a senior boy who was editor of the school magazine:

> The concert ended with a dramatic climax. T. N. Williamson took the title part in a scene from *Dr Faustus* by Christopher Marlowe. The presentation of this scene showing Faustus's last minutes alive was excellent, and Williamson, with a depth of emotion, and skilful use of tone and timing, carried his audience with him in a way which would have done justice to many a more experienced actor. This performance was a fine note to end on, and the audience did not fail to respond to the efforts of Williamson, and to the effective production.

David Parry recalls that, at Easter school camp in Wales, he and Nicol did their best to entertain the group by staging a sketch he calls *A Ventriloquist Act with a Difference*. Nicol played a convincing dummy while Parry, the ventriloquist, sat on his knee.

The school has uncovered a poem by Nicol, dating from 1952, at one such camp at Bryntail in the Welsh hills:

An Elegy on a Country Residence

'Llanidloes!' came the croaking shout,
The school's contingent tumbled out,
As through the station we did tramp.
To make our way up to the camp,
The wise ones hurried on ahead,
To get the comfortablest bed:
But not so smart, I lagged behind.
The long rough country lanes did wind.

Had this pilgrimage no end?
'Left wheel ahead, another bend!'

Up to the 'cucumbers' we drew;
'I'm dizzy, Dai, I'm telling you.'
'The camp,' a shout that made me smile,
It died, 'three quarters of a mile
To go.' I rallied and began to trot;
But by this time I'd had my lot.
The camp now loomed into my view,
A welcome sight, I'm telling you.
I slumped down to the Nissen floor.
— I'd got the bed beside the door!

I'd come in last the others laughed
To think that I'd be in the draught.
My bed and I were knocked about
Whenever anyone went out.
It scraped the floor with a frightful din,
Whenever anyone came in.
'Fetch that' 'Take this' 'This should be sent'
And next the door, twas I who went.

That night I tried to close my ears,
And sleep in spite of yells and jeers;
And every night I was kept awake
By Nissen night-jar and camp corncrake.
Next day I drew no peaceful breath,
The camp-squad worked me near to death;
And dinner time was misery,
I thought the cook would poison me.
But still I dared not make complaint,
The mine-shaft threat was my restraint.

The second morning made me shiver,
I learned that we were for the river.
We scrambled down the slopes of Bryn
To the river and tumbled in.
We're lucky no one has to quote,

Of swimming in that icy moat,
'They went down to the river side
And there committed suicide.'
I took a breath, and with a leap,
Flung myself into the deep.

I sank immediately, alas!
And thought my end had come to pass,
'Help! Help!' was all my strangled shout,
And two tough fellows dragged me out.
Next a walk all strides and jumps,
It nearly wore my legs to stumps.
Then mountain races – these quite good,
Until I tumbled in the mud;
And as I found I'd sprained my wrist,
The base-ball match was one I missed.

We went to town before departing
To see the School's Old Boys imparting
A beating to Llanidloes Town;
Our rugger team deserves a crown.
The last day came alas, alack,
We were leaving, going back
To Birmingham, back to the city,
I really thought it quite a pity.

The Easter camp's had me perplexed,
But summer is for me the next;
We shall have a different cook
And warmer water in the brook;
There'll be less mud and work to do,
And I have learned a thing or two,
I'll choose a bed upon the floor
Rather than that next to the door.

(Nicol Williamson, 5s, 1952)[10]

Tony Croft sensed that Nicol enjoyed the spotlight, 'We remember him as making the very most of any opportunity to act or display his ability to read lines and use his fine voice. The school (immediately postwar) was ill-equipped for stage productions but Nicol would make the most of whatever could be used.'

Tony Garnett also remembers Nicol's acting talent, 'He and I played all the leads. He was a brilliant mimic and his impersonations of various members of staff delighted the boys, if not the teachers when they caught him.' Luke says his father told him that he always had a riposte if he was scolded. 'Williamson, you will hang,' one teacher told him after a bout of mischievousness. 'Yes, in the National Gallery!' young Nicol replied.

Garnett was in the 'A' stream while Nicol was in the 'C' stream, indicating that Nicol was perhaps not studying very hard. (According to David Parry, the initial 'streaming' at Central was for two years after which pupils were divided into different classes, mostly based on interest and ability in languages.) Garnett also recalls that Nicol was a loner, a description that would stick, 'I was always an outsider on the edge of the group', Nicol said of himself during this period.

Nicol was determined to be an actor even though Hugh expected him to become a metallurgist. In 1953, Nicol passed an audition to the Birmingham School of Speech Training and Dramatic Art. Nicol recalled his father simply said to him, 'Good luck. I'll be here if you need me.'

Nicol seldom spoke about his three years at the drama school and didn't seem to value such institutions, 'They can teach movement and voice production. All the rest of it is a finishing school for the daughters of rich executives,' he told a journalist in 1969 – perhaps a remark that holds less true today. Nicol must have made a good impression, however, because he was chosen to play the lead in the students' showcase open-air production of Euripides's *The Trojan Women*. Two renowned exponents of Greek theatre and movement, Ruby Ginner and Irene Mawer, directed the piece. Also in the play, cast in the male role of Astyanax, was 7-year-old Christine Burn who became a continuity announcer.

In 1956 Nicol was lent to Birmingham Rep to play unpaid walk-ons. Albert Finney was already halfway through his first season as a professional. (Nicol and Finney – a brilliant contemporary to whom Nicol was often compared – never acted together. Finney had enjoyed a head start over Nicol, having successfully dodged National Service.)

Under the false impression that Easter Monday was a holiday for actors, Nicol missed a performance and was fired. The management gave him the option of playing one more night if he apologised to the cast. Yet Nicol preferred to leave instantly. 'I told myself, I'm after that mountain, this little hill is nothing to trip over,' he recalled.

Nicol then spent two years in Aldershot as a gunner in an airborne division. A forceful nature served him well. 'Somebody once told me I was very good at what he called personality blackmail,' he later told Kenneth Tynan.[11] 'The phrase means "play ball with me or I shall exude such a dislike of you that you will simply feel dreadful".'

Yet Nicol was far from unpopular. Several fellow National Service recruits wrote to Nicol's son, Luke, with happy memories. Dennis Buckland remembered Nicol as a great pal:

> I was fortunate to be a friend and colleague of Nic Williamson, the young National Serviceman. Nic and I served in the 33rd Parachute Regiment RA. Nic would keep us guys quiet and entertained with his wonderful story-telling, piano-playing, and his endless practical jokes, and it was obvious to all of us that he was an exceptionally talented guy. It is well documented that Nicol Williamson was a great actor, but also Nic Williamson was a great guy to serve with as two young National Servicemen.

Carol Alexander also wrote to Luke:

> [Nicol] and my husband Rob were in the army together as young men and became quite good friends. Rob played guitar and he and your dad used to 'entertain' at local pubs and made quite the team. Rob has never forgotten him and always followed his career with great interest and always admired his tremendous ability as an actor. Many wonderful memories and stories will live on in our family of Rob and Nicol's army escapades.

Peter A. Murray also recalled his time with 'big Nick Williamson, the ration storeman' in the 33rd Paras. 'He was just known as big Nick, a 6ft 4in friendly chap.'

Signing on with the Paras took some gumption. ('And that is soooo Nicol because he had a fear of flying, so he joins the Parachute Regiment to try and overcome his fear. See the courage he had?' notes his first wife, Jill.) Nicol did fourteen parachute jumps in total.

After his discharge Nicol wrote to the management of Dundee Rep which hired him to play a pirate in *Sinbad the Sailor*. Three months' unemployment followed. He was about to audition for a job as a crooner when a telegram invited him to return to Dundee. Scotland's fourth-largest city, on the north bank of the Firth of Tay, was home to a prestigious repertory company, founded in 1939, which had continued to perform weekly rep throughout the war years.

Nicol appeared in thirty-three productions during his seventeen months at Dundee, most of them staged by Anthony Page. It was a rich and varied training ground for actors. Among the company were Glenda Jackson, Edward Fox,[12] Anna Way and Lillias Walker. Jackson remembered Nicol as formidable but distant, 'He was an extraordinary person and actor but he was very hard to get to know as a person. He wasn't particularly sociable.'

Nicol struck up a firmer friendship with Edward Fox even though they came from very different backgrounds. 'It was always clear that Nicol possessed gigantic acting talent and indeed was immensely gifted,' Fox recalls. 'I was in many productions with him at Dundee and it seemed impossible for him to be anything other than remarkable and sometimes magnificent.' Fox also remembers that Nicol 'was fond of making gigantic-sized dramatic gestures, I think to amuse himself and us, his friends.'[13]

Local boy and, later, distinguished actor Brian Cox, ten years younger than Nicol, has vivid memories of Nicol's time at Dundee:

> Nicol was the first 'live' actor I ever met. Actually it was more of an invasion than a meeting. It was 1961. I was 15 years old. I was on my way to my first ever job interview at the Dundee Repertory Theatre in (aptly enough) Nicoll Street.[14] The lady in the box office told me that I had to enter the theatre from the Stage Door in Rattray Street. As I mounted the narrow staircase to the main stage and auditorium I became aware of some kind of fracas on the landing above. I would have to cross this landing to get to where my meeting would be taking place. Suddenly I found myself in the middle of a fist fight between a rather effete red-faced bow-tied individual and a tall lean 'viking' blond. The language was the last thing I expected to hear in such an auspicious setting more in tune with the streets where I grew up. I immediately recognised the 'Viking' as the actor whom I had seen the week before at a school matinee of *Love from a Stranger* giving, even to this day, the scariest performance ever … And here, before me, besting the brawl, was the very same actor. As I emerged out from under the brawl I was greeted by another thespian who was exceedingly amused at my bewildered and slightly terrified expression. 'It's alright, darling. They're just a little over-excited after a night on the bevy and no sleep. Not to worry.' This was the actor Gawn Grainger.[15] And that was my introduction to Nicol.

Cox recalls an early example of Nicol's irritation with noisy theatregoers and his ability to silence them. The most memorable incident would be at Stratford more than a decade later:

> Even more scary and impressive was the way this actor quelled a rather rowdy audience of schoolkids by walking to the front of the stage and saying in the deadliest and quietest voice imaginable. 'When yoooouu have all feeeenished … I will continue … But … not … unteel … then.' And he stood there and waited

… and waited. Until the noise in the auditorium diminished to nothing. From that point on, you could have heard a pin drop.

Cox says it was a privilege to watch Nicol for the next six months until Nicol left Dundee. He particularly recalls Nicol as Clive in Peter Shaffer's *Five Finger Exercise*, as Peter Cloag in *Marigold* and as Jack Manningham in the Victorian melodrama *Gaslight*:

> Nicol was exemplary in every role he played, showing an astonishing range well beyond his years. He for me, more than any actor of that generation, set 'the bar' of standard to be achieved as an actor. But also I will always remember his kindness and consideration towards me in my inaugural years at Dundee. For that I am eternally grateful.[16]

Repertory required actors to learn parts quickly, mount a production lasting no more than a couple of weeks, and then move on. Peter Gill, later a distinguished director, thinks that Anthony Page deserves special credit for staging so many complex, even controversial, plays – with actors frequently playing older parts. 'Now the ice has been broken but in those days it was really something,' he told me.

Reviews in *The Stage* show that Nicol did well at Dundee. Highlights of Nicol's work included playing Sir Walter Blunt in *King Henry IV*, directed by Raymond Westwell. In Dickens's *Great Expectations*, adapted by John Maxwell, and directed by Page (in which Edward Fox played Pip) it was noted that Nicol, as Joe Gargery, 'provides humour and pathos'. Co-star Kate Binchy later recalled Nicol was 'terribly good and touching and radiated kindness' in the role.[17]

Nicol also played Harold 'Mitch' Mitchell in *A Streetcar Named Desire*, directed by Anthony Page. Lillias Walker played Blanche Dubois, Trevor Martin was Stanley Kowalski and Glenda Jackson was Eunice Hubbell.

In Victor Rozov's *In Search of Happiness*, a rare translation of a Russian play – set in a Moscow residential block – *The Stage* wrote that 'Nicol Williamson once again proves his worth to the Nicoll Street Company with his interpretation of Fyodor, the eldest son, full of frustrated ambition'.

Nicol also won good reviews when he appeared with Prunella Scales (most famous as the monstrous Sybil in *Fawlty Towers*) and Michael Culver (best known for *Secret Army*) in *The Curious Savage*, John Patrick's comedy about a rich old widow. Kate Binchy remembers Nicol's skilful improvisation in this play, fiddling around with a pack of cards in an ingenious way each time.

The Stage also praised Nicol's performance in Dennis Driscoll's 'rib-tickling comedy' *Man for the Job*. 'Lillias Walker's portrayal of the domineering Maggie with a heart of gold is delightful, and in Nicol Williamson and Gawn Grainger as Walter and Amos she has two wonderful foils.'

Nicol was already demonstrating his skill as a song and dance man. Dundee Rep staged a special variety show every Christmas. *The Stage* noted that 'the outstanding personality is Nicol Williamson who plays the fox and shows that, if he had not chosen repertory, he might have done well in cabaret. His singing, dancing, wit and piano playing are entertainment in themselves'. In addition to being a great all-round entertainer, Nicol also had a wonderful sense of humour. Time and again, friends and colleagues, including everyone at Dundee Rep, recall the fun.

If Nicol is remembered for just one production at Dundee, however, it was for a modern version, written by John McGrath, of Chekhov's *The Seagull*. McGrath's play broadly followed the original but moved it to twentieth-century Scotland. A famous couple – a West End actress and an author – arrive in the Highlands for the summer. The actress's son, Duncan (Nicol in a revamped depiction of Chekhov's aspiring playwright Konstantin Tréplev) tries to fulfil his ambitions as a writer, encouraged by a stage-struck local girl, Shona, played by Kate Binchy.

Duncan is derided for his literary attempts despite his obvious ability. In the end he attempts suicide. 'You must go to the edge,' Nicol later told Kenneth Tynan. 'You must look over the brink into the abyss.' It seems that Nicol did just that. Nicol jumped into the River Tay. The cast had to follow him and extract him from the mud. Yet, as Kate Binchy recalls, although the incident happened during *The Seagull*, it was unconnected to the play. It's one of those tales (wearisomely) embellished by the press. Nicol was in one of his bad moods – 'volatile, disgusted and upset' in Binchy's words – but the water was only knee-deep and he was in no danger. More a drunken manifestation of irritation than, as the press had it, a suicide attempt.

Brian Cox has another explanation for Nicol's behaviour:

Lindsay Anderson had come to see *The Seagull*. Lindsay was casting his film *This Sporting Life*.[18] And I believe Nicol was interested in playing the central role. There was a first night party at the house of two of our main rep supporters, Syd and Sylvia Gillies. The house was on Osborne Terrace, a street in Dundee that runs down to the Tay. Lindsay, in his very 'Lindsay-like' fashion, apparently ignored Nicol. A lot of drink was taken and Nicol, in a fit of pique bravura, much to the alarm of all present, ran out of the house down to the Tay and jumped in. But, of course, the tide was out! Nicol ended up crotch-high in the muddy sand.

Binchy, by contrast, remembers an example of Nicol's composure during *The Seagull*. It was a stage mishap that might have flummoxed another young actor. Yet Nicol handled it deftly:

> In the play he's supposed to come in and throw a dead seagull (which he'd supposedly shot) at me while I'm lying on the 'lawn'. The props people were meant to have taken the seagull out of the freezer to allow it to thaw. This time they forgot. There was a crashing noise offstage while the seagull was retrieved. There was a huge pause before Nicol came on to the stage and chucked the seagull at me. It was covered in icicles and made a horrendous noise as it landed. Yet somehow Nicol and I managed to carry on, ad-libbing through the scene.

Peter Gill remembers seeing *The Seagull* and thinking that 'the tall, rangy, blond-haired young man' (Nicol) was 'a revelation'.[19] *The Stage* commented that 'as the sensitive Duncan, Nicol Williamson controls his role well, full of hope and fear'. The seagull made no comment.

Binchy cites the camaraderie and hijinks, fuelled by copious amounts of booze. Everyone was working hard but they found time to party. Women were banned from certain pubs – and licensing laws were stricter back then – but the company skirted this by either going to St Andrews or becoming honorary drinking members of a ship's 'mess' on the River Tay. Binchy says that Nicol got on well with everyone. The company continued to meet post-Dundee, when they had all moved on, in most cases down to London.

Yet Binchy is not surprised that Nicol's demons became a problem:

> He could be very neurotic. I remember when we all went swimming in London, to a pool somewhere in Chelsea. He wasn't comfortable in the water at all. We were urging him to try to get over it but at one point he thought he was going to drown. So we had to swim at either side of him and he grabbed hold of us. He later said there'd been a bad incident while he'd done National Service, where he'd been thrown into the water.

Binchy says it was clear that Nicol was an astonishingly gifted actor. The demands of repertory on a young actor (just 24 in Nicol's case) were immense, 'You don't often get the feeling that someone so young could handle so many parts.' She doesn't disagree when I say that 'Nicol was in a league of his own' but draws a comparison with Albert Finney with whom she acted in *The Party* alongside Charles Laughton, 'Albert was more "normal", which in this context I don't mean as a reflection on his talent. I just mean that he was more *grounded* than Nicol.

Actors are often very nervous people below the surface and Nicol – wonderful actor though he was – was no exception.'

Anthony Page recalled Nicol as 'being real in the midst of a lot of people who were obviously acting'. It was this bare-it-all vibrant quality that distinguished Nicol from his peers. His performances were freshly minted and spontaneous. If his characters were working-class and beaten down, then Nicol made you feel the despair, smell the grime and sweat. It was a gift that would propel him quickly to stardom.

2

THAW GETS NICKED

'The chip on his shoulder was so vast it dug right down into a great inner cavern.'

Sarah Miles on Nicol Williamson

Nicol was now away from Dundee and transported to a bohemian life in London. 1962 was a breakthrough year for British 'realist' films. *This Sporting Life, A Kind of Loving, The Loneliness of the Long Distance Runner, The Servant* and *Billy Liar* – all these were either going into production or just about to be released. This crest of class-based movies bypassed Nicol who would not get his first leading movie role for another six years. Instead, he was to become a stage star with a fearsome reputation – *the* magnificently charismatic *enfant terrible* of the London theatre.

People might have assumed that Nicol was happy just treading the boards, but it simply appears that he wasn't offered a substantial film role. It would have been different if Anderson had chosen Nicol to play Frank Machin. Instead he had to wait until *The Bofors Gun* before he played someone of similar intensity and rage.

Around this time Nicol met John Thaw who was to become his closest friend. Thaw was 20, having attended RADA when he was just 16 where he had to endure having his Manchester accent scrubbed out of him.

Thaw would later go on to enjoy spectacular TV success on *Redcap*, the iconic seventies series *The Sweeney* and, later, *Inspector Morse*, ironically provoking some envious glances from Nicol. Thaw was essentially a private, shy man, more reserved than Nicol and less flamboyant, but, like Nicol, he enjoyed a drink and they shared a similar sense of humour.

Nicol moved into John's flat in Highbury, which he also shared with his old RADA buddy Tom Courtenay and set designer Terry Bicknell. By now Thaw was

dating Sally Alexander, the young actress who became his first wife. Sally had met
John while working as his Assistant Stage Master (ASM) and understudy when
he appeared with Laurence Olivier in the play *Semi-Detached* at the Royal Court.
Nicol would join John and Sally for supper and drinks in pubs near the theatre, in
the Salisbury, in after-hours drinking clubs, or in Sally's Kensington flat. Sally recalls
that Nicol was a constant caller – frequently with Anthony Page. Visits continued
after Nicol married Jill Townsend in 1971 and after John and Sally separated when
John would go round with daughter Abigail.

Sally recalls their friendship:

> John and Nicol were close friends for a while – they admired each other's work,
> made each other laugh and they were both vivid mimics. They endlessly discussed
> plays, directors, work they were doing, or hoped to do, as well as other actors.
> There was always much laughter as they swapped stories, admired Hollywood
> films and comedians (especially Max Wall and Ken Dodd, favourites of John's).
> Nicol sang and played the piano by ear. His hero then was Al Bowlly[1] – he'd
> sing to anyone who would listen. John's passion was classical music as well as
> jazz, Bach, Vivaldi, organ and cello concertos, but he indulged Nicol's repertoire.
> Somewhere I have photos of us sitting on the sofa, Nicol looking as though he's
> in mid-song! He would often sing rather than speak; especially after a few drinks.
> He was happiest at the piano.[2]

Nicol was cultivating a reputation for outrageous behaviour. When John married
Sally in June 1964, shortly before Nicol's huge success in *Inadmissible Evidence*, he
performed a real party piece. Sheila Hancock later recounted the story in her book,
presumably based on John's account:

> Nicol Williamson behaved, as was his wont, disgracefully at the wedding
> reception. Auntie Beat and the family watched aghast as he leaped into the pool
> in his underpants, took them off and squeezed them dry into the champagne
> glasses waiting to be served. Since his student days he had become even more
> of a melodramatic madman after a few – no, a lot – of bevvies … John admired
> him profoundly and they were devoted friends. Drink could make Nicol cruel
> and dangerous but certainly outrageous.[3]

Sally says they were different personalities:

> John was quieter, more internal, ran deep. He loved to be made to laugh, and to
> make others laugh, but was gentler in his humour than Nicol. There were several

quarrels. Once John would not answer the door to Nicol. I was shocked. 'The door is there to keep people out, Sally,' he said. I asked him why he would not speak to Nicol. He – John – was intransigent, but not forever. Just for a while.

As for Nicol's character and his impression on others, Sally says:

He could be wild, extravagant in speech and gesture. But he was tall and lanky and deep voiced, and loud, and thought he could charm – he could on occasion. My mother and sisters loved him. Singing, leaping on to the piano or into the swimming pool were par for the course for him.

Laughter united John and Nicol. Dining out was always a raucous occasion. Luke Williamson relates that his father told him that they were once in an exquisite Italian restaurant when Nicol delivered a splendidly timed quip that made John choke on his food. So much so that John doubled up against the wall and eventually had to go outside to clear his windpipe. As John staggered around trying to regain his breath, a posh Daimler pulled up and a guy emerged, dressed to the nines and wearing a tuxedo. Just at that moment John threw up over the pavement. Nicol ran out to check on John and witnessed the whole scene, 'Stay away from the seafood linguini!' Nicol told the immaculately attired diner.

Meanwhile, away from all the boozy camaraderie, Nicol's stage career was starting to take off. In 1961, director Anthony Page persuaded William Gaskill to cast Nicol in *That's Us* at the Royal Court, his debut at the theatre, and in *Arden of Faversham*.

Trevor Nunn, then a Cambridge student, was writing reviews for a magazine called *Broadsheet*. He caught Nicol in *Arden of Faversham* during its pre-London touring dates, one of which was in Cambridge. 'I remember commending the actor Nicol Williamson who was playing a character called Shakebag, telling the student readership that here was a talent to watch, a star in the making.'[4]

Penny Taylor, who worked at Peter Crouch Associates, remembers Nicol turning up at the agency office in Soho Square at around this time, seeking representation, 'He was very shy, very shambly. He had a giant grey overcoat on. Peter kept him waiting for an hour. He was very patient.'

Nicol appeared at the Royal Court in January 1962 in *A Midsummer Night's Dream*. Kenneth Tynan, later to record his impressions of Nicol in a marathon essay, wrote that 'without Colin Blakely's blustering Ulster Bottom and the help provided by Nicol Williamson's shame-faced Thisbe, the laughs would be few and crudely provoked'.

Of *The Lark*, a critic in *The Times* commented that 'the best performances come from the most offbeat bits of casting – Nicol Williamson as Warwick'. The same critic also praised Nicol's performance in *Women Beware Women*, Thomas Middleton's Jacobean tragedy about a poor man wooing a rich woman.

Nicol also played Satin in Maxim Gorky's play, *The Lower Depths*, in a Royal Shakespeare Company production with Julian Glover, Margaret Tyzack, Wilfrid Lawson and Prunella Scales in the cast. Lawson was to be a particular favourite of Nicol's – the old actor was by then in the depths of alcoholism and his antics fuelled many a story.

In June 1963 Nicol appeared with Sarah Miles in Henry Livings's *Kelly's Eye*, a gritty northern two-hander, at the Royal Court. Miles, who has penned several volumes of memoirs, devotes a lot of space to Nicol in her account. Miles's first impression was that Nicol was a bit too much:

> He was the epitome of the angry young man. He was a tall bear of a man, with fine curly blond hair. I never managed to work out how much of him was a Scot and how much a northerner. The chip on his shoulder was so vast it dug right down into a great inner cavern. Rehearsals weren't easy. Nicol, being such a powerful personality, repeatedly undermined the director's authority. 'He's an arsehole,'[5] was all he said.
>
> The chemistry in the rehearsal hall grew worse and worse until Nicol began not to show up at all. This made me nervous because I hadn't had much theatre experience. We both had whacking great parts and the first night was getting uncomfortably close. Sadly my character completely relied on Nicol's. Such is a woman's lot. Although I had a long journey ahead of me on preview night, I felt I'd done a fairly good job. I had a few friends in who thought so too. Henry Livings was delighted, and that gave me enormous encouragement. Nevertheless I wanted the first night out of the way so that I could relax into the character and start enjoying it. I was on my way in to see if Nicol had any notes for me when I saw him disappearing round the corner towards the stage door, arm in arm with Anthony Page – a clever young director. These two sneaking off together didn't worry me at the time; I knew they had worked together and respected each other's talent enormously.
>
> On the following night, however, the final night, Nicol had a completely new character, doing completely strange business at completely different places all over the stage. I'd go to a particular spot to start a scene, only to spy Nicol on the opposite side of the stage, whittling some wretched piece of wood, for instance, or about some other business he'd never done before. What with my fear of crowds plus a full first-night audience to tame, I needed every ounce of courage to stop myself from wanting to bury not only my head, but my whole body in the sand dunes. How I got through it I don't know. It was, without doubt, a most

unfeeling thing to do to someone with so little experience. I closed my dressing room door and wept.

I didn't bother to read all the reviews, having got the gist after the first few. They blamed the play more than either Nicol or me, but that wasn't the point, which was that I'd lost respect for Nicol. Whatever greatness he may have been blessed with was no excuse for what he'd done.[6]

The reviews were actually complimentary. *The Times* said, 'Nicol Williamson builds Kelly into a figure of Samson-like proportions whose long passages of lowering inertia and explosions into ruthless action carry massive authority.' R.B. Marriott, writing in *The Stage*, judged that 'Kelly's character is very well drawn and the part is played with tremendous effect by Nicol Williamson'. Malcolm Rutherford in *The Spectator* said that Nicol had given 'a superbly brooding performance'.

Also in the cast, as the narrator, was Arthur Lowe, later cast as Hudson in *Inadmissible Evidence*, who became Sarah's shoulder to cry on, 'I was terribly young and having quite a lot of difficulty with Nicol. It was a horrible situation but Arthur was very supportive of me,' she recalled.[7]

Incredibly, despite this inauspicious start, Nicol and Sarah eventually became lovers. The trigger was an extraordinary, unforeseen 'entrance'. Sarah had locked her magnificent Pyrenean mountain dog, Addo, in the dressing room. One night, her dresser had left the door open and the dog bolted out on to the stage. Somehow – and for the uninitiated it would seem impossible – they managed to integrate Addo into the proceedings. Miles recalled that once Nicol found out she hadn't let her dog out on purpose, he grew warmer. She discovered an altogether more complex man:

> He was a mysterious chap, such a mixture of contradiction, conflicting moods, emotions and talent. It was partly because he pretended not to give a damn about anything – although he did hugely underneath – and partly because he appealed to the snob in me that I found myself, reluctantly at first, drawn to him.

How does one charm a woman? By singing, of course! One evening Nicol took Sarah to the house of a friend who had a piano:

> Nicol sang his way right through to my bones … I let myself be wooed by his mellow singing voice. Such a magical sound that gradually it moved away from my ears, and down towards my heart, where it got tangled up with fashionable new-wave yearnings together with my inverted snobbery.

Nicol moved into Sarah's house in Hasker Street, Chelsea. Meanwhile, he had captured the critics' attention with his portrayal of Sebastian Dangerfield, the drunken, layabout Dublin law student in *The Ginger Man*. 'Nicol Williamson is giving a performance of extreme interest', said *The Times* of the Croydon production of November 1963. 'Mr Donleavy's central character is not really a very interesting person, for if Sebastian Dangerfield has depths they are hidden too efficiently to be discovered. Nicol Williamson gives him an incisive intelligence which exercises itself in tearing everything into very small fragments.'

The Times critic was just as enthusiastic when the production moved to the Royal Court. Nicol, in a part played by Richard Harris on stage and Ian Hendry on TV, was hailed for an exceptional performance:

> We must hope he will remain long enough to give those who have not yet discovered this actor, nor experienced his strange power to suggest that a character capable of becoming many things chooses and determines to remain just that what he now is, a fresh opportunity of doing so.

Patrick Phillips, QC, then a frequent theatregoer, remembers the power of Nicol's early performances:

> I first saw Nicol Williamson at the Royal Court in the early sixties in a succession of plays such as *Kelly's Eye* and Mike Donleavy's *The Ginger Man*. I was immediately smitten by his playing and told anyone who would listen (few did) that he was an actor without compare. Only after his arresting performance as Maitland in John Osborne's *Inadmissible Evidence* did other people take notice. His acting had an intensity and a power like a tsunami. He commanded a stage like no other actor. He was irresistible.[8]

Nicol was already making his mark on the small screen. His TV debut had come in 1962 in a Henry Livings play about life in the RAF, *Nil Carborandum* – his performance in the same play earlier that year at the Arts Theatre was hailed as 'outstanding' by *The Stage*. He also played Pierre in a TV production of *War and Peace* – 'the most striking performance comes from Nicol Williamson', noted one critic.

But it was *Z Cars* that brought wider attention. In the episode *By the Book*, directed by Anthony Page, Nicol was a villain. Brian Blessed noted Nicol's early star quality, 'Many stars appeared in *Z Cars* over the years. In fact, I think they queued up! One of the most outstanding was Nicol, and he was playing a rather unsavoury and repellent character too. I thought he was a young genius. A very clever outstanding actor.'[9]

Meanwhile the fun with Nicol and Sarah Miles was continuing at Hasker Street. They were bemused by each other's background. Miles wrote:

I was as unsociable as ever, which was fine by Nicol since he had no desire to mix with showbiz, the so-called establishment or society. He was a surprisingly gentle lover, home-loving even to the point of making it up with Addo. But clichés aren't clichés for nothing and like any other lovemaking, it could never reach its peak when he was pissed. Thankfully this was not commonplace during the first few months, so everything was as it should be with a new love – as long as I turned a blind eye to tantrums. Sadly these became more regular as the months passed and I found it disconcerting to be powerless while witnessing him either wrestling with his dark evils, who were hell bent on attacking the world, or encircled by angels, allowing him to be as soft and tender as a lamb, frequently even bordering on the sentimental. He was usually found to be in the kitchen in a striped apron, cooking some magnificent Scottish hotpot, spoiling me rotten, he was a great cook.

Nicol's penchant for getting into fights made life difficult. One day Nicol was walking down Hasker Street with a friend when he claimed to have heard a builder insult them. Nicol demanded an apology. When it didn't come he threw a brick at the builder, causing a crack of broken glass. The builder descended from the scaffolding. According to Miles, the builder was the size of Arthur Askey.[10] Nevertheless he laid Nicol out with a single punch! Miles had to drag Nicol up to the top of her steps, helped by a neighbour, where she threw a bucket of cold water over him.

Sally Alexander admits that Nicol could be rambunctious, 'He definitely had a self-destructive streak. Dangerous to himself more than others, though others might be carried in the wake of his destruction.'

Was it thwarted ambition that riled Nicol? He was hoping to get film roles worthy of his talent. Miles reported that Nicol grew annoyed when she won an important part in *Those Magnificent Men in their Flying Machines*. Worse still, the director Ken Annakin had cast Miles after seeing her in a short film called *The Six-Sided Triangle* in which Nicol had co-starred. Yet there was no offer for Nicol. She felt that Nicol would only accept the best roles, which, as we shall see, probably harmed his career.

Around this time Peter Hall offered Nicol a long-term contract with the Royal Shakespeare Company. Nicol's old English teacher, Tom Reader, urged him to accept but Nicol declined. 'He [Tom] told me I should learn to use the system. I said that wasn't possible for me – I wasn't patient enough. I went home and turned Hall down.'

In her memoirs Sarah Miles relates some alarming incidents in Cornwall. She describes how her mother reacted to one of Nicol's visits:

As the evening wore on, Nicol allowed the maudlin and cantankerous side of his nature to emerge – a tedious state of affairs and sadly common among drinkers. Mother sat there stiff as a board while Nicol meandered on and on about his childhood. It might have been riveting but neither mother nor I could follow his inebriated gist.

In a good mood, Nicol would entertain revellers in a local Cornish pub:

Each night Nicol sang and each night the pub filled up a bit more. He was the genuine article, blossoming into the gentlest of pied pipers and mesmerising all around him with his talent. Oh, to have that ability! To open your throat with such ease and let your sound come tumbling out. The whole village, having found its voice, joined in one massively heart-lifting sing song.

Miles's account alleges that Nicol accused her of not wanting to marry him because he was working-class. Ironically, she claims that that was perhaps the only reason she was with him! He took to sleeping on the lawn after Sarah had banished him to a spare bedroom when he was drunk. Another night, according to Miles, an enraged Nicol began breaking up the spare room. Sarah scaled the roof in order to access the room from an outside window. What followed sounds frightening:

An enormous ego such as his, combined with fury, is a veritable time bomb. Losing all sense of what he was doing, Nicol charged at me like a raging bull. I fell backwards out of the window and went on a journey at some speed down the roof. Thank god for gutters, for without them I wouldn't be here to tell the tale. As I hung there miles from the ground and miles from the spare room, I looked up to see what Nicol was doing about my 'attempted murder'. Even worse than committing murder, surely, is not checking to see if your victim's dead. There was no sign of him. He didn't even come to the window. As I looked down at the gravel far below, a great sadness crept up through me … I knew of Nicol's personal agony, a pain stronger than childhood memories, deeper even than an obvious lack of nurture. But I'd come to the conclusion that my days as Florence Nightingale were over.

Nicol emerges from Miles's account as a bruised soul. They say that the most exciting stars are usually those with an air of danger. What will they do next?

By that yardstick Nicol was certainly in the major league of excitement! (Burt Reynolds once claimed on a TV chat show that a key litmus test for male stardom was whether you would let your daughter go out with the actor concerned. If the answer was 'no', then the would-be suitor was probably set for stardom!)

We should also remember that Miles's account is entirely hers and hers alone. (Luke Williamson recalls that his father had no recollection of this event at all when a friend told him about Miles's book. To which the friend retorted that Miles was 'barking mad'. Luke does, however, concede that Nicol probably did a lot of crazy things when he was young.)

Nicol was certainly acquiring a reputation for professional 'aberrations'. Around this time Michael Winner (the director most famous for the *Death Wish* franchise) was staging a London theatre show. It was called *Nights at the Comedy*, a pub variety show at the Comedy Theatre. In the line-up were veteran comic Jimmy James and a young Jimmy Tarbuck. Nicol had a part too. Winner recalled:

> Williamson had a habit of leaving shows. He did the first few previews of this show extremely well and suddenly [he] was gone! His agent said to me, 'he's gone to Glasgow where he thinks he's a reincarnation of McGonagall', a very famous Scottish poet. The agent said, 'You'll have to go and get him back.' I said, 'I'm not working for British Rail. I'm certainly not going up to Glasgow.' So we replaced Nicol.[11]

Perhaps Nicol felt the variety show was unworthy of his talent. Fortunately, two theatrical roles came that would establish him as the most exciting British stage star of his day. And one, in particular, was to provide a recurring channel for his anger. Bring on Bill!

3

INADMISSIBLE BEHAVIOUR

'Did you see him? Actors should be a little mad.'

Jason Robards on Nicol Williamson in John Osborne's *Inadmissible Evidence*

Bill Maitland was a 39-year-old alienated lawyer, unhappily married, hating his job and fatherhood, festering in failure and self-loathing, self-destructive and wrecking everyone and everything in his path. Maitland was also, as written, a scourge of youth and their values – a disillusioned sot surveying the debris of his life. It was John Osborne turning into (early) male menopause and looking for fresh targets.

Critics loved *Inadmissible Evidence*. Terence Rattigan, supposedly the antithesis of Osborne as a playwright but actually an ardent admirer, praised it as not only Osborne's 'fullest and most moving work' but the finest play of the century. Perhaps Rattigan was trying too hard to compensate for his own genteelness. It was, I think, a great part rather than a great play. Maitland was the whole story with the other characters just offshoots.

Leslie Halliwell later described the film of *Inadmissible Evidence* as 'an anti-humanity soliloquy' and that's a fair summary of the play too. Osborne was challenging just about every value that bourgeois Britain held dear – that a comfortable home, a meaningful profession, marriage and parenthood would shore up a man's life in middle age. Osborne was saying, 'Wait a minute – here's someone who has all these things and yet he's unfulfilled. So what else is there?' And yet these *are* the values that anchor most people. So at the end of *Inadmissible Evidence* we can't help but feel that Bill is to blame for his own failure.

Maitland, as Osborne imagined him, was dissatisfied with everything that life offered by way of consolation at its halfway point. Nicol – for this very reason – was not first choice. He was only 27, already with a reputation as a fearsome stage actor, but surely too callow for Maitland? Assistant director Peter Gill remembers that Freddie Jones was first considered for the part at the Royal Court in the summer of 1964.

According to William Gaskill, it was Anthony Page, who had already directed Nicol in *Z Cars*, who was responsible for launching Nicol's career and persuading John Osborne to accept Nicol as a 39-year-old.[1]

Osborne recalled how they discovered Nicol, 'At the end of the afternoon Anthony (Page, director) brings on his dark horse: Nicol Williamson. Nicol is in costume. It takes flight. This 27-year-old pouting, delinquent cherub produced the face to match the torment below the surface. He's much too young but no matter. He is old within.'[2]

It was Page's catch but, as Nicol later revealed, Tony Richardson, with whom Nicol had an on-off relationship, tried to sabotage it. Richardson sent Page a cable saying 'Nicol Williamson a very bad idea STOP nothing more than a good rep actor …'

Yet Nicol proved the doubters wrong. He was always able to conjure torment and self-loathing, sharing as he did some of Maitland's contempt for respectable values. 'He lives in the jungle', the playwright John McGrath later said of Nicol, someone who trod a fine line between creation and destruction.

The few video excerpts of his performance (on Broadway) reveal Nicol's power. The 1968 film version, though magnificent, does not quite do justice to the sweating, heaving, thrusting nature of Maitland's brutal, orgasmic self-loathing – like an accelerating locomotive, driving forwards, never relenting. Yet in Nicol's combustible, enraged performance something deeply moving does emerge. Anthony Page said, 'The play creates its own rules. It's a dramatic poem about a man's measure – the quintessence of dust, the heroic situation, passion and fierce irony and the guilt, weakness and shabby reality.'

Peter Gill remembers a difficult initial rehearsal period because Nicol did not learn lines easily. Rather, his technique was to work from inside out and *then* master the script. So Nicol was constantly under stress; in Gill's words 'he was a terrific actor but hard to handle'.[3] Nicol later said the character was a composite, constructed from various people he knew. Gill thinks Maitland was partly based on well-known lawyer Oscar Beuselinck, a view shared by Nicol's one-time agent, Lionel Larner.[4]

Gill remembers that Marianne Faithfull was originally set to play his daughter in the production.[5] Natasha Pyne then took over. Sheila Allen was his wife and Arthur Lowe played the loyal clerk, Hudson.

The first production of *Inadmissible Evidence* opened at the Royal Court on 7 September 1964. Milton Shulman in the *Evening Standard* praised Osborne's writing for its 'supple virility and thrusting drive'. Ronald Bryden in the *Observer* focused on Nicol:

> He fills every cranny of Maitland's portrait with knowledge: the nervous sweating, the lurching jocularity, the sick waves, tangible as nausea, each shift and terror transparent, while amassing the twitching motive and counter motives into a semblance of individual solidity. He gives failure a face crystalline enough to reflect our own.

R.B. Marriott in *The Stage* wrote that:

> Nicol Williamson ... is splendid as Maitland. The character is exceptionally demanding, on-stage continuously with scores of facets and a multiplicity of feeling. Mr Williamson grasps and keeps the centre as he should, then moves from a brilliant display into a realm of creative interpretation that persuades us that this is 'the thing itself'.

Alan Brien[6] described Nicol as 'reacting with stony gargoyle gloom, now with glowing sexual conceits, his face twitching with nervous energy and then collapsing like a sinking soufflé as he listens to his own voice'. It was also Brien, writing in the *Sunday Times*, who penned one of the most unforgettable descriptions of Nicol, '... eyes like poached eggs, hair like treacle toffee, a truculent lower lip like a pink front step protruding from the long pale doorway of his face'. (Brien was one of the few critics Nicol liked. Coincidentally, Ian Holm also described Nicol's eyes as looking like poached eggs – or perhaps he 'poached' the description from Brien!)

Theatre director Roland Jaquarello judges Nicol's performance as the greatest he has seen in a modern play:

> It had spontaneity, passion and danger. Caught in the pincers of time, Nicol's Maitland was a man who looked back with despair and forward with trepidation. It was an interpretation that brilliantly captured the worst fears of middle age. It's difficult to think of the play without Nicol.[7]

Paul Sidey, later a prominent publisher, recalled that 'if the seats in the auditorium had been wired with electricity, the audience could not have failed to be zapped by the legendary high voltage of Williamson's performance when he really let rip'.[8]

Osborne was so impressed with Nicol's portrayal of Maitland that he praised him as 'the greatest actor since Brando' – a mighty comparison to live up to. Osborne later told Richard Eyre that the only notes he gave to Nicol urged him to 'treat every other line as if it had just come upon you by surprise, as if it had just invented itself. That is the way, the only way in my opinion, to treat this complexity of text'.[9]

When the play transferred to the Wyndham's Theatre in March 1965 *The Times* compared it to *Who's Afraid of Virginia Woolf?* as 'another claustrophobic study of moral breakdown'. It also noted that 'John Hurt "subtly doubles" the parts of the office junior and the homosexual client but, of course, the evening still belongs to Nicol Williamson, whose frenziedly brilliant performance has gained in variety and shape since its first appearance'.

Hurt, a brilliant actor whose passing in 2017 was rightly marked by generous tributes, was an interesting contrast to Nicol. Hurt excelled at playing twisted, embattled characters. Picture him writhing on a torture table in *1984*, gravely ill in *Champions*, wrongly accused in *10 Rillington Place*, hideously deformed in *The Elephant Man*, chest-bursting in *Alien*, as the traumatised long-term prisoner in *Midnight Express*, or the eccentric Quentin Crisp in *The Naked Civil Servant*. Maitland was a tormented creation too but you could never imagine Hurt playing him. Hurt simply lacked Nicol's indefinable gravitas and force.

Natasha Pyne, just 18 at the time, and an admirer of Nicol's since watching him in *Z Cars*, recalls Nicol's performance as 'frighteningly real and truthful'.[10] She doesn't share Gill's recollection that Nicol took some time getting into the part; she believes that he became 'older' very quickly. Pyne noted Nicol's mastery of the sub-text as well as his extraordinary power, rivalled only, she says, by Richard Burton in *Taming of the Shrew* in which she played Bianca.

Eleanor Fazan was in the play at the Wyndham's Theatre and also played his wife in the film. She noted the eerie (anguished) parallel between Nicol and Maitland:

> Nicol was a troubled soul. He would throw himself into a role and commit himself totally. Everything – on stage and personally – for Nicol was about absolute intensity. He was such a commanding presence on stage, and during *Inadmissible Evidence* we became great friends. We used to have supper in an Indian restaurant. Nicol always ordered the very best wine. That, I am afraid, was the problem: he drank too much.[11]

The Indian restaurant in question was almost certainly Ashoka, just fifty metres or so from the Wyndham's Theatre. It was there that Nicol first met Trevor Nunn, later a distinguished RSC director:

> I had discovered Ashoka years before, and frequently occupied a late night table for one there after work at the Aldwych Theatre,' Nunn recalls. 'I began to notice, each time I was in the restaurant, another habitué, also invariably at a table for one

… Nicol. He would finish his show, get changed, probably sign some autographs and then manage the one-minute journey to the restaurant.

We nodded in well-mannered English recognition a couple of times, and then, throwing caution to the wind, I went over to his table the next time our late night dining habits conjoined, and introduced myself. Nicol said my name before I did, he urged me to join him, and thereby, began a delightful, and immensely fruitful friendship.

It was here that Nunn first suggested to Nicol that he play Coriolanus, a part to which he was ideally suited. But it would be a few years before it happened.

Nicol, riding on the back of wonderful reviews, was entitled to enjoy his curry. But not everyone, of course, thought *Inadmissible Evidence* was fantastic. Theatre critic Leo Lerman described it as 'endless and dispiriting … who wants to sit through a nervous breakdown lasting almost three hours?'[12] John Gielgud, known for his comical indiscretions, blurted out his opinion at a dinner party he hosted. One of his guests was a distinguished playwright. Gielgud was talking about recent plays he'd seen, 'That actor – oh dear me – young, Scottish, most unattractive … he was in that long, terribly dull, boring play. Oh, dear God, of course, you wrote it.'[13] His guest was, of course, John Osborne.

Nicol's father was his usual phlegmatic self when he came to London to see his son in the play. Nicol introduced Hugh to George Devine,[14] the director of the Royal Court. Devine turned to him and said, 'Your son's doing very well, isn't he?' Hugh replied immediately, 'Yes. That's what he's there for.'

In between the two performances of *Inadmissible Evidence* at the Royal Court and the Wyndham's Theatre Nicol had also appeared in Ben Travers's 1925 farce *A Cuckoo in the Nest* about adultery and divorce. Anthony Page insisted on casting Nicol rather than Daniel Massey who was the original choice.[15]

Also in the play was John Osborne, Arthur Lowe from *Inadmissible Evidence* and Alan Bennett – like Osborne, later to become far more famous as a playwright. Bennett described the production as a disaster, 'Nicol Williamson, who played the lead, was no farceur and seldom wrung a laugh from the audience, whom he chose to intimidate rather than entertain. Very shaky on the words, he would pause lengthily, snarl "yes?" and stare malevolently at the stalls until the prompt came.'[16]

The Times also thought Nicol was miscast:

Equipped with a monocle and nasal accent he (Nicol) sweats through the night's humiliations, soaked muddy and trouserless for the final debacle with Mrs Bone, in a way that arouses nothing but distress. It is a performance that destroys the belief that the act of farce depends on taking things seriously.

That was quickly forgiven when Nicol was cast in Samuel Beckett's *Waiting for Godot* which opened on 31 December 1964. Anthony Page had first suggested a revival at the Royal Court with Nicol as Vladimir, Alfred Lynch as Estragon and Jack MacGowran as Lucky. Beckett turned up at rehearsals and was unhappy about progress. Nicol retained his London barrister's accent for the author's reflective tramp. 'Where do you come from? Is that your natural voice?' asked Beckett, and when told that Nicol was Scottish, asked him if he could not use his natural non-London intonation.

Beckett became happier as the days passed. Eventually he told John Calder that he was ecstatic about Nicol's performance. 'There's a touch of genius in that man somewhere,' Beckett declared. Not surprisingly, according to Calder, from that moment on, 'Beckett was Nicol's God'. Calder added, 'Nick was extraordinary. I have never heard anybody do Vladimir's speech, so that it ended up as a trumpet call … The "I can't go on" was screamed with a trumpet voice.'

Waiting for Godot was such a success that it was extended by three weeks. Roland Jaquarello recalls:

> Some people think that Nicol was only good playing deranged characters. This wasn't the case. His Vladimir with a soft Scottish accent was a sensitive portrayal of a lonely man, full of pathos and humour. It was my favourite production of the play so far, with all the clarity and simplicity associated with Royal Court productions of that era.

Critic Martin Esslin also recalled Nicol's skill, noting that every time Vladimir wanted to laugh, Nicol's features were distorted by pain. 'A wonderful expression of the play's genre, which, after all, is subtitled "a tragi-comedy",' he noted.

Nicol was so good at projecting anguish and morbid dread that Beckett felt a kinship with him. 'He and Beckett used to talk about things like the void and the death of the ego a lot,' said Nicol's son, Luke:

> And it was always driving him to dark depths. I think Beckett was so glad that someone else had the same fears that he would aggravate them in Dad to make himself feel better. That's my feeling, of course. I don't know that to be true. I never met Sam, but Dad loved him … They were moths circling the same flame.

Nicol had scored a spectacular double whammy of success. *Inadmissible Evidence* continued in 1965 at the Wyndham's Theatre. Conjuring up an emotional collapse night after night, in what was virtually a one-man show, took its toll. One time Nicol stopped the play because of latecomers. On the evening of 20 May, he staggered offstage with chest pains. He did, however, return for the second act. At the curtain call he accused the management of overworking him to the point of collapse. He also offered theatregoers a refund if they were dissatisfied. Wednesday matinees were promptly cancelled.

Nicol fired repeated broadsides against the producers. Natasha Pyne remembers that she was offered a role in a TV play and asked for three nights off. The management refused, telling her she could either leave the play or stay. She left. She was told that Nicol made a speech from the stage after her departure, attacking their decision. On-stage diatribes were to be Nicol's hallmark.

Yet Nicol loved live performance. He once told Kenneth Tynan he felt 'elated before going on stage. There's also the chance of getting that extra ingredient, that jab of adrenaline. When that happens you do things that can scare you stiff.' And scares others to boot! During *Inadmissible Evidence*'s run at the Wyndham's Theatre, John Calder invited Nicol to take part in a Beckett reading at the Shakespeare Memorial Theatre in Stratford on a Sunday night. Nicol insisted on Beckett's personal direction.

According to Calder:

> Nicol's single-minded enthusiasm was such that he cancelled both his Saturday performances of *Inadmissible Evidence*, then playing at the Wyndham's, and sent on his understudy – who also had to play the whole week following, because Williamson, having returned from the rehearsal in France on the Monday, then disappeared for the whole week.

Nicol had spent several days in France, visiting Beckett at his home in Essy, outside Paris. Nicol later wrote about the experience in an extended essay *The Beckett Piece*, which is also available as an audio recording. The account reveals Beckett's Spartan, even monastic living conditions. It also displays Nicol's gift for mimicry, capturing the playwright's gentle, lyrical accent and his eccentricity – driving around in a dilapidated Peugeot – culminating in a visit to a painter's birthday party. It's even more illuminating, however, for revealing Nicol's constant battle against depression, craving for drink and fear of pending collapse.

But the friendship was sealed. Nicol, as well as Billie Whitelaw, Patrick Magee and Jack MacGowran, became Beckett's favourite interpreters. Calder describes what happened on Nicol's return:

> The day before the Sunday performance at Stratford, when I had made emergency changes in the programme, he appeared at my flat to rehearse, and took the audience by storm the next day, throwing the other readers into confusion by

his innovations. Patrick Magee[17] said that he would never again appear on the same stage as an actor so selfish.

Yet Beckett's admiration for Nicol was undiminished. (When Albert Finney took the lead in *Krapp's Last Tape* at the Royal Court in 1973, Beckett was disappointed by his performance. 'He had as much poetry as an ashtray,' Beckett reportedly said of Finney. He always regretted that Nicol hadn't played the role instead.)

We shouldn't forget that Nicol was still very young, just 28, and perhaps it would have been odd if some of the praise had *not* gone to his head. Director Lindsay Anderson recalls a meeting with Nicol, who was perhaps still smarting from being passed over for *This Sporting Life*, from a diary entry dated 12 June 1965:

> As Nicol (Williamson) sat there, maniacally detailing how Peter (O'Toole) and Richard (Burton) had made the wrong decisions, how Tom (Courtenay) was infinitely limited, how Alfie (Lynch) wasn't good in *Godot*, how he saw through Anthony (Page), saw through Tony Richardson … with sinking heart I felt myself again falling victim to these monstrous egoisms, these more-or-less charming children, these cracking bores …[18]

Nicol's waywardness was on display in a controversial television play by John Hopkins, *Horror of Darkness*, depicting a complex love triangle. Glenda Jackson and Alfred Lynch played young lovers and Nicol was a gay lodger causing waves with his unexpected arrival. The theme of latent homosexuality was unusual for the time. 'A powerful, unrelenting performance is delivered by the main cast of three (a mixture of half-smiles, hysterical outbursts and louring close-ups) – Williamson in particular,' wrote Tise Vahimagi on BFI ScreenOnline. *The Times* reported that the play 'provided Glenda Jackson, Alfred Lynch and Nicol Williamson with opportunities for impressive, nervously strained acting which they accepted very effectively'.

Glenda Jackson had acted with Nicol at Dundee Rep. She still viewed Nicol as extremely gifted but troubled. 'Nicol simply disappeared for the two-day rehearsal period,' she recalled. 'We wanted to rehearse properly but it was impossible without him. When he returned it didn't show in his performance at all but *we* had carried the burden.'[19]

Jackson believed that even back then Nicol's 'offstage life was taking primacy', not just his obvious love of drinking and partying, but the psychological problems that dogged him.

Nicol had also appeared in a television play *The Day of Ragnarok* by John McGrath who had written the Scottish version of *The Seagull* and with whom

Nicol would memorably collaborate later in the decade. The play, which starred John McGrath's wife Elizabeth MacLennan (who had also appeared at Dundee Rep), Pauline Boty and Wendy Richard, centred on women staging a protest in a London park after the announcement of a nuclear war. First shown in January 1965, most of the forty-minute film has no dialogue, just a voiceover at the beginning followed by sound effects and a music score by Dudley Moore.[20]

Nicol was working extremely hard during this period, perhaps *too* hard. David Cregan's play *Miniatures* about life in a comprehensive school was given a one-off Sunday night performance at the Royal Court in April 1965, with a cast including Jane Birkin, Lindsay Anderson, Graham Crowden and Nicol as a deranged music teacher. Nicol, in character, ripped a record player apart and hurled the debris into the wings! He also won excellent reviews for *Sweeney Agonistes* in which he played Sweeney as part of an evening honouring T.S. Eliot at the Globe Theatre.

Meanwhile, Nicol took *Inadmissible Evidence* to America, opening at the Belasco Theatre in New York at the end of November 1965. It was Nicol's first trip to New York. Peter Sallis, best known for his part in *Last of the Summer Wine*, inherited the original Arthur Lowe parts – playing the judge who sends Maitland down in the dream sequence as well as his clerk. Sallis took Nicol to Jimmy Ryan's in Manhattan, a popular venue for Dixieland jazz. 'He thought it was great,' recalled Sallis, 'and once or twice they let Nicol sing. He had a pretty good voice. In fact, he made an LP and pretty good it is too.'

Lionel Larner, who became Nicol's agent, also recalls Nicol's love of 1930s jazz, citing bandleader Ray Noble, and Noël Coward and Gertrude Lawrence in *Private Lives*, as favourites. Another friend who used to go with Nicol to Jimmy Ryan's described how Nicol 'would always sing for his supper. He's a gravelly, blues shouter really. There's nothing modest about his talents'.

The US run was marked by an infamous showdown, one of those incidents which – no pun intended – punctuated Nicol's career. He later said there was usually one every five years. Legendary Broadway producer David Merrick, fearing that the near-on three-hour play would deter theatregoers, demanded cuts. Page refused and Merrick threatened to fire Page after the initial Philadelphia[21] try-out. Nicol defended Page and fisticuffs ensued. Nicol later gave his account to Kenneth Tynan:

I was a holding a glass of Budweiser. Suddenly I remembered how José Ferrer had thrown champagne over Fred MacMurray at the end of *The Caine Mutiny*. He didn't chuck it at him, he flicked it forward like this, like throwing a dart. So I said, 'I won't stoop to spit in your eye' and let him have it with the beer. Then

he sort of rushed out at me and I stuck out my fist and he was on the floor. The
funny thing was that nobody in his entourage tried to attack me or help him.

Sallis offers his own account in his autobiography:

> As I went towards his [Nicol's] dressing room a man came out whom I half
> recognised as one of David Merrick's management team and, as he went past me,
> he was almost in tears, he was shaking his head and saying, 'He didn't oughta have
> done it'. I thought oh didn't oughta have done what? I got to the dressing room
> and knocked on the door and Peter Murphy, a friend of Nicol's helping to dress
> him and generally look after him, opened the door and said 'You can't come in'.
> I said 'But what's going on?'
>   'I can't tell you. I can't tell you. Just wait in your dressing room. Somebody will
> come along in a minute.'
>   … I said to Peter Murphy, 'Where's Nicol?'
>   'He's gone, he's gone. He's left for London.'
>   'What do you mean, he's left for London?'
>   He said: 'There's been a row, he's walked out and now he says he's going back
> to London.'
>   I said: 'Well, not without me he isn't.' I chased him out of the building and I
> saw him going down the street. He was hatless and coatless and just striding off.
> I ran after him and I caught after him and I said, 'What are you doing, what are
> you doing?!'
>   He said: 'That man. That man. I've just hit him.'
>   'Who have you just hit?'
>   'That Merrick.'
>   I said, 'Why?'
>   'He wants to cut the show.'
>   'Do you mean to take it off?'
>   'No, no, no, he just wants to cut it and I'm backing up Tony, so I hit him.'[22]

Osborne refers to the incident in a scattergun diary note for 9 November 1965:

> Anthony Page is no good at handling gangsters like David Merrick. Showdown
> backstage tonight with Merrick and Nicol Williamson squaring up to each other
> like old-time fairground pugilists. Merrick told Nicol Williamson, 'Page is fired'.
> Nicol Williamson replied, 'You can't fire the fucking director without telling me'.
> They are both quivering with fear. St Valentine's Day massacre. Nicol discovered
> next morning at the railroad depot singing *mammie*.[23]

A rumour emanated that Nicol had also thrown Merrick into either a dustbin or the Hudson. Untrue on both counts. Strangely enough – and a little-known footnote to the Merrick fisticuffs – twenty minutes *were* pruned off the play and, subsequently, Nicol admitted that Merrick might have been right and that his performance had improved. Lionel Larner thinks that Merrick, flamboyant producer that he was, would actually have thrived on the incident. Anything that generated publicity for his shows was a bonus.[24]

Merrick was not the only person Nicol quarrelled with. Merrick later asked Nicol to take a salary cut. 'I refused and so he talked to Tony Page and Page came to see me and absolutely begged me to accept it. It was pathetic. I haven't forgiven him for that and never will,' Nicol subsequently told Kenneth Tynan.[25]

Yet the cast *did* agree to take a 30 per cent pay cut. Sallis recalls being told by an American actress in the cast that *they* – the American performers – had no choice. Tom Prideaux, writing in *Life* in January 1966, noted the struggle to fill seats:

> After a batch of mixed reviews and facing Broadway's usual holiday slump Merrick feared the play might not survive and asked the actors to take salary cuts. They did and Osborne waived all his royalties, waiting to see if business picks up. If Broadway's audiences don't support this play, they should be ashamed of themselves.

It turned out, they *did* support it. *Inadmissible Evidence* was a success but perhaps not the *rip-roaring* hit everyone expected, especially since Nicol was nominated for a Tony Award for best actor. (Hal Holbrook won for *Mark Twain Tonight*.) It transferred from the Belasco to the Shubert, playing 166 performances before closing at the end of April 1966. The American critics were a bit sharper in nailing the play's shortcomings. Prideaux commented:

> His [Osborne's] Bill Maitland, of course, is a thoroughly implausible dramatic character. Any man with his penetrating gift of gab, his insights into himself, would never collapse into such a miserable slough. When he discourses elegantly about being 'irredeemably mediocre' it just doesn't wash … but if Bill, with all his sins upon him, is a little too bad to be true, he is not too bad to make good, vigorous theatre.

Prideaux's observation was perceptive. Most jerks go through life without realising they are jerks. The unusual aspect to Maitland was that, according to Nicol, 'he was aware of what he was, which was the awful thing about him'.

Peter Sallis noted Nicol's consummate skill, especially the speed of his acting:

I have never known anyone whose mind worked at such a rate … his was ahead
of you. He was thinking out what the woman was and saying it in the next
millisecond; he was thinking out each phrase, yet he spoke with a rapidity and a
poise that you knew was absolutely genuine. In other words he hadn't just learnt
it and was gabbling it off. He knew exactly what he was saying at any particular
point … it was an indication of the volatility of his mind. And as for emotions,
he could create more atmosphere with a flick of his wrist than most actors can
in a month of Hamlets.

Sallis added, 'I did just this one play with Nicol and the movie of the play and he
was wicked towards me but I didn't resent that at all. I felt quite chuffed that he
thought he could do it. What an actor! What an actor!'

Lionel Larner became Nicol's agent and friend around this time. Nicol was
always ringing Larner and inviting him out for drinks with new friends. Larner
recalls, 'When I signed him up it was a real coup for me but would people have still
felt that way if they had known all about his shenanigans?' Larner felt that Nicol
was a 'gigantic talent … you couldn't take your eyes off him, he was just magical'
and yet, perversely, he was underrated and would remain so. He believes that Nicol
was – in a phrase that occurs with some frequency throughout this book – 'his own
worst enemy' although, doubtless, some actors may contest that![26]

More than fifty years on, Larner remembers Nicol fondly, while acknowledging
he was a handful:

I had a wonderful time with him. He was an exciting star but very unpredictable.
I was always dragging him out of bars. Today he would probably be classified
as a manic depressive … What he really needed was a blockbuster movie to
establish him, but it never came. If an actor is extremely talented without fame,
then they need luck and timing. As it was, he couldn't quite get away with some
of his behaviour because he never made it to the front tier and the competition
was too strong. He was always resentful of the 'pretty boys' – guys like Robert
Redford – but essentially I think he was a creature of the stage, although he did
flawless impressions of Bogart and John Wayne.[27]

Larner also recalls, 'If someone said something to me in an offhand way he was
ready to punch them out!' Nicol would also arrive in Larner's office at all hours
for unannounced visits, often collapsing on to his sofa for a heart-to-heart. Larner
feared that Nicol would barge in even if he had an important meeting.

Yet when Larner wanted to contact Nicol, he had no luck. Nicol didn't like the phone. Kenneth Tynan and Ian Holm also noted Nicol's reluctance to answer calls. Holm wrote:

> I recall him phoning jazz clubs in New York and staying on the line for 30 minutes or so while the band played requests for him. This was the only time I can recall him using the telephone with any degree of enthusiasm. Mostly he regarded it as a sign of weakness to answer a ringing phone, and quite often he would even refuse to identify himself when calling people, who would then have to guess to whom they were talking.

At some point an exasperated Larner had to make a decision. 'Nicol liked me very much but he took up all my time. I started to wonder – do I continue to represent Nicol and part company with all my other clients?'

Meanwhile, something more interesting than bust-ups over cuts to text or pay was happening. Also in *Inadmissible Evidence* was a gorgeous 20-year-old American RADA graduate, Jill Townsend, cast as his daughter, Jane. Lionel Larner, also her agent, got the part for Jill. There was just one caveat. Her character had her back to the audience the whole time; Larner insisted that she should face them. And, of course, the critics all commented on her beauty.

Jill auditioned wearing a foxy pantsuit and brown boots, and Nicol remembers thinking, 'Screw me, who's this?' Jill Townsend was born in 1945. Her father was ex-Avis and American Express executive Robert Townsend. She later claimed to have been drawn to acting by her maternal grandfather, composer-conductor Frank Tours,[28] who was musical director of several Irving Berlin shows.

She had wanted to act from the age of 8 when she saw Mary Martin playing Peter Pan on Broadway. Jill commented of that time:

> I soooooo wanted to fly. Mother said I had to become an actress to do that. It was either being an actress so I could fly … and/or later juggling that with an interest in forensic science which I still have. I did a summer stock (like rep) when I was 15 and then joined the drama club at boarding school (Dobbs Ferry, New York) where my English teacher thought I had talent and said that RADA was the place to go.

Jill and her grandmother sailed to England in July 1963. Unfortunately, they missed auditions by one day so Jill had to wait until November to try again. Meanwhile, she attended a language school, studying commerce, manufacturing, typing and economics in French, Spanish and English. She thought that if acting didn't work out she could get an interesting job involving travel. But she passed her audition and joined RADA in January 1964. Just ahead of her, in the year above her, was Ronald Pickup. 'I didn't meet him but I'll always remember how good he was in RADA production,' she recalled.

Jill fell in love with another student, Donald Sumpter.[29] 'Before my last term my mother freaked out and got me back to the States promising I could go back and finish. But she never had any intention of allowing me to return. I was so angry! That autumn, instead, I got the part of Nicol's daughter on Broadway.'

The sexy blonde in the boots made quite an impact on the leading man. Jill recalls her first glimpse of Nicol:

> I remember walking into the stage door entrance and seeing him on stage. I was just waiting in the wings, to be called to do my audition. Nicol later told me that he had looked into the wings and he had seen his future wife! When he said that I did wonder if Tony Page knew that or had a say in the matter because, on reflection, he never gave me notes on rehearsal so I don't know if that was Nicol saying to him – 'I must have that girl'.[30]

Jill had heard of Nicol's great reputation but had never seen him on stage. Just 21, the word 'overwhelmed' sums up her feelings:

> I couldn't afford to go to the theatre while I was a student but I'd heard about him from *The Ginger Man* and the other important theatre of the time. Working with him, rehearsing with him on stage, you felt he was an extraordinarily gifted person. He had this fire within him that was fascinating and confusing at the same time.

She was an innocent at the time:

> I came from a family that didn't give me much of a perspective on the outside world. Then I went to an all girls' school, then RADA. And then I met Nicol, a huge presence when he was on stage, and also when we were courting. I was overwhelmed by him, confused because I didn't understand a lot of the energy he had within him. I'd never experienced anything like that before. I was swept up into his world. He'd take me out to dinner. I'd have a bowl of spaghetti and a glass of milk. I'm not a drinker and never really got into alcohol at all. He'd say: 'You're not ordering spaghetti and milk again!' He'd take me out to an Indian restaurant and shove a lime pickle into my face. I'd say 'it's too spicy' and he'd say, 'no, you'll love it, trust me!' We had a lot of laughs, a lot of fun at the beginning.

I learnt about eating avocado, that I could drink a half glass of red wine with a meal. I learnt so much. He was amazing. He swept me off my feet pretty instantly. I've always been quite shy so I'd prefer to be behind someone. It never really bothered me that I was seldom seen when I was with Nicol. I liked watching him too. And he was also a very kind person, extremely well read and intelligent. And I loved books, so we had reading and things to talk about.

Lionel Larner recalls that Nicol had become 'insanely possessive of her … it was rather like a Scott Fitzgerald tormented love affair'.

The press had it that Jill bailed out of the relationship because she felt smothered by Nicol. Yet Jill tells a different story:

> We were still doing *Inadmissible Evidence* in New York. One morning, Nicol told me that an old girlfriend from England was coming over to stay with him and I had to move out. That's what did that in. That was heartbreaking for me because I'd been scooped up into this amazing presence and then he was gone. I was then asked to be in a movie in California. I don't know how many weeks were still left of my contract on *Inadmissible Evidence*. Paramount somehow brokered the arrangement whereby I left the production a few weeks before the end and then could go out to Hollywood to do this film. During the film I got a part in a TV series, *Cimarron Strip*. I would say 'I won't consider that for under x amount' and they would give me the sum I'd asked for. But, of course, it was never enough – my mistake! Nicol then flew out and contacted the studio to try to renew things with me. I said that I didn't want to see him. I'd been tossed over. So the director – the great Sam Wanamaker – had to spend hours with him, talking to him.

Jill had already had an early taste of Nicol's dramatic mood swings *before* their split. It was a cold winter's night in January 1966:

> After a performance of *Inadmissible Evidence* I was driving back to my parents' home in Long Island with Nicol in the passenger seat. He'd had way too much to drink and insisted I take him to the beach. He tore into the freezing cold water and I had to get him out of there. I took him back to my parents' house and put him in the guest room. The following morning Nicol, who was very confused, started interrogating my father about what had happened. My father eventually drove him back to the train station.

Yet this was nothing compared to what happened when Nicol found out that Jill was spurning him. 'I almost destroyed myself. I got extremely drunk and drove a car at top speed down a hill full of hairpin bends', he told Kenneth Tynan. Nicol, who didn't have a licence, crashed off the road into someone's patio, spending a week in hospital. Jill is not sure whether this episode, which somehow expands on the retelling as they tend to, was directly linked to her 'rejection'. But her version corroborates that Nicol came close to killing himself. 'I'm not sure of the circumstances but he was at someone's house up on Mulholland Drive, got their car keys and then drove himself home and then went off the cliff. I think it was part of some rage that had been there all along.'

Kenneth Tynan later alleged that Nicol tried to 're-live' this episode, with Larner and Oscar Beuselinck's wife in the car. Yet Larner vehemently denies this, saying there was no way he would *ever* have agreed to have been in a car driven by Nicol!

It would be several years before Nicol and Jill would resume their romance.

Meanwhile, from madness offstage to madness on it. As if to confirm that Nicol had a special gift for playing tortured characters, he played the part of a lonely civil servant, Alexei Poprishchin, driven mad by poverty and rejection, in Sussex Playhouse's production of Gogol's *Diary of a Madman*. The Sussex run was just six nights.

The Spectator commented on his portrayal of the seedy civil servant:

Nicol Williamson is one of those rare actors who, as a hardened professional once said of Davy Garrick, could act as a gridiron and you'd believe him … shut up in his room at night, driven slowly insane by poverty, humiliation and the grinding monotony of the Russian civil service, he comes to believe he is king of Spain and ends in an asylum, stripped, starved, beaten and tortured at intervals with a primitive cold water shock treatment.

The Stage said that 'this gem of a play needs the talents of Nicol Williamson to cut the facets which bring it to brilliant life. His marathon performance never falters as he leads us along a devious path through disturbed alarm to distressing horror.'[31]

Irving Wardle compared Nicol's portrayal to another hellraising actor – who received a fatter pile of press cuttings than Nicol – Richard Harris. Yet, Wardle declared, Nicol surpassed him:

It was last played professionally in London four years ago by Richard Harris and although I admired that performance more than most people it is much outclassed by the present version. What Mr Williamson makes us realise within the first minute of his arrival – spitting on his cuff to shift a stain and cheerfully making tea – is that Alexei Poprishchin is a real man and that no matter how far he descends into madness by the end it is real human material that is being destroyed. The performance is thus much funnier and much more painful than its predecessor.

Vivienne Griffiths was Nicol's assistant and dresser for the Sussex production:

This was a one-man performance, a tour-de-force which involved numerous rapid changes of costume. My main task proved to be making sure Nicol Williamson actually got on stage. This was no mean feat as he was prone to moods not unlike the character he was portraying. It was particularly traumatic on the night the London critics were due to attend; Nicol Williamson disappeared shortly before the performance was due to start and was only found and persuaded to appear just in time.[32]

Griffiths later expanded:

One of the reasons why *Diary of a Madman* was such an ordeal for Nicol Williamson was the huge number of lines that he had to learn in a very short time. It was a one-man show, so stood or fell by his ability to deliver these in a compelling and convincing way, as his character deteriorated into madness.

The play was set in a book-lined study, and Nicol's character spent a great deal of time either looking in the books or writing in his diary. A solution to the line-learning was for some of them to be typed out and pasted into the books; others were hand-written and placed in his diary. For some reason, it fell to me to be in charge of this responsible task. The worst part was that Nicol nightly tore up the lines inserted into his diary, so every evening before the performance, I had to rewrite the lines and ensure that they were put in the correct place. The possibility of making a mistake or forgetting to do this was terrifying to both me and Nicol.

I was more than a little scared of Nicol. A big man, he was physically intimidating and also took some enjoyment in unnerving me with his actions and comments. I was a 'shy, cloistered' young woman, only just 18 years old by the time of the production. As Nicol's dresser, I had to get used to seeing him in various stages of undress, and at times he seemed to delight in walking round his dressing room naked. Modestly, I usually tried to avert my eyes. One evening, he caught sight of me having a surreptitious peep at him and asked me, rather gleefully, 'Haven't you seen a naked man before?' As I was almost totally inexperienced at this time, the answer was 'no', but I did not give him the satisfaction of a reply.

After Nicol's near no-show on press night, the director, Walter Eysselinck, suggested that Nicol's then girlfriend spend more time in Brighton to give him confidence. I remember her as being a somewhat stereotypical actress in appearance,[33] wearing a fur coat and big sunglasses, but she was really friendly towards me. One evening, she turned up in Nicol's dressing room while I was there and he was naked, and told me, 'Don't mind Nicol. He just likes to shock people'. That made me feel a lot better.

In retrospect, I feel very lucky to have had the chance to work closely with an actor of his standing. Despite some difficulties, the production was a huge success and Nicol's acting was brilliant. It gave me a small taste of working in the professional theatre, an experience that I took with me later into theatre-in-education work as an actor-teacher.[34]

By the time the performance had shifted to the Duchess Theatre in London, Irving Wardle wrote, 'Nicol Williamson sticks consistently to this reading, spitting out the diary entries with pedantic venom and rising into the climaxes with an underdog snarl.'

Significantly, *Diary of a Madman* was another one-man tour-de-force for Nicol who was on stage throughout the one-and-three-quarter hours' production. 'The play is more exhausting than I thought it would be but it's a satisfying exhaustion,' Nicol told *The Illustrated London News*:

It's a strain on the mind because of the relentlessness of it, and it becomes tiring. There are no periods of relaxation from having someone else on the stage. But I like the play. It has everything in it: unconscious pathos, tragic drama, high comedy. At least we certainly hope for laughter, if uneasy laughter. There's more variety in this character than in Maitland. The vocal, emotional and physical range is greater. You can see seeds of this character in yourself … the play is very hard work but I enjoy it. You begin to invent, to have ideas, to enter into the past. I'd get bored with most West End parts in five days. But I won't get bored with this.

Anthony Page was again at the helm for the London production and they clearly respected each other. 'I enjoy working with him and understand his approach,' said Nicol. 'This means that the rate of work is more intense and much quicker. We've worked this character out together. It's a fusion of our ideas and instinct.'[35]

Facile wisdom had it that Nicol had a special gift for playing lunatics. He was so convincing in *Diary of a Madman* that a couple of psychiatrists asked him to repeat the portrayal for their students as 'an absolute study of breakdown from the beginning of paranoid schizophrenia'. It was simply that Nicol was so good at heavy roles. After *Diary of a Madman* Nicol was offered (what he perceived to be) similar roles. 'Film companies have a habit of saying "we have a good script for you" and you find it's just a cheaper version of what you've done before. They wanted me to play a policeman who goes off his head. It was a ghastly script and I said so.'[36]

Nicol always professed to hate television. Luke remembers that his dad told him he believed it an 'inferior' medium. Among the TV roles Nicol turned down were the lead in Dennis Potter's *The Singing Detective* – eventually taken by Michael Gambon – and, probably, the lead in the same writer's *Karaoke* and *Cold Lazarus*, eventually played by Albert Finney. (Nowadays, Luke believes, Nicol might have been tempted by something that would have been given sufficient scope and depth, like *Game of Thrones*.) Yet, fortunately – going back to 1968 – he *did* agree to a TV version of John Steinbeck's *Of Mice and Men*, the classic tale of two California drifters during the Great Depression. Nicol played Lennie and another big name from the period, George Segal, was George.

Director Ted Kotcheff, later most famous for the movie *First Blood*, recalls Nicol as delightful. He does, however, remember strange panic attacks Nicol was having in which he imagined 'another Nicol' looking at him, 'a disembodied version of himself'. Kotcheff said that Nicol had a novel interpretation of Lennie. Because the character had learning difficulties, he told Kotcheff that he would like to play him as a child. So he did just that, going up to Segal on his hands and knees. The director concluded it 'was a great idea'.[37] And so it was. Nicol gave – in the words of his first wife, Jill – 'a truly heart-breaking performance' as Lennie. As always, Nicol nailed the American accent so perfectly that nobody guessed he was British.

Segal, who had delivered memorable performances in *Who's Afraid of Virginia Woolf?* and *No Way to Treat a Lady*, loved the experience:

I had seen *Inadmissible Evidence* by the time we did *Of Mice and Men*. So I knew what a great actor he was and was delighted for the opportunity to work with him. He was a dream to work with. We both shared a love of early jazz music and I believe he was an accomplished ragtime piano player. He was a truly gentle man of profound modesty and a withering sense of humour. He abjured all the ballyhoo associated with show business. I knew that he suffered from severe anxiety attacks but they never got in the way of the work. We shot the show at the NBC colour studios in Brooklyn and worked all night on the last day so at 9 a.m., after a night's work, Nicol, Ted and I went to a batting cage on Coney

Island. I remember Nicol smashing every single ball pitched at him, putting Ted and me to shame. What an eye that guy had![38]

Nicol's performance left a strong mark on a young boy watching it on TV. 'I was 10 and it was one of the most moving performances I've ever seen. He was a wonderful Lennie. From then on, I would make it my business to watch any movie that he was cast in,' recalled Brian Kirkland.[39]

Nicol's fan base was growing. But did the camera like him? Nicol had never been tested in a leading role.

4

TAKING FILM BY STORM

'When I saw the look on his face (those poached egg eyes staring balefully at me) I thought he was going to kill me.'

Ian Holm

Playing misfits came easily to Nicol. The part of O'Rourke in *The Bofors Gun* seemed ideal for him – he had already acquired a ferocious reputation as a rebel. The danger in playing such a nutter was that the portrayal would obliterate everything else. Thanks to Nicol and director Jack Gold,[1] teamed for the first time in this story of barrack-room bullying, it retains its credibility.

The Bofors Gun was based on the play *Events While Guarding The Bofors Gun*, written by John McGrath[2] especially for Nicol who was 'hot' after *Inadmissible Evidence*. But Nicol couldn't do the play. McGrath then suggested Nicol for the film. Jack Gold recalled, 'Nicol Williamson was a well-known stage actor with a terrifying reputation. People said "who's in this?" And I said "Nicol Williamson" and they looked at me and made the sign of the cross over me.'

Nicol's psychotic National Service squaddie, stationed in Germany, rails against bourgeois values of self-improvement and aspiration, in particular the desperate, pitiful determination of a rookie bombardier (David Warner) to have a quiet final night with his section before an anticipated promotion. Warner is the gentrified, mild-mannered Lance Bombardier Evans, baited by Nicol's vitriolic Gunner O'Rourke who's angling to be put on report.

There are two ways of seeing Evans, perhaps a deliberately ambiguous character. You could see him as genuinely compassionate, trying to placate his subordinate and keep him out of trouble. You could also posit that Evans has no interest in O'Rourke's wellbeing at all, faking concern when he's only thinking of his own pending promotion. On this reading Evans is reluctant to discipline him simply to save his own reputation. If he really had O'Rourke's interests at heart he would have put him on report – and indeed *should* have done because O'Rourke is so obviously a danger to himself and others.

Provoked beyond reason, Evans still refuses to sanction O'Rourke, 'If that bloke had a decent chance he'd be perfectly alright.' Yet from O'Rourke's first appearance – bullying, swaggering and complaining about 'weaklings, bedwetters and hypocrites' and showing false deference to the bombardier – it's clear that another chance would *not* redeem him. He is hell-bent on self-destruction, scornful of compassion or redemption. Evans has the chance to do the right thing but is determined *not* to take it.

The Bofors Gun is British ensemble acting at its best. Peter Vaughan offers authoritative support as a firm, dignified sergeant whom Evans is desperate to appease. Of course, Evans wants to appease *everyone* and, in so doing, tragedy ensues as O'Rourke goes on a bender, self-harms and finally, for reasons not entirely clear, save for his self-loathing, succeeds in killing himself and scuppering Evans's dream of promotion.

John Thaw played Gunner Featherstone, O'Rourke's drinking partner in the movie, and – as we have seen – Nicol's best friend at the time. Thaw, still only 25, had just had huge success on TV in *Redcap* and had recently divorced his first wife, Sally. Nicol had allowed Thaw, who was facing a huge tax bill, to move into his new flat in Bloomsbury. (Luke recalls Nicol telling him that Thaw never paid a bill!) During this period Nicol, Thaw and Ian Kennedy Martin, future creator of *The Sweeney*, were still inseparable drinking buddies. An excerpt from a book about *The Sweeney* reveals the happy hellraising:

> They would meet for mad nights out, often starting at Covent Garden theatre restaurant, the Ivy, or else at maverick restaurateur Peter Langan's Odin's in Marylebone, where the owner could sometimes be found drunk under a table clutching an empty bottle of champagne. Nicol Williamson was the trio's devil may care ringleader. 'They were nights out not to remember,' laughs Kennedy Martin. 'I was pissed out of my mind for eight years, 1962/3 to 1970.'[3]

Perhaps their off-screen friendship helped Thaw and Nicol in their performances. All the actors do well in *The Bofors Gun*, not only a claustrophobic, tense British Army film, but also a twisted, inverted psychological battle. You can feel the tension – not to the same extent as, for example in *The Hill* – but it's not far off. Whereas in *The Hill*, Ian Hendry's psychotic Sergeant Williams terrorises the underlings, in *The Bofors Gun* O'Rourke terrorises his superior.

Warner is every bit Nicol's equal in this film but it was Nicol who had the tougher part. Kenneth Tynan later wrote:

> The satanic Irishman is so bombastically over-written, his madness and death wish are so heavily signalled ('I should not be at large', 'I hate all goodness', 'I'm not long for this world') that the part can hardly be played without being over-played. Nicol did his best and it was far more than enough.

Filming took place in the winter of 1967–8 with rehearsals in an old army barracks near Stevenage on a six-week shooting schedule. Peter Vaughan recalled:

> It was a brilliant piece of work and became a great art-movie success. We all worked for minimum expenses and a percentage when the film went into profit. Universal Pictures taught us a sharp lesson here, for despite its success not a penny profit ever came our way. I think they call it creative accounting, or something like that.[4]

Gold later commented that he thought the six-week shooting schedule was a luxury:

> It was only during and afterwards I discovered it was anything but a luxury and we got through it in six weeks, shooting four or four-and-a-half minutes a day which is more than the average for a picture and it just worked. We just kept on because I didn't know that one shouldn't.

It was the first of five collaborations between Gold, who became known as primarily a television director, and Nicol. He became one of Nicol's doughtiest defenders, praising his professionalism and talent. Nicol would always be well-behaved with Gold. That didn't detract from Nicol's 'difficult' image, of course, it merely meant that Nicol chose other people to be difficult with. (John Thaw 'loved' Gold too, according to Thaw's first wife, Sally.)

'Nothing could have been easier or nicer,' said Gold of his time with Nicol. 'He was totally professional, very responsive, very amusing, a great guy to have around. I've done two films with him,' said Gold after he had also directed Nicol in *The Reckoning*. 'I've worked with him in various tense circumstances over seventeen, eighteen weeks, and there was nothing but pleasure all the way.'

Gold, penning a tribute after Nicol's death in 2012, expanded:

> Directing him was a constantly surprising process. He was quick to understand

even a hint of a suggestion. There were rapid and subtle changes of expression, his antennae as finely tuned as his performances. He liked the challenges, the technicalities, the rigours of filming … but if ever there was a piano handy, he was immediately seated there, singing ballads, blues, rock, jazz. He loved the great musicians and improvisation. I think that, latterly, that is where his heart truly lay.[5]

Warner also praised Nicol's professionalism. Nicol's final scenes in *The Bofors Gun* called for him to undress and kill himself. 'It was a tough shoot and freezing cold and Nicol Williamson … had to take off his shirt and stand there. I don't know how he did it.'[6]

Co-star Barry Jackson remembered that Nicol could be dangerous company. Nicol challenged him to a game of darts with a difference. While one placed his hand on the dart board, the other would throw round it. Jackson went first, and duly threw round Nicol. Then Nicol went and threw the dart straight through his hand. Jackson smiled and said nothing. Weakness could never be displayed in front of Nicol.[7]

Nicol had also cultivated quite a reputation as a practical joker. It was his extraordinary gift for mimicry that always served him well – and, of course, that is very difficult to convey on the page. Jack Gold, keenly aware that everyone should learn about marching and manoeuvres, had arranged a four-day boot camp for his players. Nicol tried to dodge it by citing his two years in the Paras. A certain Sergeant Major Britten was brought in to 'drill' the actors. Nicol, affecting the clipped delivery of the upper-class officer, buttonholed Britten beforehand and convinced him that he (Nicol) had been an officer. So much so that Britten addressed Nicol as 'Sir!' Nicol told him that he thought the actors would need more than three or four days' drilling. 'I'd suggest a week,' Nicol told him. 'And, in particular, watch that one over there,' he added, pointing at Thaw in the distance, 'because he's *very* bolshie.' Nicol then said, 'I'll slip off now and I hope everything goes well. Carry on, Sergeant Major!' Nicol got into a car and left the set. 'Where's he goin'?' asked Thaw. The last thing he heard was the sergeant major shouting at John Thaw, 'Get back into line, you 'orrible little man!' Nicol, true to form, was absent while the others were put through their paces. He also stayed away from home to avoid calls from an irate Jack Gold!

Nicol's drinking sometimes gave him a harder edge. Also in the cast was Ian Holm playing a (Protestant) Irishman, Gunner Flynn, the only one who respects the bombardier, earning O'Rourke's contempt. Holm recalled a boozy evening from around this time during which Nicol took a shine to his then partner, Bee (Bridget) Gilbert:

There was always a dangerous edge to him [Nicol] and his savage, often cruel powers of observation were acutely sharpened by drink. He, Bee and I used to eat together so often that it became a sort of weekly ritual. Then, one night, during a meal out, he got terribly drunk and after an hour or so of noisy philosophising from him I went to fetch the car. When I arrived back at the restaurant there was no sign of him or Bee. Bee later said that she had also been very drunk and couldn't recall much except that quite early on in the evening Nicol Williamson had declared his love for her and promised to make an honest woman of her. He had been very prickly with me all evening and he could be *very* prickly. And although I had put it down to drink, maybe it was also connected to his amorous designs.

He must have bundled Bee into a taxi while I collected the car. I knew that he had what I shall call a soft spot for her and guessed that he had gone back to his flat. We were all the worse for wear, the lines between intent and tomfoolery blurred by drink. What followed was a kind of gruesome, though comic, burlesque. Having located them, I played the part of the jealous lover by shouldering open the door, shouting something Edwardian and melodramatic like 'think of the children' and then marching her out into the night air. When I saw the look on his face (those poached egg eyes staring balefully at me) I thought he was going to kill me.[8]

In character as O'Rourke, so it seems.

The distinguished film critic Pauline Kael criticised the film and Nicol's performance, writing that his character's 'self destructiveness was so wildly, flamboyantly out of scale – his Irishman was such a drunken, satanic brute that one simply couldn't imagine how anyone could help him and one's sympathy shifted to the corporal'.

Yet Kael had called it wrong. Nicol could only play the part as written and O'Rourke was a suicidal, drunken, psychotic mess. The character, just like in *The Reckoning*, was working-class Irish Catholic, presumably hating the British ruling class, Protestantism, and – perhaps even more so for its hypocrisy – any (affected) concern for his wellbeing. And any sympathy we have for Warner's character at the beginning quickly ebbs.

It's a powerful film of the type that British actors do so well, if a shade wordy and melodramatic, but Nicol was rewarded with a BAFTA nomination for best actor. Reviews for the film were more mixed.

John Russell Taylor in *The Times* said:

It is difficult to see who comes out better in a conflict between an idiot and a lunatic. Nicol Williamson plays the lunatic O'Rourke with electric intensity, which is about all anyone could do with a role with few gradations and no seeming existence before the start of the film.

Vincent Canby wrote, 'Nicol Williamson seems to have a special genius for defining in coherent terms the state of mind of a man who has slipped his moorings and is sailing towards the outer limits of sanity.'

Halliwell called it a 'fascinating, but often crude and eventually rather silly expansion of a TV play chiefly notable for its excellent acting opportunities provided by its unattractive but unrecognisable characters'.

Nicol had cemented his reputation on the back of *Inadmissible Evidence* which remained a shadow hanging over every performance. Filming such a sensational play was a gamble but it worked out well. Thank God for the decision, otherwise what would remain of Nicol's magnificent performance save a few clips set to melodramatic music on YouTube?

Anthony Page, who had directed the original production, also directed the movie which starred Jill Bennett as Liz, Peter Sallis as Hudson, Isabel Dean as Mrs Gamsey, Eileen Atkins as Shirley and Ingrid Boulting, who wins a couple of lines here as his estranged daughter.

Acting such a thunderous part on film called for a subtle downsizing of technique. Nicol, a much more sensitive screen actor than Kael ever realised, toned down certain gestures and inflexions. The extraordinary oscillations of his stage performance, turning from a domineering bully into a tearful wreck, are still here, but slightly filtered.

The screenplay takes us to London streets, even a strip club, but it's the same Maitland – breathless, bewildered, boozy, panic-stricken and pill-popping. It's Nicol's vocal range, betraying the character's passive/aggressive swings, which conveys the descent. His is not a poetic voice – like Burton's, for example – but it can shift from raging to whining in a millisecond.

Maitland still repels everyone around him. His son wants to go to boarding school, his daughter won't travel with him in the same train compartment, his secretary is sick of him, taxi drivers and lift attendants ignore him. He is bored by his family, lost in lust, but emotionally blocked. He even fails when tentatively consoling the distraught would-be divorcee, Mrs Gamsey, or when jotting down the story of his gay client.

Some scenes in the film of *Inadmissible Evidence* are Nicol's best on celluloid – fully justifying another BAFTA nomination for best actor – in particular Maitland's final encounter with his daughter. He berates her for her insensitivity and then fantasises about how their relationship could have developed – with a hint (perhaps?) of incestuous lust:

> I always used to think that when you are the age you are now, I'd take you out to restaurants for dinner, big restaurants like I used to think posh restaurants were like, with marble columns and glass and orchestras. I thought we'd be rather like a grand married couple, a bit casual with lots of signals for one another, lots of waiters would pass by and envy us and when we got back to the table we'd look at each other with such pleasure we'd hardly be able to eat our dinner.

Nicol switches from wrecker to wreckage in seconds. He then explodes before collapsing into a heap. At the end when Maitland is corralled in an isolated office, kicking bundles of legal papers, it seems like hubris.

Perhaps the only fault with the film – and also a criticism of the original play – is that it is too obviously a one-man show with the other characters just foils for Maitland's spleen. A.H. Weiler commented, 'You also feel, for all Maitland's mental trauma, that his bullying and badgering has created a bleak universe. Despite Nicol Williamson's expertly bitter, tortured and sustained repetition of his stage creation of Maitland, one leaves the theatre feeling that this is a bleak world Maitland created for himself.'

Halliwell called it an 'interesting and surprisingly successful transcription of a difficult play'. Michael Billington in *The Stage* wrote that Nicol 'confirms that he has a screen presence to match his stage personality. He brings out beautifully the "fibbing, mumping, pinched little worm of energy" that is inside Maitland'. Stanley Kauffmann said that 'a play that was conceived as an increasingly bad dream has been made into a grittily detailed, naturalistic film'.

Perhaps that was the finest compliment for a screening of what was essentially a theatrical experience. Nicol's Maitland never ceases to be believable – an extrapolation, maybe, of the mental collapse many of us glimpse but ultimately avoid. The dreary black-and-white photography adds to the sour mood.

Nicol later said he never saw the film. 'But when it was finished I said to the cameraman, "Am I any good? Am I as good as Spencer Tracy at his best?" because these are the boys who really know. And he said I was, so that was enough for me.'[9] Certainly Nicol deserved an Oscar nod for *Inadmissible Evidence*. His omission was shameful.

The comparison with Tracy was well taken. Both had great concentration and presence. (Katherine Hepburn, who greatly admired Nicol, once told him that he reminded her of Tracy.) Significantly, neither had matinee idol looks. Jack Gold commented:

Nicol Williamson hasn't the most attractive face in the world. But because of this, or despite this, you're constantly aware of him as a human being. You have to watch the things that are going on in those eyes, or behind the eyes which were extraordinarily expressive. Also he has a quality which I think great stars have – the quality of danger.

In other words, not the matinee idol looks that bring legions of swooning women to the cinema, more a riveting intensity.

Ingrid Boulting recalls Nicol's signature card – middle of the night phone calls:

He fascinated me with the confidence he exuded as an actor. We remained friends. He and Jill would often visit me for tea in New York in the early seventies. Nicol could be intimidating but he did not scare me. I remember him calling me at all hours of the night (fuelled by having had a few drinks) and going on about things. He seemed tormented in the way that brilliant people can be. [10]

Portraying Maitland in *Inadmissible Evidence* was emotionally demanding, to say the least. Around this time Nicol appeared on *Frost on Saturday* [11] and expanded on what was to be a lifelong obsession – an overriding, sometimes all permeating fear of extinction. Nicol gave a darkly brilliant, galloping reading of Samuel Beckett's *All That Fall*. He told Frost that he thought about death constantly, throughout the day:

I don't find it a pleasing prospect … what concerns me is sudden death, one can eventually come to terms with death itself … I don't think there is anything else except complete oblivion. What makes me angry, panic stricken, is the thought that one won't fulfil in life all the things one can do and in an exciting way, the threat of sudden death that cuts you off before you have made any kind of statement, mark or contribution at all.

Nicol added that his morbidity stemmed not from a classic death wish, rather more of a life wish, and horror at the idea of leaving loved ones and friends.

Sir John Betjeman, by his side, said he empathised with Nicol's horror of extinction. Yet when Frost turned to the audience and asked how many people – mostly it seemed middle-class and middle-aged – thought frequently about death, only a few hands went up. More an obsession of actors and poets, so it seems! But the Frost programme was interesting for revealing Nicol's intelligence in considering serious issues without flippancy or the need to joke – so much the bugbear of modern TV.

Since Nicol garnered so much acclaim for acting heavies – and he was clearly a man of oceanic depths – it was easy to forget that he was also a versatile light comedian. That's how he bagged the lead in *Plaza Suite*, Neil Simon's 1969 Broadway comedy, directed by Mike Nichols, in which Nicol took three different roles. Maureen Stapleton and George C. Scott were the original stars (Scott would appear with Nicol several years later in *Uncle Vanya*) but Scott suddenly had to leave for an eye operation. Several actors were approached to take over during Scott's six-week absence – including José Ferrer, Martin Balsam and Fritz Weaver. They all declined.

According to Neil Simon:

No one wanted to follow in the footsteps or reviews of George C. Scott. Mike Nichols then came up with an original idea. Nicol was an English actor who had already made his name in London and New York. He was a brilliant actor and could also do a perfect American accent. We sent the play to Nicol; he read it and agreed to do it.

Three days later he was in New York rehearsing. He needed about a week or ten days to get ready ... in the meantime actors' equity in America protested our choice of using an English actor in an American part. We assured them we had tried every possible American actor of appropriate stature and were unable to come up with one. Should we close the show and put their American actors out of work because of the equity ruling? They finally agreed but there was a large contingent of actors who were against our move. We watched Nicol Williamson in his final dress rehearsal and he was quite wonderful.

That night, as he was about to make his debut in the part, irate members of actors' equity picketed the show outside the theatre, most of them carrying placards. One of the young actresses who was carrying a placard – which I didn't find out until many years later – was Marsha Mason, someone who would eventually play an important part in my life. The curtain went up with Maureen Stapleton alone on stage. She received her usual acknowledgement from the audience, then had a six-minute scene with the bellboy.

Then Nicol Williamson made his entrance. As he did, a young man stood up from his aisle seat. Obviously an actor from equity who was unhappy with our choice and began to sing the star spangled banner at the top of his lungs. The audience was confused and annoyed and began to hiss the man to be quiet. The play onstage stopped completely. A police officer came in and ushered the young man out just as he finished ' ... and the home of the br-a-a-a-a-ve'. The curtain went down, then after a few moments went up again. Maureen repeated her scene with the bellboy and Nicol made his entrance on stage. The audience gave him a standing ovation![12]

Nicol loved the experience. 'I thought it would be fun to do a slick, marvellous modern American comedy in New York with very little rehearsal. It was fun and it worked.'

For once it wasn't Nicol causing a brouhaha. And further commotion was to arise that summer, when filming started on Tony Richardson's *Laughter in the Dark*, Nabokov's novel of blindness, in sight and in love, originally set in thirties Germany and mysteriously updated to sixties London. Nicol was coming into his own. Yet he still needed a really great film to seal his success.

5

FUN IN THE SUN

'The thing about Nick is that he really likes the jungle. That's where he lives.'

John McGrath

Richard Burton, then at the height of his fame, was initially cast in *Laughter in the Dark*. Shooting started in July 1968 with Burton filming scenes at Sotheby's. Earlier in July the press had noted that Elizabeth Taylor had bought a £50,000 Monet painting. Tony Richardson had directed Burton before on the film of *Look Back in Anger* and also in *A Subject of Scandal* and they had seemed to get on.

On 9 July, however, Burton was fired. Rumour had it that Burton had arrived late on set, accompanied by his adopted daughter Liza. Richardson had apparently bawled at Burton and Burton had bawled back. According to Matthew West, for Woodfall Films, 'Several other occasions of unpunctuality were taken into account when it was decided to replace Burton. I think this is the nub of the dispute.'[1]

Burton was never a fan of Richardson's after that – perhaps unsurprisingly – forever adamant that he was one of the most overrated directors around.[2] To judge from *Laughter in the Dark*, a dazzling mix of directorial blunders, Burton may have had a point.

The part was then offered to Nicol who accepted but, he later said, his salary was a 'twentieth' of Burton's. When Nicol arrived on the set he was strangely nervous, perhaps because he sensed a collective disappointment at the departure of an international superstar, the ultra-charismatic Burton. Nicol played wealthy art dealer Sir Edward More, a character several years older than himself, who abandons his wife (Sian Phillips) for a voluptuous cinema usherette. The nymphet, played sexily but monotonously by Anna Karina, only values his chequebook and continues seeing her boyfriend, Herve (Jean Claude Drouot), one of Edward's former employees. They even dally on a beach near him and then again before his – by this time blind – eyes in a Majorcan villa.

Nicol might have been nervous because he had been rushed into the role. According to Peter Bowles:

> Nicol Williamson, who was considered by his contemporaries, including me, to be the most exciting actor of his generation, took over the part on very, very short notice. He can hardly have had time to read the script, let alone the book on which it was based. (Sometimes that's a good idea!)

Nicol was rarely at ease playing an aristocrat. According to Bowles:

> He was taking over from Richard Burton and was arriving to make love to a very disappointed Anna Karina, who I honestly doubt had ever heard of Nicol. I knew Nicol from various carousals in pubs and parties and I liked him and by the end of the film we became close friends. On the way back to London after his first day of shooting he asked me if he was going to be okay in the part. Being Scottish he was particularly worried that he wasn't managing the Queen's English. I reassured him in every way and was flattered that he had sought my opinion.[3]

As it turns out Nicol had few problems with the accent, more with the flawed script that depicts his art dealer as a total buffoon. Nicol's acting is fine, his expressive, roving eyes gleaming with desire. Yet Edward is such a fool not to see Margot for the materialist bitch she is, that he soon loses sympathy. It's so obvious she loves the trappings, not him, and his naivety grates.

The ludicrous script – accompanied by melodramatic, portentous piano music – just depicts Edward as inadequate. 'It's a judgment on me!', he says, phlegmatically, when he hears of his daughter's death. In Spain the action gets even more risible. Margot and Herve continue their passionate affair while Edward sits on the shore, clad tip to toe in white, too self-involved to notice. He'd only catch on, one feels, if they screwed right in front of him!

Edward, as written, seems a master of the banal. 'Every time I see an ice cream, it reminds me of where I met Margot,' he says at one point. Ha bloody ha!

The plot becomes even more far-fetched after Edward is blinded in an accident. Does he never suspect that Margot is still seeing Herve, even after being duped once? They retreat to a secluded Majorcan cottage and he is sequestered in his bedroom, abandoned by Margot. Yet still he suspects nothing. Doesn't he sense Herve's body odour? We're asked to believe that he never guesses there's a ménage à trois, even when they all share lunch. These, however, are Richardson's shortcomings.

Early on in the filming, Nicol, as was his style, started to test Tony Richardson, perhaps laying markers.

Peter Bowles recalled:

> The first day of shooting had, in fact, been the reshooting of the scenes at Faringdon House in Oxfordshire[4] and once again our splendid hosts gave us a wonderful lunch, served by their staff. Nicol, to everyone's horror, suddenly said, with tremendous venom. 'Tony, why do you speak with that ridiculous false whining camp accent? It's very affected. I want to know why you do it because I think it's silly.' We all received it like a blow in the face, especially Tony. But he gave one of his neighing laughs. 'Oh, come along, Nicol, I don't know what you mean and I certainly don't know why you're saying it.' It was very embarrassing for everyone. As far as I remember, Nicol got up and left the room. I think what Nicol was up to was domination, driven by insecurity. He was going to deliver the first blow by insulting and embarrassing Tony now, up front, straight away, full frontal, with everyone to hear and witness it. He felt he couldn't be fired, I suppose, and he wanted us all to know he was not to be trifled with, that he was dangerous and he was.

Perhaps a good retort would have been that Richardson spoke in a camp accent because he made camp films. Nothing in *Laughter in the Dark* rang true. It's enjoyable as a kind of silly Brit in the sun satire, circa late sixties, but nothing more profound than that.

The funniest sequence takes place on the beach as Nicol's character and the cheating couple keep altering the position of their deckchairs. Also in that scene, as a friend of Edward who reveals all about Margot and Herve's frolic in the water, was Philippa Urquhart. She tells how Richardson cast her:

> I was on holiday in Deya, Majorca, staying at a pensione owned and run by Rupert Graves (son of Robert Graves the poet and author). There were two other actresses staying there, Sheila Reid and Antonia Pemberton. One morning at breakfast Rupert announced that there was a film being made nearby. The director Tony Richardson, was looking for an actress to play a small part in it, and would we be happy to be collected there and then and be taken to the director's apartment? We were driven there immediately. Tony gave each of us a script, went inside and left us sitting on his balcony to have a look at it. Then he called us in

one by one to read the scene. After a bit he reappeared on the balcony and said (he had a lovely slightly camp sort of lisp): 'I thought you were all very good, but the best was Philippa'. So I got the job.

I was given water skiing lessons for a day, but that wasn't nearly enough and I never got very good at it. The scene with Nicol was shot on a beach, with a crowd of onlookers so close that it was rather off-putting, for me anyway. Nicol had enormous nervous energy; he was almost shaking with it. Tony wanted me to be a bit tipsy. My character lets the cat out of the bag in that scene. But I wasn't giving him what he wanted, so he called for some ice cubes and told me to stuff as many as I could into my mouth, and then do the scene. I only managed to get two in, but it seemed to work! Clever director. No fuss, no shouting – just ice cubes!

The major thing that I remember about Nicol was that he was incredibly nervous, or so it seemed. I got the feeling that he was as put off by members of the public on the beach, who were crowding around watching us, as I was. He was a very strong presence, not at all relaxed, completely caught up in his need to concentrate on the scene.[5]

The denouement to *Laughter* is ludicrous. The now blinded Edward, corralled in a hillside villa, is taunted and teased by Herve as he stumbles around. Herve keeps blocking his path with cactus leaves. The Bowles character, his brother-in-law, suddenly arrives in search of Edward and tells him he had seen a stranger at the scene. Nicol then realises the deception and tries to murder his cheating lover. Perhaps by then Nicol knew the material was risible because Bowles found him in a mischievous mood. As he describes it:

Because Nicol is such an exciting actor he could at times be unexpectedly volatile and I had a personal experience of this in a two-handed scene we had together. Nicol's character is blind at this point in the film and he was using a walking stick to get around. The scene was outside and it was a tracking shot, which means the camera was following us on rails. It was the first take. We had rehearsed the dialogue but not the unexpected improvised attack. On 'action', after the first few lines of dialogue, Nicol attacked me. It was an explosion of maddened violence with his heavy walking stick. Fortunately I was an expert in judo and immediately and instinctively defended myself by parrying the blow from Nicol. As I turned him into the air I realised that I must somehow break his fall or he would be hurt as I landed on him. I aborted the perfect Tai Otoshi and screwed around so that he fell partly on top of me. It saved him from what probably would have been serious harm, as his violence had been so propelled.

I was ok and the film still had a leading man. Tony thought it was the funniest thing he had ever seen. 'Oh Nicol, you are naughty, now we will have to do it again.' After we had brushed ourselves off, Nicol Williamson looked at me with unblind eyes and I knew he would never try anything like that again – at least not with me.

Laughter in the Dark was not well received. Michael Billington was the most generous:

> We already knew that there are few actors around better at conveying unquiet desperation but the reassuring thing here is that he creates a character who is completely at home nudging up the prices at Sotheby's or giving arts talks on television. He more than makes up for the unsurprising performances of Anna Karina and Jean Claude Drouat as the conspiratorial lovers.

Pauline Kael, correctly, found the film jarring and blamed Richardson:

> Tony Richardson is, however, a strange mixture of intelligence and insensitivity, a director with terrible lapses of judgment and *Laughter* was one of them. One could never quite be sure what the tone was meant to be, or whether it was alright to laugh out loud at what appeared to be funny.

Leslie Halliwell called it 'an unsatisfactory adaptation of a novel with a very specialised appeal: conventional swing London settings only confuse the spectator'. Philip Strick hit home when he said, 'it fails to create the slightest interest in its trio of repulsive characters'.

Kenneth Tynan thought Nicol was miscast:

> Nicol seemed ill at ease playing a member of the ruling class and in several early scenes he looked like a sheepish butler in his own house. The authority that should have gone with the character's wealth and rank just wasn't there … he was too easily flustered, too perceptively dismayed.

Tynan, however, acknowledged Nicol's skill in depicting blindness. 'It isn't easy to forget the scene in which he weeps, his fingers fumbling for a cigarette, as Karina describes the view of the mountains and ocean that he can't see.'

As for Karina, she said recently that 'it was a mistake for Tony Richardson to change the setting from pre-war Germany to contemporary London with all the miniskirts and bling!'[6]

If Richardson was perhaps overrated as a director, then Jack Gold was almost certainly underrated. *The Reckoning*, Nicol's curiously forgotten foray into the revenge genre, and his second film with Gold, was a thumping good story. Shot in the autumn of 1968, it contains themes that permeated the sixties: class warfare, the questionable morals of the materialist society, the north/south divide, the conflict between old and new values. John McGrath wrote it and so, with Gold at the helm, it was the same team as on *The Bofors Gun*.

Nicol played Michael Marler, a tough, Irish self-made London city businessman who has married 'well' – as they say – into an upper-class family. He enjoys tigerish sex with his posh wife (Ann Bell) who finds his roughness a welcome contrast to her genteel family. He likes speeding through his idyllic-looking (but spiritually bereft?) adopted turf of Virginia Water with its sprawling detached houses and even more detached residents.

Everything falls apart when Marler learns that his father has died after a beating in a pub. He drives back to Liverpool. A voyage of rediscovery ensues as he revisits his childhood home – 'I feel as though I've gone back twenty years' – reunites with his family, reconnects to the earthy values he once scorned and questions his acquired lifestyle. Has he sold out? He despises his wife's prissy dinner party guests and even hates her. 'That Anglo-Saxon bitch. I could happily smash her face in.' A happy marriage, then!

Several British films of the late sixties have an obligatory scene involving a disrupted dinner party. Bored, disgruntled husband resents upper-class tedious table talk, usually gets drunk – swigging from the bottle – and either sullenly retreats into a corner, as in *Inadmissible Evidence*, or, as here in *The Reckoning*, raises hell. But, of course, Marler is devious and streetwise, qualities that helped him rise to the top in British business and will also help him to carry out the honour killing of the lowlife who decked his dad.

The Reckoning has themes explored more softly in *Charlie Bubbles* – self-made successful man returns up north – and more harshly in *Get Carter* where the Caine character returns to Newcastle to avenge his brother's death. At its heart is the Pygmalion-like experience of a man torn between two worlds. Some of the most powerful images have Marler traipsing through derelict areas of Liverpool with its terraced housing and street kids rummaging through rubble. Likewise, in Virginia Water, as he peruses the trendy shops while schoolchildren march past, noses in the air. (Direction from Gold – 'look as snobbish as possible!')

Of course, we shouldn't forget that Marler is Irish Catholic. Just like O'Rourke in *The Bofors Gun* – although not to the same extreme – he hates Brits. He sings nationalist anti-Imperialist songs and reverts to his authentic 'oirish' persona when drunk at his wife's 'velly' British dinner party. It's more honest 'up north' where people get pissed openly, spill their beer and have a punch-up while watching the wrestling. But at least they retain some semblance of spirituality; there's a crucifix in his childhood room together with, coincidentally, an authentic picture of Nicol as a child.

All this could be seen as clichéd fifty years down the line. Are we supposed to sympathise with Marler? The revenge is morally questionable. Should he really kill his father's murderer? Perhaps a punishment beating would be more appropriate. Not that it matters because Marler gets away with everything.

Nevertheless *The Reckoning* was a well-made film with a cast of old reliables, Rachel Roberts as a love interest and Joe Gladwin as a drunk. The script offers some self-insight as Marler ponders his predicament. 'It's like a bad joke about Sicilian gangsters.'

Nicol enjoyed the part. McGrath, speaking in 1970, recalled, 'Nick's commitment to the character was real. He identified with it so much that he nearly over-balanced the picture. Nick reminds me of Wilfrid Lawson. He gives off the same sense of danger and he doesn't give a damn. More than anything, I'd like to see him playing Macbeth.'

Tom Kempinski, later a distinguished playwright (*Duet for One* and *Separation*, among others) – and cast as Nicol's associate Brunzy – recalled an amusing exchange before the drunken cocktail party scene. As they waited outside this huge posh house, Bentleys parked outside, Nicol caught Kempinski eyeing the vehicles. 'Picture Kempinski looking at the things he'll never have,' said Nicol. Kempinski adds it would have been a shrewd observation from Nicol at the time. 'He thought I was a bum and it was so accurate.'

Kempinski continued:

I regarded Nicol as a great actor – certainly on a par with O'Toole or Finney – with a destructive flaw. He was also a marvellous pianist and a wonderful singer and would sit down at the piano between shooting … he was an expressive and brilliant actor but he had this flaw concomitant with great actors. After all, there's a relationship between genius and madness. And the deeper meaning is this. All great artists have damaged childhoods but when you have a damaged childhood it breeds imagination. What would have happened if it hadn't turned out like this? … I also recall a certain cynicism … always a sign of hurt, but he could also be enormously witty and funny.[7]

Gold remembered that at the end of filming, Nicol, who liked 'stirring', was presented with a six-foot wooden spoon. He also noted Nicol's unerring talent for comic impersonations of everyone around him.

Many critics thought *The Reckoning* was a notch above *The Bofors Gun* and perhaps, technically, it's more accomplished – with a cynical anti-hero people could relate to. John Russell Taylor said:

The film, written by John McGrath, and directed by Jack Gold marks a considerable advance on their first collaboration *The Bofors Gun* … the film is excellently acted, soberly but confidently directed and unexpectedly enjoyable, and some of the little scenes, like the hero's incredulous morning after realisation that everyone expects him to kill a man himself, or the little footnote his wife provides to their after all rather satisfactory marriage, have a sharp feeling of unrehearsed truth.

Leslie Halliwell called it an 'interesting melodrama of a man disgusted with both bourgeois and working-class values, slickly made and fast moving'. Michael Billington noted that:

I wouldn't say it greatly extends his range but it confirms that there are few actors better at displaying a blend of external aggressiveness and inner discontent … in fact, burning my critical boats, I'd say it was one of the most compelling debuts I've ever seen any actor make in the cinema.

The Reckoning was an underrated film, just as good in its own way as *Get Carter*, but perhaps more complex. Nicol's character is always riveting if sometimes objectionable. But as our hero says at the end, 'If I can get away with that I can get away with anything.' This could stand as some kind of statement on Nicol's life. Nicol himself cited the film as an example of his best work.

This clutch of films, especially *The Bofors Gun* and *The Reckoning* and the film of *Inadmissible Evidence*, established Nicol as a first-rate screen actor. Significantly, in both *Inadmissible Evidence* and *The Reckoning*, he plays older than his age. Many actors in those days seemed more mature than their years. But these were powerful breakout performances.

Pauline Kael, usually a shrewd observer, took Nicol to task in an essay for *The New Yorker*, entitled *English Bull*, in which she slayed him for being, in effect, too forceful and crude. She charged that Nicol was not only the proverbial bull in a china shop but not even a particularly adroit one at that:

Nicol Williamson is a violently self-conscious actor whose effect on the camera is like that of the singers who used to shatter crystal. Nicol Williamson is always 'brilliant' and 'dazzling'. He is brilliant, he is dazzling – yet he's awful. You feel as if he were trying to reach out of the screen and strong arm you. The great movie actors know when to cool it and how to relax on camera and just be. By his fifth movie, it's just about impossible to take his snarling and whining seriously; it's just the Williamson routine … he is probably the worst major and greatly gifted actor on the English-speaking screen today … Nicol Williamson has no centre as an actor, no core to his characters, nothing one can trust and fall back on. You never have the sense of how his characters would be if things were going well for them.[8]

Kael was one of the most respected critics around and Nicol did read her article. That review, Nicol later told Kenneth Tynan, was 'like POW'. Kael especially liked Brando and Newman, both overtly 'naturalistic' mumblers and sexy T-shirt types.

If you look at some of Nicol's later performances, particularly in *The Human Factor* and *Black Widow*, they were totally different, beautifully modulated and subtle. In *The Bofors Gun* and *The Reckoning* he played forceful characters because that's what the characters were like. But, as Brando said, 'you can't act unless you are what you are' – in other words actors bring some of their own personalities to their roles.

Penelope Gilliatt,[9] John Osborne's third wife, remarked of Nicol, 'Nick likes jousting with people. But he jousts to win. And, of course, he's the congenital nay-sayer.' Nicol was coming into his own and about to challenge for the prestige prize. Until then the ultimate Hamlet had been Gielgud or Olivier. Nicol was about to change all that.

6

CAGED TIGER

'The trouble with people like Walter Kerr is they can't forgive me for making Hamlet someone who is insufferably alive.'

Nicol Williamson

Great though Nicol had been in *Inadmissible Evidence*, and in his first three major screen roles, the legend surrounding Nicol really took off with his Hamlet. His Prince was quite simply revolutionary. We could say that Nicol tore up the rule book. Perhaps this would obviously stand as a metaphor for Nicol's whole life. Or maybe Nicol never knew there even was one?

Until then Hamlet had traditionally been played by genuflecting to the verse, stressing the lyricism and meter. Gielgud, 'the greatest actor in the world from the neck up', had been the finest practitioner of this musical interpretation.

Olivier's Hamlet is a little less musical but doesn't ignore the rhythm. Burton's Hamlet – and recordings of his 1964 performance are available on YouTube – was a beautiful volcanic eruption, sexy and meaningful, but also inherently rhythmic.[1]

After Burton there seemed to be a gap while people decided who was to fill their shoes. Nicol would have been aware of the great Hamlets of the past, of course, but he certainly wouldn't have imitated them or, even, been much influenced by them. According to Michael Pennington, who played Laertes in the stage and film version, 'he was very much his own man'.

Many years later, in 1996, when Nicol played John Barrymore in his one-man show, *Jack*, Barrymore offers his thoughts on portrayals of Hamlet. We can assume that Nicol – although speaking through Barrymore – shared these observations:

American audiences had been subjected to years of posers, prettifying attitudes, passing it off as great acting. [Launches into an exaggerated, rather prissy Gielgud/

Olivier hybrid impersonation for effect.] That's not acting, that's like sticking a finger up your arse for Chrissakes. A good actor is like a good stripper. You have to lay everything bare arsed naked, show it all, your innermost self, your soul within the role, however much it pains or offends others or yourself. That's when your balls clank, that's stardom. You play the line of your character by understanding his words and his heart and the words automatically become the music, your ally, because it's alive; it's real, it's sense, not posture.[2]

Nicol, as Barrymore, was talking of a bygone era, of course, but this was also his view of certain contemporaries who, he believed, were too dandified. Luke Williamson, Nicol's son – although not even a twinkle at this point – remembered having long conversations with his father about Shakespeare. Nicol's opinion on Shakespeare was crucial to our understanding of his approach to Hamlet. 'He thought that Olivier represented much of what was wrong with Shakespeare … the over-flowery speech disconnected from the actual meaning,' said Luke. 'Dad's Hamlet was much more visceral and claustrophobic. When you hear him speak you don't have to think too hard about what he's saying; it's all so understandable. He thought Shakespeare had gotten to a point where it was people reciting lines for the sake of the lines rather than the feeling and meaning.'[3]

Tony Richardson, who had directed Nicol in *Laughter in the Dark*, had decided to stage a production at London's Roundhouse. Built in 1847 on Chalk Farm Road to the north of Camden Town, the Roundhouse had been conceived as a railway engine shed with a turntable for the London and Birmingham railway. A circular structure, gloomy, damp and cavernous with large wooden beams, it smelled of creosote.

Anjelica Huston hoped to be cast as Ophelia, although in the end the part went to Marianne Faithfull with Huston as her understudy. She recalled:

Nicol Williamson, a tall laconic Scottish actor, played Hamlet with a nasal twang and partial lisp; this was not affectation but Nicol's natural speaking voice. And without doubt broke through some conceits as to how the Great Dane should be played. Tony and Nicol rarely seemed to agree and Tony munched nervously throughout the period of rehearsal. Anthony Hopkins was playing King Claudius and Judy Parfitt was Gertrude and their chemistry was powerful. But after the show was up and running Nicol would on occasion leave the stage without warning. This was always an interesting moment for the rest of the cast who without benefit of a curtain, would trail offstage after him into the wings in mute embarrassment.

Nicol was also an amazing actor and had a very strong presence. He was always entertaining to watch. One night, the tip flew off his fencing foil in the graveyard scene and out into the audience. Nicol calmly stopped the action and asked if everyone was ok. Then crying 'on with the show' he fell to the ground as Michael Pennington, playing Laertes, immediately stabbed him. Marianne and I were both flirting with Nicol. We spent some time in his dressing room between shows.[4]

Marianne Faithfull, like many stars who worked with Tony Richardson, was not especially flattering about him:

He had a Machiavellian streak. He wasn't just a bisexual narcissist living his life. He was a director which gave him licence to indulge in serious game-playing. He was bitchy, sarcastic and ruthless. In other words, your typical director. I got very little direction from him. He just let me talk out there and vibrate – but I did get a lot of manipulation. Directors will do almost anything to extract the reactions they want from you. At some point I figured out that my affair with Nicol Williamson had been set up by Tony … Tony wanted to get that charge out of the two of us on stage. We would make love in Nicol's dressing room before going on stage.[5]

Faithfull said that Nicol helped her a lot with the technical side of performance, learning the correct meter. She noted that Nicol read his in a run-on North Country lilt meter 'but for that to work the rest of us had to do ours in iambic pentameter'.

Hamlet opened in February 1969. Author and film historian Kevin Brownlow remembers the first night when there was a typical 'Nicolish' episode:

Nicol said 'To be or not to be … oh fuck!' and walked off the stage. Then you heard Richardson in the audience say, 'Come back, Nicol'. And at that point in the play, you didn't even have Marianne Faithfull to look at while he was off-stage.[6]

Despite that inauspicious beginning, most British critics were ecstatic. Irving Wardle in *The Times* described Nicol as 'our finest actor under 40' and continued:

Hamlet is supposed to be actor proof but other much-admired young stars have been defeated by it. His is also the first performance I have seen that escapes the shadow of Gielgud and annexes it as his own territory. He does this principally through force of temperament and passionate attention to the feeling behind the lines.

Michael Billington said:

It lacks irony, delicacy, gentleness. Its virtues, however, plea trumpet-tongued on its behalf ... It informs the lines with a bristling, bruising intelligence and is constantly showing Hamlet to be testing those around him ... and it provides the rarest of all sensations, the feeling that the actor rejoices wholeheartedly in his presence on the stage! Some actors take the stage by default. Nicol Williamson takes it by storm.

Michael Pennington, playing Laertes, recalled Nicol's innovation:

He could, and did, play Hamlet on a couple of bottles of wine without dropping a stitch and, on another occasion, a few hours after a serious car crash ... the violence of his performance was much discussed but not enough its nimble humour and the tentative benevolence that he brought to the scenes with the players and the gravedigger.

Nicol walking off the stage should not, according to Pennington, detract from his brilliance. 'Nicol's work was electrifying, of course, self-lacerating but deft, technically awesome and ferociously disciplined. Most of what is written about his unreliability is utter tosh.'

Roland Jaquarello thought it a Hamlet for its generation, 'Rebellious, contemptuous, cynical and angry with flashes of ironic humour'. Nevertheless some 'snobs' took exception. 'Somebody chalked up "Prince of Darlington" on one of the surrounding flats,' he recalled. 'Probably an upset aesthete who wanted a more obviously traditional, poetic Hamlet. Nicol certainly made the part his own and his Hamlet was impressively unpredictable and vulnerable.'

J.C. Trewin, in *The Illustrated London News*, also criticised the coarseness in Nicol's enunciation, something echoed by American critics:

It is the voice that troubles me. Harsh and rasping, it is no doubt the voice of our period, a period that too often rejects beauty of tone and suggests – in some form of inverted snobbery – that an actor of vocal splendour must be listening to himself. Surely there is no reason why sense and sound should be at war?

Trewin acknowledged, however, 'that my personal discontent was not shared by the Roundhouse audience'.

Tony Richardson felt that Nicol's acting deteriorated during the run. Just before the production was due to go to America, Richardson returned from a Riviera holiday to see the final performance. He disliked what he saw and called a company meeting, singling out Nicol for particular blame. Nicol later told Kenneth Tynan – with deadly emphasis imitating the original showdown – how, in turn, he cornered his director and told him off for reprimanding him so openly. 'I said to him, "I'm not going to ask you not to talk to me like that again. You-will-NEVER-talk-to-me-like-that again."'

Richardson later offered his own version of events. 'When it opened in February 1969 *Hamlet* was an enormous hit and received international plaudits. Nicol Williamson was recognised as his generation's Hamlet; without illusions, yet humorous and ironic, capable of instant rage and mockery and with a sad existential resignation.'

But, he believed, Nicol became progressively undisciplined:

> He was soon over the top in his own acting and reckless of other people's feelings. Soon after the opening, he was already overacting shamelessly, although he didn't know it. I attacked him for it. He never forgave me but in the early days when I knew him he was terrific. [7]

At least by then they had Nicol's Hamlet on celluloid. Richardson's movie was shot at the Roundhouse in fewer than ten days. Nicol subsequently revealed he had been paid the 'princely' sum of $2,400. Nicol later said the movie was intended to be 'claustrophobic … because it really is about people trapped in a sort of a prison'.

His screen Hamlet was likened by some to a caged tiger, a good analogy for someone like Nicol who always seemed restless, prowling, pacing up and down hotel suites and sound stages, someone who could never keep still.

The darkness of the venue, the damp stone walls and flickering candles conjure up the gloom of Elsinore. The film captures Nicol's electric stage performance and corroborates the reviews. Nicol says the lines as if they had just occurred to him. His is a nasal, treacly voice in contrast to Hopkins's more majestic 'reciting'. Few seemed to notice that Judy Parfitt was obviously too young to play Hamlet's mother but, ironically, Nicol is at his most moving with her – sobbing and whining.

The famous monologues, those played for maximum effect by the likes of Olivier, Gielgud and Burton, are downplayed by Nicol. For example, his 'what a piece of work is a man' speech, delivered to Rosencrantz and Guildenstern, is rendered as a series of comic asides, addressing them in turn, his head bobbing to and fro like a spectator at a tennis match. It's a deliberate choice to strip the poetry and play it 'straight' or, as rather in this case, for comic effect.

John Russell Taylor thought the film captured the essence of Hamlet, 'Though there are moments when his diction grates a little, his reading makes such overall sense of the part that it does seem inescapably the Hamlet of the present.'

Pauline Kael, however, disliked it, saying his Hamlet lacked sex appeal:

Nicol Williamson's surly Hamlet is more in the American spirit; his acting is all pathos and vituperation, snarls and tantrums. Yet he isn't really strong; he's such a weeper. Bearded and with a nasal twang, he's deliberately, wretchedly unattractive. He stares so much he's in danger of wearing out his eyeballs. Hamlet's speeches, as Nicol Williamson delivers them, lack beauty … it is shot almost exclusively in oppressive close-ups, without concern for locating the players in terms of where they are or what they are to each other.

Kael then delivered a final salvo, and one often quoted since, that might have floored Nicol but boosted a young rival's career no end, 'Anthony Hopkins, though he is a very young Claudius, has a handsome Burton-like authority but he's so much more appealing than Nicol Williamson that one rather wishes Claudius was left in peace to rule the country, since Hamlet is obviously unfit.' (Doubtless, Nicol would have disagreed. Luke told me that 'Anthony Hopkins is a lovely guy but Dad didn't really rate him – *at least back then*; he felt he was a collection of mannerisms'.)

Anjelica Huston later wrote that she had hoped that Richardson would offer her the part of Ophelia when *Hamlet* went to the US. In the end, however, it went to Francesca Annis, one of Nicol's favourite leading ladies.[8] Constance Cummings now played Gertrude and Patrick Wymark, who died the following year, was Claudius.

Hamlet premiered at New York's Lunt Fontanne Theatre on 1 May 1969 and ran for fifty-four performances before going on to Boston. Some hinted that Nicol should be grateful to equity that the British company had been allowed to appear on Broadway virtually intact. Nicol was having none of that. 'Without me there would have been no production of *Hamlet* and I wouldn't do it unless I could play with the actors I want to play with,' he said.

The American run was marked by an infamous incident, constantly cited in Nicol's obituaries, when, on 23 June, the opening night at Boston's Colonial Theatre, he walked off the stage at the start of Act 2.

Stage manager (now producer) Howard Panter later recalled Nicol's exit. 'The first night was going very badly. The audience was restless. There was a lot of rustling. There was a bit of corpsing on stage and the performance was deteriorating.'

Lionel Larner, Nicol's agent, remembered it differently:

> It was incredible. He flung a goblet clear across the stage and marched off. The management argued with him for twenty minutes and then he came back and told the audience he didn't feel at his best and he thought they were being cheated. He said they could have their money back if they wanted. As it happened, they didn't and so he went on with the show.[9]

Larner expanded on the incident many years down the line:

> That was a night I'll never forget. The producer, Norman Twain, had gone for a walk. When the curtain came down after Nicol's exit I went straight to Nicol's dressing room where I found him with his head in his hands. He told me that he just couldn't bring the company up, couldn't lift it. He also told me, to my horror, that this was his last performance on the professional stage. Ever. Of course, I told him that he really should get back on to the stage.

After the curtain descended, Panter addressed the audience and tried to calm things down. Nicol eventually returned about fifteen minutes later and said, 'I deeply apologise. There are times when you get to a certain point, when you can't really care about going on any further. My voice is gone. I'm giving a bad, bad, bad performance. I hate everything I've done tonight.'

Panter believed this was no flippant fit on Nicol's part. 'Everyone was so shaken that the concentration was very sharp. I don't think it was a stunt at all. He was deeply depressed.' Ben Aris, playing Rosencrantz, later recalled, 'He had the chutzpah to stop mid-stream. When he came back it was a million times better than it was before.'

Larner remembers the whole incident wisely. Nicol had been carrying Hamlet for months; he had done several recent TV appearances and was simply exhausted. The press followed Larner back to the Ritz and he tried to reason with them. 'If Maria Callas had done this in *Tosca* you wouldn't have been surprised.' Yet, somehow, with Hamlet, it was different. People expected actors to be robots.

Fortunately, back in the sixties, actors' indiscretions were tolerated more than today. Patrick Wymark, for example, was a notorious drinker who made the likes of Richard Harris or, indeed Nicol, seem small league. Many at the time worried more about Wymark's reliability than Nicol's. Journalist Stephen Claypole recalls:

> In 1969, when I was the New York correspondent of *The Evening News*, I took a visiting Fleet Street executive, Phil Wrack, to the legendary bar at the Algonquin

Hotel. Sitting rather rigidly in the corner was Patrick Wymark who was playing Claudius downwind from Nicol Williamson's Hamlet …

After a couple of the most entertaining hours, Wrack and I somehow levered Wymark into a yellow cab and got him to the stage door within minutes of curtain-up. At the end of a four-city tour Wymark contacted me to thank me for the lift. It gave me the chance to ask him about the evening, in Boston, when Williamson had hurled a goblet across the stage and stopped the performance, protesting that he was an inadequate Hamlet.

'Inadequate?' snorted Wymark. 'Nonsense. I breathed on the bugger!'[10]

It would be silly to deny that Nicol's penchant for walk-offs damaged his reputation. One 'enraged' theatregoer, W. Cunliffe, even wrote to *The Stage* to complain:

Mr Williamson only seems to tackle the most strenuous of parts, but if he is unable to sustain a run he should either limit his appearances to a few performances as he did in *Diary of a Madman* or concentrate solely on film work, where the audience will not suffer by the occasional outburst. Can you imagine the theatrical knights storming off stage? Surely some of the classic parts – Othello, Lear, for instance – must draw on an actor's resources in the same way.[11]

The letter prompted a spirited defence of Nicol from another theatregoer named Lesley Denny:

I feel I must say in defence of Nicol Williamson that he is succeeding in something few other great actors have even attempted: in sustaining and enlarging the creative act at each and every performance, often every day of every week, over a period of six months or more. Besides the obvious physical strain such playing lays upon the actor, there is also the greater danger of overwhelming 'tiredness of the spirit' as Mr Williamson puts it. Creating something new and fresh for the audience at every performance is something that should only be encouraged and complimented for it is very rarely seen these days, even in rep. And it is creditable that Mr Williamson should have the courage of his convictions to walk off the stage when he himself believes he is not giving a 100 per cent performance.[12]

The walk-off notwithstanding, American reviewers liked his Hamlet but were less ecstatic than the Brits. One of Nicol's favourite critics was Ted Kalem[13] of *Time* who captured the essence of what Nicol was trying to do:

He cuts through the music of the Shakespearean line to the marrow of the meaning … some actors occupy the stage, a few rule it. Some actors hold an audience – a few possess it. Some actors light up a scene. A few ignite the play. These combustible few daze with the x factors of acting – intensity, intelligence and authority. There is a royalty apart from the role and when an Olivier, Gielgud, Nicol Williamson or Irene Papas tread the stage, their fellow actors are as rapt as the audience.

John Simon, in *New York* magazine, railed against Nicol's voice, accent and appearance. Read today, his comments seem like extreme snobbery:

> It remained for Nicol Williamson's Hamlet to suffer from an acute sinus condition … Add to this the accent. It has been called Midland, North Country and Cockney with a loose overlay of culture. Only Henry Higgins could correctly place it South of the Beatles or North of the Stones and identify the veneer as grammar or council school. But even Colonel Pickering could tell it isn't Hamlet.

Simon went on to refer to (Nicol's) 'equine head with the mad Viking locks jiggling behind the nape and neck; the unweeded, piratical beard and brushwood moustache; the obstreperously lower class features. The gangling skulking body; the legs, not exactly spindly but with more than a hint of octopus about them – all this is unsettling and finally disruptive.'

Also less complimentary was Walter Kerr:[14]

> The voice is a quick twang, the sort of sound a man might make if he spoke rapidly while carefully pinching the bridge of his nose. The performance as a whole seems one given by a museum guide who obviously knows what he is talking about but is severely crippled by a blocked sinus.

Nicol told Kenneth Tynan, 'He [Kerr] reviewed my voice, not my interpretation. Jesus Christ, I was trying to make an interesting noise, not a beautiful one. The trouble with people like Kerr is they can't forgive me for making Hamlet someone who is insufferably alive.'

Nicol later said he felt that;

> American critics wanted a cardboard figure, someone out of costume history. They're more right-wing than the average London audience. They're used to seeing a company do *Hamlet* well dressed and well spoken. They think that's what Shakespeare is … I wanted to offer more in terms of reality. So you could see

people in real situations. But I don't ignore the meter or verse. I use the poetry to say something. As for my accent, nothing was terribly princely then.

Audiences, however, generally loved Nicol's Hamlet and a whole new generation became interested in Shakespeare as a result. The crowds gathered nightly outside the stage door to get an audience with their idol. Actor Ron Fassler, then just 10 years old, tells a charming story in his book:

With little knowledge of who he was at the time (let alone his reputation), I had no idea what was potentially in store for me going backstage to meet Williamson. I was so fired up and excited by what had just transpired that as soon as the curtain came down, I ran from my box seat and raced to the stage door. Arriving breathless, I was met by a brusque doorman who blew me off 'Wait outside,' he said.

This was a first. What happened? Was my kid charm wearing off? Maybe I wasn't as irresistible as I thought.

After a long wait, during which time about two dozen people had gathered on the sidewalk surrounding me, the doorman popped his head out, looked straight at me and in the same gruff manner said, 'You!'

I looked back at the others as if to say, 'So long, suckers.'

Once inside, my new friend pointed upstairs. 'First door on the right.'

I went up, knocked, and a deep voice ordered me to enter. And there was Nicol Williamson, an imposing sight at 6ft 3in. He barely looked up while attending to buttoning his cuffs, a cigarette dangling from his bottom lip.

'Hello.' Then, looking past me, he asked, 'Where are your parents?'

I said, 'At home.'

A look of surprise crossed his face. 'You came by yourself?'

'Yeah,' I said. 'I couldn't get anyone to go with me.'

Williamson laughed. I didn't realise I'd said anything funny. It was the truth. No one I asked was interested.

'Did you enjoy the show?'

'Oh yes. Very much.'

'Did you understand it?'

'I think so. I do have one question. When you saw the ghost, did you really see him or was that in your mind?'

Williamson stared me down. For a moment, I believe he considered having a real conversation with me. But after a brief deliberation, he smiled, went back to his cuff-buttoning and said, 'I think I'll leave you to consider that.'

He then signed my programme with a flourish and I was on my way.[15]

Another theatregoer, Frank Corrado, who saw Nicol's Hamlet in Boston, compared Nicol to Burton in terms of vocal range:

> The only voice to rival his on stage in my experience was Burton's, also in *Hamlet* in New York in 1964. If Burton's voice was an organ, [Nicol's] was a trumpet with overtones of the richest clarinet … in the midst of the 'What a piece of work is a man' speech, he reached down and picked up a scrap of paper that had somehow deposited itself on the stage, and without missing a beat of text, and somehow in total character, drop-kicked the random scrap into the front row. It was a curiously sublime moment.[16]

Another fan, Stella Rodrigues, recalled the influence of Nicol's Hamlet. 'His performance triggered my immense love for Shakespeare's plays and I will be forever grateful to him for that.'

When the play had ended Nicol seemed keen to downplay the acclaim. 'Even if there is such a thing as the greatest actor I don't think it's important. It's important what you do, not what they call you.' Yet, in interviews, he sometimes criticised other venerated actors:

> I've seen Guinness,[17] Olivier and Scofield. After a couple of times each I can tell you how they do it … The public is very easily gulled. You hear them say, 'Oh, wasn't he great?' when an actor has buried a scene under an avalanche of technique with the most dreadful … I have ever seen. The public always wants what it wants but I'm not able to give them that kind of satisfaction. I would never pander to the public. Once you do, you become a star and then you belong to the public and they have every right to you. However, I'm not going to be shoved around by tinpot Hitlers. Let them work out their neuroses with their own shrinks … critics are necessary for some things but too much importance is placed on them. In fact, they sometimes lie about shows they have seen.

Nicol's performance at the Roundhouse was certainly seen by the British Prime Minister. The result was an invitation rarely extended to a British performer.

7

NICOL AT NIXON'S

'That star is here tonight – the man the Prime Minister says is the greatest Hamlet.'

President Richard Nixon

Long before Donald Trump swept all the awards for the most hated occupant of the White House – indeed until 'the Donald' annihilated all historical contenders – chief villain for liberals everywhere was President Richard Nixon. And this was while Watergate was still an anonymous Washington building, i.e. before the real scandals broke.

Nixon was never a movie fan. Kirk Douglas tells in his autobiography *The Ragman's Son* of how Nixon confused Burt Lancaster's movie, *Trapeze*, for his own. Yet Nixon had a canny eye for good publicity and liked to surround himself with famous Republican supporters – John Wayne, Frank Sinatra, and Dean Martin – and even managed, far more incongruously, to get a controversial hug from Sammy Davis Junior and a meeting with Elvis during his presidency.

In March 1969, Nixon had visited the UK as the guest of British Prime Minister, Harold Wilson. The two leaders broached peripheral issues such as the Vietnam War before turning to the real 'hot' news – the production currently being staged at the Roundhouse. Wilson apparently told Nixon that the greatest Hamlet of his era was Nicol Williamson. Nixon had never heard of Nicol but remembered Wilson's words.

The following January, Nixon started staging a series of performances called *Evenings at the White House*. The entertainment would begin at around 8 p.m. lasting about an hour, followed by a reception and dancing. The first to appear was long-time Republican Red Skelton, followed in February by the cast of the Broadway musical *1776*. And who to ask for March? Nixon, recalling his conversation with Wilson, invited Nicol. The idea was that Nicol would perform, mainly, excerpts from *Hamlet*. Nicol accepted and travelled to Washington for rehearsals accompanied by critic Kenneth Tynan who later penned his observations of Nicol's eccentricities in a 15,000-word essay called *Nicol Williamson: the Road to the White House*. The account was originally written for the *New Yorker* and then published a few years later in his book *The Sound of Two Hands Clapping*.

Releasing details of 'intimate' conversations earned Tynan the enmity of Nicol – a 'cunt' being Nicol's favourite epithet for the renowned journalist. Although exactly what Nicol thought Tynan would do with his observations – just jot them down in a secret diary? – is anyone's guess. Tynan had been the foremost theatrical critic of his generation, the first person to say 'fuck' on British TV, so publishing his impressions of Nicol was hardly surprising. (Luke, reflecting on the whole 'reportage', understands his dad's anger but believes that Tynan made some 'good observations'.)

Tynan's account affords us an intimate insight into Nicol's psychology, notably his refusal to back down when he feels affronted, whether by directors, actors or critics. According to Tynan, 'he has a sly but well-organised urge to dominate whatever group he finds himself in'. The most obvious question, however, was why Nicol, someone of 'presumed liberal convictions' (Tynan's words and Nicol does not demur), would agree to entertain Nixon, then regarded as an ultra-conservative. 'I wouldn't act in South Africa,' Nicol told Tynan, 'but, otherwise, anything goes.' (Luke told me that he believed his dad was apolitical and that he certainly didn't vote in the last twenty years or so of his life.)

The wonderfully indiscreet essay is laced with amusing vignettes. Take Nicol's classic (alcoholic's?) self-delusion. 'I have low blood pressure and a low blood-sugar count. Sometimes I get terribly dizzy. I drink to prevent myself collapsing.' 'I never booze before acting' – yes, Nicol said *that* – and a wonderful explanation of his fracas with David Merrick, 'As I a rule I detest people who get into fights.' Yes, he said *that* too! 'They are thunderously boring, and that kind of behaviour is fantastically undesirable but Merrick had to be insulted and insults must be delivered with style.'

Nicol also reveals much of his work credo: his dislike of long engagements, his belief that actors act too much (despite describing himself as 'the ideal subject for a director') and perhaps an over-discriminating attitude to offers. For example, Tynan notes that Nicol had declined $400,000 to play Enobarbus in Charlton Heston's film of *Antony and Cleopatra*,[1] as well as the part of the elder son opposite Laurence Olivier in Mike Nichols's prospective production of *Long Day's Journey into Night* at the National Theatre. (There appeared to be no hard feelings. Before he departs for Washington with Nicol, Olivier warns Tynan, 'Be careful, or that man will magic you!' Sarah Miles wrote in her memoir, 'Olivier thought he [Nicol] was an actor of spectacular ability, but was wary of Nicol's inability to work within a team.') Tynan ultimately concludes that Nicol, despite his roustabout behaviour, is a depressive by nature. 'He is never exultant or euphoric. His relaxed moods are respites, temporary, you feel, from an unassuageable melancholy.'

Tynan recalls Nicol's binges, monumental hangovers, and last-minute ambivalence about performing at the White House ('I should never have accepted', he says at one point) as well as an account of suicidal driving and his disdain for possessions. 'As long as his food, drink, shelter and transportation are paid for, he has no financial ambitions,' says Tynan, noting almost as an aside that Nicol's favourite wines are great Moselles, burgundies like La Tâche and Grands-Echezeaux, as well as the finest champagnes.

Nicol's big day arrived on 19 March 1970. By then Nicol had insisted that *Times* critic Walter Kerr, who had criticised his Hamlet, should not be in attendance, so Kerr withdrew.

Lionel Larner's assistant, Ro Diamond, who was present throughout the show, recalled that right up to the performance there was discussion about the content. Nicol was determined to include other writers, not just speeches from *Hamlet*. 'He always did the opposite of what other people wanted and, of course, he always loved to sing,' said Diamond. She remembered arriving at the gates of the White House. 'Are you the entertainment?' asked the guards on duty. 'Yes, and a pigeon will fly out of my pocket,' replied Nicol. Diamond was impressed that Nicol complimented her on her new mink coat – 'what a divine coat!' – in the run-up to such a momentous evening.[2]

Nixon explained to his assembled White House guests, who included chat show host Dick Cavett, British broadcaster and current ambassador to the United States John Freeman, Secretary of State Henry Kissinger, and actress Ellen Holly, why he had chosen Nicol. The President recalled his conversation with Wilson:

> Everyone wondered what we were talking about. Now I can tell you. The Prime Minister was telling me about a great new star they had on the scene. He said that the new star was probably the best new Hamlet. He said: 'You should see him in London.' I said 'I can't stay another day.' So because I couldn't stay in London, that star is here tonight – the man the Prime Minister says is the greatest Hamlet.

Nicol performed speeches from Arthur Miller's *Death of a Salesman* (perhaps this critique of the American Dream was a sop to Nixon's critics),[3] Maitland's attack in *Inadmissible Evidence* on the uncaring coolness of the young (doubtless this would have chimed more with Nixon's world view given the haranguing mobs demonstrating against him on campuses), an extract from T.S. Eliot's *Little Gidding*, an erotic poem by E.E. Cummings, excerpts from Beckett and various songs: *Baby, Won't You Please Come Home?*, *Dunsinane Blues* and the winter lyric from *Love's Labour's Lost*.

Writer Edward Allan Faine described Nicol's performance thus:

> The king and queen [Richard and Pat Nixon] finally entered to prolonged applause and seated themselves front and centre … suddenly a heralding blast by the WGJB [The World's Greatest Jazz Band] – the evening's performance was about to begin. First up, a short mock-Elizabethan overture by the band. Thus summoned, fellow player Nicol Williamson, wearing informal brown slacks and a blue cashmere shirt with a paisley scarf tied casually at his neck, sauntered forth to issue a Shakespearean soliloquy. In a voice characterised as a North Country nasal twang (*Washington Post* drama critic Richard L. Coe) or, alternatively, a quick twang, the sort of sound a man might make if he spoke rapidly while carelessly pinching the bridge of his nose (*New York Times* drama critic Walter Kerr), Nicol Williamson essayed Hamlet's speech to the players. 'Speak the speech I pray you, as I pronounced it to you, trippingly on the tongue.'
>
> A proper bow, polite applause and another WGJB fanfare followed. Nicol Williamson then limned a Samuel Beckett poem, followed by another rather silly fanfare with two howling clinkers that caused Bob Haggart[4] to go bug-eyed with shock. If the mock-Elizabethan overture and the musical bridges sounded lame, it was because a dumbstruck Haggart had been told to compose and arrange them only two days before. They were purposeful, though, giving the entertainment time to catch his breath and rearrange his thoughts. At this point, some in the audience – one could only imagine – adjusted their high expectations for the evening downwards. Patience would be rewarded, however. A return to the bard: Williamson as Hotspur, confronted the King as in Henry IV, Part 1, 'England forever and always.'[5]

Tynan recalled that Nixon's face was 'rigid and expressionless but he was staring straight into Nicol's eyes'. He recorded that Cavett enjoyed the show, likewise Kissinger, and that Freeman was particularly 'knocked out' by the Beckett. The Nixons excused themselves early as was their custom. (Perhaps there was another reason. The Cambodian government had collapsed the same day after a coup and the new Prime Minister had issued an ultimatum to North Vietnamese forces to leave the country, ushering in a dangerous new phase of the Vietnam War.)

Nicol continued the party. 'This should be an evening that swings. We should all have fun and get boozed. And I hope to God we don't wake the people upstairs,' he told the audience. After the evening wrapped, Diamond said that they all headed to a popular Washington restaurant called The White Castle for hamburgers. Tynan was still in tow, scribbling notes the whole time.

A few days later Nicol received a letter from the President:

> Your magnificent performance in the White House on 19 March surpassed even the exceptionally favourable advance notices which I had received, and I want to express my thanks to you once more for your generous gift of your time and talent. Your presence made a spectacularly successful evening deeply memorable as well.

Earning plaudits from Nixon was a mixed blessing in a business in which 'appeasing' such a conservative figure was hardly hip. As such, Nicol was brave to accept. Luke believes that Nicol, although no reactionary, retained, not exactly a soft spot, but a sliver of warmth for Nixon.

Nicol had also proved popular with his fellow musicians. Bandleader and composer Bud Freeman reflected in his autobiography that:

> Nicol had very little time to prepare for the tremendous amount of material he had to remember. I played at all the rehearsals. They were tedious and difficult, and I didn't have to remember anything. Nicol is one of the finest men I've ever met; he's unselfish, charming, kind, and considerate.[6]

If people thought that Nicol was rowing back from his 'bad boy' image, however, they were soon put right. A few months later, Dick Cavett, one of the more intelligent talk show hosts, who had attended the White House event, invited Nicol on to his programme. First up was Nora Ephron, journalist and screenwriter – later famous for *Silkwood*, *When Harry Met Sally* and *Sleepless in Seattle*. Nicol was the second guest. At some point, however, Nicol declared he was tired of waiting and left the green room.

A chat show host running out of chat was like a newsreader live on air finding out there is no news. Or a presenter at the Academy Awards losing the envelope – or, should we say, being given the wrong envelope? Cavett had to endure a heart-stopping hiatus of improvisation. 'Nora and I, having used up all our good stuff and at the point where I was supposed to say "my next guest", now faced what felt like a Sahara-wide half hour of remaining airtime to fill.'[7] Cavett admitted he later fantasised about poisoning Nicol.

Away from that madness, perhaps Nicol's most significant revelation to Tynan had been that he was no longer interested in being the world's greatest actor. As if to prove his point, the rest of 1970 was a surprisingly fallow period for Nicol who also claimed he was broke. 'I'm committing professional suicide telling you that,' he confided to *Chicago Tribune* journalist Carol Kramer. 'People, especially in this city, will say: "He's finished." But I couldn't care less. My own security is knowing that I will always be employed by directors who want to work with me and will insist on it.' Nicol also refuted the 'difficult' label. 'All you have to do to find out if I'm temperamental is to talk to any of the directors I've worked with.'

Then, that summer, a wonderful reunion ushered in the happiest period in Nicol's life. Nicol managed to get the whereabouts of Jill, who was in London at the time, and dialled her number. Jill continues:

> My father was about to turn fifty and didn't want to know. He borrowed a friend's sailing boat to go round the Aegean so nobody would find out. My mother and I and one of our sisters went back to the UK where my parents had rented a little apartment in Goodwin's Court in Covent Garden. One day, in August, the phone rang. Only my parents and my cousin knew my number and so I was unprepared. I heard this man's voice, saying 'hello' but he wouldn't identify himself. I said 'hello, you're calling me, so can you say who you are?' Then he said – 'no, you're calling me'. It was Nicol.

Nicol and Jill, after four years apart, were back together and, of course, how typical of Nicol, famed for his eccentricity on the phone and tendency to ignore calls, to be so proud as to pretend that Jill was calling *him*!

In early 1971 Nicol took a part in a 'light' film, in the sense that's it's very much a hit-and-miss affair, *The Jerusalem File*. Jill accompanied him to Israel. What drew Nicol to this labyrinthine depiction of post Six-Day War politics, a subject lost on most cinemagoers, is unclear. Jill thinks that Nicol wanted to work with the director, John Flynn, and the acclaimed director of cinematography, Raoul Coutard, who became a good friend.

Nicol plays a professor of archaeology who seems to have the ear of every influential person in Jerusalem, including Shin Bet police chiefs and the upper echelons of the Israeli military. The boyfriend (Bruce Davison) of one of his students (Daria Halprin) is engineering a secret peace meeting between leftist Israeli peace groups and moderate Palestinian factions. The sub-plot is the romance between Davison and Halprin, innocent love which stands no chance, of course, once they get into the doomed world of Arab–Israeli politics.

The plot is complicated and uninvolving, dismissed as 'Zionist propaganda' by *Time Out* because it depicts the Arabs as instigating all the bloodshed. The pleasure lies in the acting, in particular Nicol's red bull performance as he crashes in and out of hospitals, museums and military headquarters. Balancing Nicol's 'young and thrusting' style is a nuanced, twitchy turn from Donald Pleasance as a mild-mannered but ruthless major and a boozy cameo from Ian Hendry as an Israeli general with a generously stocked liquor cabinet.

Director John Flynn later recalled the film, shot on location:

> I met writer Troy Kennedy Martin (*The Italian Job,*[8] *Kelly's Heroes*) and we became pals. He rewrote a bad script called *The Jerusalem File*, making it quite good. I signed on to direct the picture, because I loved the script and it was a chance to return to Israel for a few months. I stayed at the American Colony Hotel in East Jerusalem, further refining the script while waiting for the production money to come in. All the foreign journalists congregated in the bar of that hotel. So I'd be sitting there in that cavern, as they called it, with all these gentlemen of the press, getting the inside dope on what was really happening in Israel.[9]

Flynn recalled that he 'never saw Ian Hendry sober but somehow he managed to function'. He also says that Nicol was drinking heavily. 'Late one night, Nicol got quite loaded and threatened to throw Bob Dylan off a hotel balcony!' Luke recalls a slightly different version, as related by his father:

> Apparently they had been assigned a member of the wait staff whose name was Abu Jheerius and he was rather adept at not being around when you needed him. Dad had taken to calling out in a sing song voice, 'Aboooooooooooooooooooooooooo Jheeeeeeeeeeeeeeeeeeeriuuuuuus' whenever he could not be found, and Dylan then checked out of the hotel claiming he 'couldn't handle Nicol Williamson's singing'.

Jill remembers Nicol and Ian Hendry sharing a lot of ouzo. She also recalls a funny story about the shooting:

> One day they were filming in the Old City and had hired lots of Arabs as extras for the day … they gave them their money up front as they requested. In the Old City, the roads are narrow with high walls … they lined the extras in places along the wall … when John [Flynn] was ready to film, he called out, 'Are we ready to shoot?' and all the Arabs ran away thinking they were going to be shot.[10]

Daria Halprin, cast as the love interest in what turned out to be her last film – even though she was only 23(!) – recalled Nicol's influence:

I was a completely novice young actor, bringing no formal training or skill at all to the table, finding myself opposite a classically trained, seasoned and hugely talented actor. Nicol was patient, generous, encouraging and kind with me. At times he was hysterically funny, gentle and vulnerable – at other times rough, and raging. Beyond the roles and the work, Nicol became a close friend. He was gifted, he was tortured and I was aware that he was a handful and then some to deal with. That he extended his authentic friendship to me, inviting me into his personal life and his home, also speaks volumes about his tender and loving heart.[11]

Perhaps unsurprisingly, given the wildness of Nicol and Ian, Halprin recalls that Donald Pleasance was a safe pair of hands:

While Nicol was a kind of bigger and louder than life presence – Donald seemed to me the wise and steady elder statesman – his was a quiet forceful brilliance. And Bruce Davison, not only talented (I remember thinking, geeez, he actually really knows what he's doing next to these guys) he was a genuinely good guy and, in my eyes, impressive in holding his own next to Nicol and Donald.

Ultimately, however, *The Jerusalem File* all but disappeared and didn't perform well at the box office. It's a ho-hum film, enjoyable for catching the different acting styles of the various players, with pleasant photography and music. Philip Strick in *The Times* thought that Nicol's final cry in the film of 'let's get the hell out of here' would have been echoed by some cinemagoers. Leslie Halliwell called it 'a muddled mixture of action and politics'.

Jill and Nicol returned to the UK where they were married on 17 July 1971 at London's Chelsea Registry Office. Jill admits that her parents had reservations. They would have preferred her to marry Evelyn de Rothschild, scion of the Rothschild family:

My mother seemed to like Nicol because he was famous. Dad thought Nicol was a madman. My opinion was that my father was just as outrageous as Nicol and the two of them drinking together (with absolute dislike for each other) was something to be avoided at all costs! Although my parents thought Nicol was nuts, they were impressed by his 'couldn't give a damn' attitude.

John Thaw and Oscar Beuselinck, among others, attended the wedding. Jill, who admits she has never relished the spotlight, felt overwhelmed. 'When we arrived at the Registrar's Office, there was all this press there … I almost didn't get out of the car!' After a formal church blessing they spent their wedding night at the Ritz Hotel. Jill's parents subsequently held a large party for the newlyweds at Club dell'Aretusa in Chelsea's Kings Road.[12]

At one point Nicol had seemed resolutely single. To Kenneth Tynan he had once quoted the opinion of his old English teacher, Tom Reader, on marriage. 'He was all against it. He that hath wife and children, he said, hath given hostages to fortune.' The implication seemed to be – at least by quoting his friend's view to Tynan – that Nicol also had misgivings about marriage in general.

Jill had been living in an apartment in Markham Square in London's Chelsea. One day she was walking around the area when she passed a 'For Sale' sign in Woodfall Street, a cozy little cul-de-sac that, coincidentally, housed the offices of Woodfall Films, John Osborne's and Tony Richardson's production company – although she didn't know that at the time. Nicol and Jill made their new home at number twelve.

Life was happily busy for a while. Jill remembers the hectic round of dinner parties and evenings out at fancy restaurants – La Famiglia in the Kings Road, Meridiana, and Ashoka, 'a wonderful Indian restaurant' (the one Nicol had frequented years earlier during the first run of *Inadmissible Evidence*). They also got into bridge. 'We went to a bridge school somewhere above a shop in Chelsea and started playing with neighbours every evening (if we weren't out with John Thaw!) … We got so good at it we never finished the school. We were a good team.'

Nicol still liked socialising with 'the boys'. Every Sunday morning he would play football with a bunch of friends in Hyde Park, the group known as the Mount Street football club who had gone to Mexico for the World Cup the previous year – including tailor Douglas Hayward, David Hemmings and Tom Courtenay. Jill would cook a large post-match Sunday roast for the players and then everyone would gather to play charades. Jill recalls that 'those were happy days indeed'.

Around this time Nicol guested on the Harry Secombe show and one critic wrote that his 'deep resonant voice reminded me a little of Lee Hazelwood' – the American country and pop singer. He also appeared on a Tom Jones special. Nothing earth-shattering was happening on the film front. Nicol appeared in *Le Moine* (*The Monk*), as a cannibalistic nobleman in a story about a monk (Franco Nero) who is sexually tempted by an emissary of the Devil. The screenplay was by the great Luis Buñuel[13] but Jill remembers the strange circumstances leading up to the shooting more than the film itself:

> The contract was in French which I had to translate for him (very strange!). We were out in the boondocks somewhere; no loos, just a hole in the ground. I don't know if the film was ever released outside France. My abiding memory was that

we flew into Le Bourget and his luggage got lost. We got into a taxi (Citroen D). We were sitting in the back seat discussing what we would do if our luggage wasn't found. Suddenly, I heard this loud crack … in an instant, I had pushed Nicol down to the floor and lain over him. I didn't know what the noise was. All I knew was that it wasn't good! The windscreen on the taxi exploded. So we continued on without the windscreen, covered in glass, out to the countryside with no loo, no shower … picking glass out of ourselves. Not a good experience, it is safe to say!

Jill and Nicol were reunited professionally – and very successfully – for Jack Gold's *The Resistible Rise of Arturo Ui*, Bertolt Brecht's parable play about a fictional thirties American mobster (who happens to bear a remarkable resemblance to Hitler) and his violent attempts to wrest control of the cauliflower racket. A satire on the Führer's rise to power, all its characters are based on key protagonists in Nazi Germany.

Peter Sellers was the original choice to play Ui. Doubtless he would have been great given his extraordinary powers of mimicry. (Luke recalls that Nicol once described Sellers to him as 'a master of physical comedy'.)

Sellers, however, eventually proved unavailable.[14] Gold then suggested Nicol. Producer Tony Garnett, a neighbour and contemporary of Nicol's at school, was initially wary:

> I was worried because my budget was very tight for such an ambitious project and Nicol had a reputation for bad behaviour. I knew him from old. In the end I went with him, partly because of my respect for Jack. I thought Nicol would not play up Jack, who created a bond of love and trust on set. He arrived word perfect, behaved with exemplary professionalism throughout and was a joy to work with.[15]

Nicol managed to elicit many laughs, capturing Ui's preening and posturing, his affected innocence and practised oratory. A broad parable, yes, but also a parody, even a pantomime. Ui is an unadulterated con man and no effort is made to conceal it. He lies, he torches and intimidates opponents, while, hilariously, acting like the wronged party.

Historians always home in, understandably, on Hitler's violence and sadism. Yet, throughout, he always claimed to be the victim of others' machinations, usually international Jewish conspirators. And so it is with Ui in Brecht's script, 'You see before you, sir, a man misunderstood and almost done to death by slanderous tongues, his name besmirched by envy and his dreams misrepresented by a world replete with Jews … if men would only yield to reason, there would be no reason for violence.'

Highlights include a veteran actor (Frank Middlemas) training Ui in everything from the length of oratorical pauses through to bearing and posture – even how to fold his arms. 'Nicol Williamson played the Hitler figure as Alastair Sim might have done – all suspicious glances and loping gait. It was a superbly funny performance', wrote Leonard Buckley in *The Times*.

It was also harrowing in its depiction of how easily people are duped, intimidated, or cowed into submission. The message is eternal. 'Do not rejoice in his (Ui's) defeat, you men. For though the world has stood up and stopped the bastard, the bitch that bore him is in heat again.'

Every event parallels Hitler's rise to power – complete with blaming a false party for the burning of Goldman's warehouse – standing in for the Reichstag, ridiculous alibis for the perpetrators and absurd accusations against innocent parties. 'I recognise the accused on account of the guilty expression on his face.' By the end Ui is a ranting maniac but still acting the wronged party, the guardian of order. 'The whole world is screaming for protection.'

In a clever touch that added to the period feel, Garnett persuaded the BBC to film in black and white. He wanted a film pastiche of a thirties Warner Brothers' gangster movie, figuring that Brecht himself, who had spent some time in Los Angeles during that period, would have been influenced by them.

Nicol viewed many film archives of Hitler. Luke recalls that it was one of the few roles that Nicol revisited with him many years later:

He had a fantastic time making it and he enjoyed the memories, and we had some interesting discussions about Brecht and Germany and how things happen. He was great in it. I was watching some *World War II in HD Colour* the other day and when Hitler was featured it was like Dad in *Ui*. It was so surreal. I felt like Hitler was my father in a strange way. He got all of it so right. I don't know how.

The critics agreed and Nicol was nominated for a BAFTA for best actor, losing to Anthony Hopkins for *War and Peace*.

Jill also remembers Nicol's uncanny impersonation of Hitler and his fondness for mayhem. One day, during a lunch break, Jill and Nicol went to a hotel in Earl's Court that also had a little Italian restaurant. Nicol and Jill breezed in, still in costume as Ui. Al Mancini, who played Giuseppe Givola, was there too. Nicol was a combination of Hitler and Al Capone with the distinctive Führer 'tache and parting. Nicol went for the jugular, imitating Hitler's guttural sniping voice complete with extravagant gestures. 'I VANT ZE MENU!' A loud silence followed.

This period, if there ever was one, was the most stable in Nicol's life. Just married and a father-to-be, he was preparing for a one-man show, a London concert called *Midwinter Spring* that would feature some of the highlights from the Nixon evening. Jill recalls that Nicol was always consulting her about what to include – never proud or feigning intellectual superiority. '"How would this go – should we have some E.E. Cummings?" He was so generous in allowing me to have input. I made suggestions on how it would sound better and he'd always heed them.'

Nicol told journalist Herbert Kretzmer of his new-found happiness, 'That's what marriage has done for me. Jill's got rid of that restless thing in me. I must say I feel terrific practically every moment of every day. I love being.'[16]

Nicol also expanded on his views about acting to Kretzmer, declaring his scorn for 'dead actors' who spurn hard work at rehearsals:

That's why they stumble and bluster about half the time. There are no rewards without work. Unless you graft, it's no good, no good at all. I find work excruciatingly painful. I take it all away with me. I worry at dinner … in bed … when I get up in the mornings, I can't let go. Then one day a light goes on, a door opens. These moments of discovery during rehearsals are the most exciting I've known in the theatre. The essential problem for an actor is to mould by painful process a character who is not himself, a separate creation. The dead actors don't really care about this. Mostly they use the play to put themselves on an ego trip. Have you noticed how they never really listen to other actors in a play? How their eyes go dead when it's not their turn to speak? Listen, I'll tell you the big secret. If you really listen you come alive and the play comes alive.

Referring to *Midwinter Spring*, which won sterling reviews, Nicol said, 'I've done so many things in theatre that have been a slog. I just wanted to have some fun too. My mother used to say, "If you get knocked down by a bus, you'll never be run over by a tram."'

Nicol's name was enough to fill 1,000 seats at London's Queen's Theatre for *Midwinter Spring*, which took its name from T.S. Eliot. Nicol read Beckett's *How it Is*, and sang *Help Me Through the Night* by Joe Walsh and *I'd Trade All My Tomorrows for a Single Yesterday* by John Killigrew. According to critic Charles Lewsen, who reviewed the concert in *The Times*, 'The message of this rather happy evening seemed best summed up in a piece in which Dorothy Parker considers every form of suicide and decides that life is marginally preferable. This was delivered with the sure rhythm and the best work of this highly intelligent actor.'

Roland Jaquarello described the evening as:

A very entertaining one-man show of song and verse. Nicol sang an excellent version of Kris Kristofferson's *Me and Bobby McGee*. It wasn't that he had a great voice, it was the feeling that he put into the soul of the song and the way he acted the story. There was a strong band on stage, a good house and a sense of fun and celebration rooted in folk, jazz, blues and poetry.

Nicol was entering a golden period, perhaps his prime as a young actor. As 1973 loomed, he was about to test himself against one of America's greatest thespians.

8

WRITING ON THE SAND

'The power of his words was actually knocking me down.'

Oscar James on acting opposite Nicol Williamson in *Coriolanus*

Some great actors resist appearing opposite talented 'challengers' for fear of being upstaged. These actors probably fall into Nicol's category of 'dead actors', those with off-centre egos and low self-esteem. The actor who knows deep down he's good does not fear competition. He knows that his game will be raised if he's tested. Nicol showed just that when he agreed to appear opposite George C. Scott in a glittering production of *Uncle Vanya*, directed by Mike Nichols.

Scott was, in many ways, the American equivalent of Nicol. Many years later, when Anthony Heald appeared with Nicol in a New York revival of *Inadmissible Evidence*, he too noted the 'bad boy' similarities. Both had prickly natures, an inherent danger and volatility, natural forcefulness and a tendency not to suffer fools gladly (or otherwise).

Scott was more aggressive than Nicol. According to his biographer David Sheward, Scott employed minders, not to protect himself from other people, but to protect other people from being attacked by *him* – such was his unprovoked rage!

Nicol and Scott were also comparable in terms of sheer talent. Scott was acknowledged to be one of the greatest American actors of his generation. When Charles Durning appeared with Scott in a 1995 production of *Inherit the Wind*, he gave a TV interview in which he described Scott as one of America's two or three finest actors. (The others, presumably, being Brando and Pacino?)

I often wish someone had recorded outstanding plays for posterity. And never more so than this production of *Uncle Vanya* starring Scott as Astrov and Nicol as Vanya, as well as Elizabeth Wilson, Lillian Gish (then 79), Barnard Hughes, Cathleen Nesbitt, Conrad Bain and Julie Christie. Ironically, as we will recall,

Nicol had taken over from Scott in *Plaza Suite* but this was the first time they had starred together.[1]

In 1972, Theodore Mann, artistic director of Circle in the Square, called Nichols and asked him if there was a play he wanted to direct. As Nichols remembers, 'I said that I'd like to do *Uncle Vanya* and I would see if George wanted to do it. That was the spine of it.' Nichols added he really wanted Nicol to do *Uncle Vanya*. 'Nicol seemed to me exactly the one to do the Vanya I perceived but Nicol had doubts because of his preconceptions of Vanya as a grey, brooding, whining spectre.'

Nevertheless Nicol agreed and rehearsals began. Mike Nichols, perhaps sensing the need to calm emerging rivalries, decided that they should be conducted from a sedentary position. Eleven beds were moved from the dressing rooms into a rehearsal room. Each actor, including minor players, lay down in the position he found most comfortable. Gish and Nesbitt placed cooling handkerchiefs over their faces while Wilson wrapped herself in a blanket.

'The rest of us lay on top of the covers, some with long-suffering looks,' Nicol recalled. 'George C. Scott sat up on his bed and did a crossword puzzle. Conrad, who does not have many lines, fell asleep.' Nicol thought the couch looked as if it was from 'an ornate Viennese psychiatrist's office and the rehearsal scene looked like something out a psychiatrist's ward!' In the end, however, he agreed that 'it was worth its weight in gold, inducing such a state of relaxation'.[2]

If there was bad feeling at the beginning, Scott was the instigator. For the first time Scott was meeting an actor who was giving him the runaround. Elizabeth Wilson recalls:

> Nicol Williamson was a wonderful actor. George was jealous. I can remember when Lillian Gish, Cathleen Nesbitt and I came in for our first dress rehearsal. We were told it had been postponed because George had gone into Nicol's room – bless his heart – and said 'what do you think you're playing – Hamlet? Come on, what's the matter with you?!' Of course, everyone was intimidated by George because of his gifts as an actor.[3]

Set designer Tony Walton recalled that Scott's jealousy spilled over into violence:

> Nicol was absolutely at the top of his game. It was truly a golden period in his life. He was sublimely happy and successful and he knew he was perfectly cast and carrying out his part spectacularly. Nicol was also someone of virtually limitless talent and had a magical vein to him. Other actors, including, for all his brilliance, Scott, were earth-bound by comparison with Nicol. He [Nicol] displayed magic

all the way through, not just in the final performance but also in rehearsals. Scott had never been challenged as an actor in such a way.

Walton claimed that Scott's temper boiled over one day in rehearsals when he sensed that Nicol, who was lying down at the time in line with instructions, was showing off, almost flaunting his versatility with elaborate gestures and extravagant flourishes. 'George ran after Nicol with one of the long oak benches that decorated the stage. He was in a fury because Nicol was so amazing. Nicol left the theatre and headed for the airport. Meanwhile, Scott went off on a massive bender.'

Walton believes that Mike Nichols even tried to bring Richard Burton in to replace Nicol.[4] Yet Nichols knew both men well. He had worked with Nicol on *Plaza Suite* and had just finished directing Scott on *The Day of the Dolphin*. He, along with some help from Jill, managed to calm things down and Nicol was brought back on board. Nichols gave a cocktail party at his penthouse high up above New York to which Nicol was invited. Somehow Scott found out about it and arrived. Walton remembers a deadly hush. Everyone was worried that Scott had gatecrashed the party to continue his fight with Nicol. It was made worse when someone handed Scott a bottle of brandy and he started swigging from the bottle.

'When Nicol arrived the whole room panicked,' recalled Walton:

> Scott suggested to Nicol that they go outside to the terrace which was about fifty storeys high. Nobody was even breathing. They left the room for the terrace. To be honest, if Scott had pushed Nicol over that terrace, nobody would have heard anything anyway. Suddenly, to our relief, they re-entered the room, arms around each other, as if they were the best of buddies, and promptly embarked on a singing contest.

Anjelica Huston also remembers meeting Nicol, and other cast members, at Mike Nichols's apartment. She recalled that Nicol played the piano downstairs all evening as the cast sang along to *Won't You Come Home Bill Bailey, Won't You Come Home?*[5] This could have been the same evening recalled by Tony Walton.

Walton believes the rivalry also stemmed from Scott's jealousy of Nicol's comparative youth and ability to stay light on his feet even when drinking:

> Nicol was in such incredibly good shape. Scott couldn't do that. When he was drinking he couldn't keep up and became aggressive. Colleen Dewhurst [Scott's wife at the time] even had escape chutes built into their house so the children could slide down them if George returned home in a drunken stupor.[6]

As opening night loomed, however, Nichols recalled more friction between Williamson and Scott:

> In *Uncle Vanya*, some scenes were great, but George C. Scott had his usual weird thing on dress rehearsal night. He said: 'I don't want to go onstage with that cunt', I said, 'Which cunt?' He said, 'Nicol Williamson.' We were great until then, but it was never quite what it had been before.

Over time, however, Nicol and Scott became amicable – two binge drinkers sensing a kindred spirit in each other. Both liked a liquid lunch. Elizabeth Wilson recalled:

> I used to have lunch between shows with George. This one time, Barnard Hughes, George, Nicol and I went out. Nicol was pretty plotzed. He saw this police car come by and he did this (making an obscene gesture at the car) 'screw you'. They stopped the car. They were going to arrest him. George had just done *Patton*. He just moved around and said to them. 'Excuse me – do you know who I am?' and the policeman saluted him, said, 'Yes, sir' and walked away.

The incident may have cemented their friendship. Nicol told interviewer Christopher Sharp:

> My wife and I see him [Scott] constantly. We have dinner with him twice a week. He gets pleasure out of making wry comments about his audiences. Last week, he was terrific. He stopped three guys who were taking pictures right in front of him. He stopped the whole show at the second act. 'Stop that or I'll come and take those cameras away from you.' The audience applauded.

Yet there were still tense moments between Nicol and Scott. According to Sheward:

> All the Circle dressing rooms were equipped with speakers so the actors could hear their cues. Scott had been getting very little laughter for what he regarded as Astrov's comic moments, while Nicol Williamson was getting more than his share of guffaws, particularly when he was clownishly pining over Julie Christie. One night the resentment boiled over and Scott smashed the speaker during Nicol Williamson's scene. The speaker was not replaced and he could concentrate on his performance.

Nicol, when asked about rumoured tension between himself and Scott, used to mimic his interviewers' frenetic questioning. 'How do you get along with GCS?'

'Wasn't he difficult?' 'Doesn't he drink a lot?' He would never give the press ammunition. 'I found George not more than utterly gentlemanly to work with.'

It's worth mentioning that between these two bulls, was the waif-life Christie who remembers feeling intimidated. 'Such an incredible company – they're so brilliant. I felt a bit as if I was a one-legged midget playing football against a team of giants,' she recalled.[7]

Actress Hilary Mason, who had played the blind psychic in *Don't Look Now* – the film that had occupied Christie just before *Uncle Vanya* – told Christie's biographers that Julie was brave to appear opposite Nicol and George, 'If you can think of two more frightening actors, I can't.'[8]

Uncle Vanya was a sellout and the reviews were magnificent. Ted Kalem in *Time* magazine wrote, '[Nichols] gets marvellous assistance from Nicol Williamson whose Vanya is compact with a mischievous, sardonic self-mocking wit that not only defines his own character, but also makes a comment on everyone else in the play. The entire cast deserves every bravo and blistered palm of applause that it gets.'

Sheward, in Scott's biography, caught the wonderful sense of competition engendered by the teaming of Nicol and Scott:

Many critics compared Williamson and Scott to pugilists, scoring who had gotten in the most devastating punches as if the play were a boxing match. *The New Yorker*'s Brendan Gill thought Scott a match for Nicol Williamson. Martin Gottfried of *Women's Wear Daily*, however, wrote that Nicol Williamson 'simply acts circles around Scott'.

Doubtless Scott would have cheerfully strangled Gottfried with a pair of knickers if he had read that! Luke Williamson also recalls his dad telling him that Mike Nichols had declared that Scott 'must never be allowed' to read the first night reviews – presumably in case the praise lavished on Nicol riled him. On another occasion, according to Nicol, George chased Mike Nichols down a beach, shouting that he was going to kill him.

Yet, in the end, perhaps honour was satisfied. Both Nicol and Scott received Tony nominations in the best actor category, losing to Michael Moriarty for *Find Your Way Home*.

'I enjoyed *Vanya*, probably because it was such an experience working with Scott. But it wasn't easy. It's quite staggering, the degree of his self-loathing,' Nicol later conceded.

Music still rivalled acting as Nicol's first love. It was also a way of unwinding. Incredibly, Nicol still had energy after a performance of *Uncle Vanya*, so he developed a ninety-minute one-man show called *Nicol Williamson's Late Show* and ran it at 10.45 p.m. for thirty performances at the Eastside Playhouse.

Luke was born during the run of *Uncle Vanya*. Jill, in the advanced stage of pregnancy throughout the rehearsal period, even wondered if she would give birth at the theatre itself!:

> The cast put a bed in the dressing room backstage just in case. I was convinced I was going to deliver my own child backstage! I was taken off to hospital one morning on the day of a matinee. Everyone hoped to announce it after the matinee performance but Luke was actually born just after the curtain call.

Nicol was at the pub Theatrical on 50th and Broadway (now Emmett O'Lunney's) when he got the news and whooped with joy and ran out of the pub to get to the hospital. In keeping with Williamson tradition, Luke was supposed to be called Hugh. Jill recalls:

> But the moment he was born – even before they cut the cord – Luke appeared as a total personality with that new name in tow. I said to Nicol: 'Honey, I've done all the work for nine months so YOU must be the one who informs them that their grandson is called Luke.' Of course, he didn't. They read about it in *Time* magazine.

Nicol was on a roll and went straight into rehearsals for *Coriolanus* on his return to London. Apart from *Hamlet* – and a 1972 radio production of *Othello* opposite Paul Scofield in which Nicol's portrayal of Iago was much praised – Nicol hadn't done much Shakespeare on stage since leaving Dundee.

The Royal Shakespeare Company production was to be directed by Trevor Nunn, who, along with Anthony Page and Jack Gold, was one of Nicol's (happy) serial collaborators. The role of Coriolanus, the soldier cum politician contemptuous of the masses and aghast at having to woo them, seemed ideal for Nicol. Yet there was a paradox here – Nicol actually was more at home with 'commoners' and perhaps, as noted with *Laughter in the Dark*, may have been uncomfortable playing aristocrats. Yet, in common with Coriolanus, he had a cloven hoof when it came to having to 'please' people.

All his life Nicol had blazed his own trail, at drama school, in National Service, in his innovative interpretation of Shakespeare. He had difficulty feigning good behaviour, indeed dissembling in any way. Just like Coriolanus, having to appease opinion was beyond him. Another of Nicol's famous dictums – 'never apologise, never explain' – could also have been Coriolanus's.

The Royal Shakespeare Company had already played a season at Stratford, with Ian Hogg as Coriolanus. Nicol was to be the new lead for the London season, supported by Margaret Tyzack as Volumnia, Oscar James as Tullus Aufidius and Mark Dignam as First Citizen. Tony Osoba, who had played minor roles in RSC productions of *Coriolanus*, *Antony and Cleopatra*, *Julius Caesar* and *Titus Andronicus* in Stratford, remembered the cast eagerly awaiting Nicol's arrival:

I was in only my third year as a professional actor and had but a superficial aware-ness of Nicol as an actor, but it was apparent from the anticipation and talk among the more experienced members of the company as we approached rehearsals with the new leading man, that this was someone to take note of – seemingly for a variety of reasons. My early recollections of him were of a bright eyed, tall but rather gangling and hunched figure with a cherubic hairstyle and a somewhat nasal vocal delivery – friendly enough but occasionally aloof when he chose to be. The occasional aloofness was not generated only towards the younger actors – it could manifest itself anytime, anywhere – Nicol generally carried an air of unpredict-ability. In fact, my recollection is that he was mostly very much at ease with the younger actors in the company and never adopting the 'I'm a leading man' attitude.

Osoba, while admiring Nicol's talent, noticed some eccentric behaviour creeping in during rehearsals:

As time passed, Nicol was every bit the professional actor, learning the lines, mostly on time, diligently rehearsing; but I remember a gradual change when he would seem restless or distracted, particularly in note sessions with the director after rehearsals. In fact, I recall one note session when the company were gathered in the front row of the stalls with Trevor Nunn perched on the leading edge of the stage delivering his notes and thoughts, when Nicol, much to the bemusement of everyone present, quietly rose up and proceeded to meander up the aisle and disappear into the front foyer, reappearing a short while later wandering around up in the circle seating area. Eventually he returned – as I recall, no explanation was asked for or given – and eventually the note session continued. The sometimes quirky and unpredictable ways of Nicol were becoming apparent – the somewhat restless spirit was never too far away. I think that Nicol was someone who could get bored quite easily and if so, never bothered to disguise it.

Nunn, however, does not recall Nicol ever walking out on a note session that he gave. This could have been more of a prank on Nicol's part, rather than a show of impatience.

Osoba also remembers another strange incident. Nicol was in his home town of Hamilton in Scotland and called in to say he would have to miss a Saturday matinee. The late Tim Piggott-Smith was his Coriolanus understudy and had to be rushed through a rapid rehearsal:

> Tim was a gifted and diligent actor and had prepared well for such a possibility and turned in a first-class performance in the face of rather daunting circumstances. I'm not sure whether it was true or not, but I remember a rumour at the time saying that Nicol had forewarned Tim the day before that he was going to miss the matinee. True or not, missing the matinee was another example of Nicol's contrary behaviour.

Offstage, Nicol was his usual unpredictable self. Osoba recalls:

> The Opera Tavern pub in Covent Garden, round the corner from the RSC's then London base at the Aldwych Theatre, was a frequent lunch venue for RSC cast and crew. I recall one such visit when Nicol, in a clear ringing voice, was regaling several of us with witty stories and slightly risqué jokes when a man approached and addressed Nicol in a somewhat scolding tone. 'Excuse me, but do you realise that you are using foul language in front of my wife?' I think we all collectively thought 'No Nicol – don't say it' but of course in a loud contemptuous nasal tone, Nicol gave the obvious reply 'Sorry, I didn't know it was her turn'. Much amusement throughout the pub and the retreat of the much flustered husband.
>
> No one could deliver a sneering put down better than Nicol – on or off stage! Of course, he had great presence onstage, for the cast as well as the audience and certainly there was no lack of concentration among the rest of the cast when onstage with Nicol – he generated focus at all times. There was always an air of unpredictability about him that also focused attention. Undoubtedly there was a hint of danger about him that concentrated the mind.[9]

Oscar James, later known as Tony Carpenter in *EastEnders*, felt overwhelmed by Nicol. 'I'm a big man but I could feel the power of his words was actually knocking me down. No other actor has ever done that to me. None. To feel the force of his words, I was moved.' And when Nicol left the stage, according to James, he took 'all the energy with him'.[10]

Actor Tony Rowlands had a small part in *Coriolanus*:

> I regard Nicol as one of the key actors of the time. Or any time. What I also really liked was his refusal to take part in the hierarchy of the company. He used

to disappear into the night after the show – so did I and a couple of chums – while the company performed a frightfully English drinks party around Trevor and Janet [Suzman]. I do remember him, however, singing Chantilly Lace at the Christmas party. I was very aware of him before the start of my professional career from his incandescent appearances in TV plays. And I regard *The Bofors Gun* as one of the great British films of the time.[11]

As for Trevor Nunn, he remembers Nicol for his electric acting but also as a great member of the company:

He was superb; heroic, temperamental, dangerous, wilful and very funny. But climactically, in the confrontation with Volumnia, his mother (played by the wonderful Margaret Tyzack), he was hugely moving. The performance was hailed, and Nicol was nominated for awards. I must admit to both relief and vindication. Such was Nicol's flamboyant reputation, many people, in and out of the RSC, had said to me, 'Don't do it ... he will destroy your company ... he won't ever be part of your ensemble ... etc.' Absolutely the opposite happened, he was immensely popular with young and old alike in the RSC ... and best of all was the relationship with Maggie [Tyzack]. Dressing Room 1 and Dressing Room 2 at the Aldwych were side by side, directly behind the stage. There was, oddly, a connecting door between the two rooms that had always been locked. Nicol and Maggie had it opened ... so they could talk and laugh and share ideas, before and after the show.[12]

The reviews for *Coriolanus* were glowing. Irving Wardle noted Nicol's expressiveness at the most poignant moments. 'The pause after Volumnia's plea seems to stretch out into minutes while Nicol Williamson's face turns to pulp. The tone he produces, of a tearful, enraged child, humiliated beyond bearing, produces the kind of shock that makes it painful to look at the stage.'

Roland Jaquarello also remembers Nicol's impressive performance and, in particular, the long exchange referred to by Wardle:

A stunning and memorable scene was between Nicol and Margaret Tyzack as a fine Volumnia, who begs Coriolanus not to attack Rome. In response to her desperate plea to end such violence, there was a tense, long silence.[13] Nicol's face contorted in agony for ages until he finally unleashed a frightening, primitive wail about her plea. It was as if the child had been touched beneath the trappings of macho authority. A great moment in modern British classical theatre.

Jill also believes that – in terms of serious drama – Nicol's Coriolanus was his finest work. (For comedy she cites his Malvolio.)

When Nicol repeated his *Midwinter Spring* concert at the same theatre, the Aldwych, Wardle was just as complimentary:

> He [Nicol] is clearly a performer who needs an occasional night off from the rituals of orthodox culture. He needs to do something for fun and he certainly achieves it here. Just as the best comedians' gags would be useless to anyone else it is hard to think of anyone but Nicol Williamson pulling off a stage anthology rooted in thirties jazz and twinning itself around Beckett, T.S. Eliot, a couple of quite tough younger poets and several comic poetasters. The only link is the personality of the benevolently gimlet-eyed performer and the fact that he is fond of all his material.

The one-man show was developed in close conjunction with Trevor Nunn who thought it astonishingly moving.

> The show worked superbly well, with Nicol proving he was an amazing all-rounder. Most unlikely of all, he included the Kipling poem *Gunga Din* – which culminates in what became, for subsequent generations, an almost joke line. 'You're a better man than I am, Gunga Din.'
>
> When Nicol got to this line, characterising a dyed-in-the-wool member of the British Raj, who finally admitted that a native Indian was a better man than he was, I swear there wasn't a dry eye in the house.

Nicol seemed to be in a mood to play classic roles. But one of his more enjoyable feats during this period saw him voicing all the parts for an audio recording of J.R.R. Tolkien's *The Hobbit*. Nicol had always admired Tolkien's work and relished such a challenging solo effort. In many ways – just as with his *Midwinter Spring* concert and later productions such as *Jack* – it suited Nicol to be in a team of … one. Nicol re-edited the original script, removing many 'he said, she said, said so and so' etc., relying on vocal character performances to convey who was saying what to whom. It proved to be a masterly recording, revealing Nicol's fluidity of expression and gift for mimicry. To this day, whenever his son Luke yearns for his father's presence, he plays *The Hobbit*.

Brian J. Hobb and Paul Simpson, in their book, *The Hobbit and Lord of the Rings*, also judged it a wonderful interpretation:

Although a one-man performance, Williamson brings each individual character to unique life (giving Bilbo a light West Country accent), making it easy for the reader to be sucked in by Tolkien's simple story. Despite featuring only one actor, Nicol Williamson's abridged reading of *The Hobbit* is one of the best audio realisations of Tolkien's younger-skewed story of Middle Earth.[14]

Other fans, too, thought it among Nicol's best work. Sam Dalladay wrote to Luke after Nicol died:

> I remember him most fondly for his voice on a tape cassette I owned as a small boy and it was him telling the story of *The Hobbit*. At the time I owned many word books. However, this one was by far my favourite and that is mostly thanks to your dad and the way he could give a different voice to all of the characters in the story (my particular favourite being Smaug the Dragon). This cassette went everywhere with me and was a companion on very long car journeys.[15]

A mastery of eccentric accents and burlesque also served Nicol well when he played Malvolio in *Twelfth Night* opposite Jane Lapotaire at Stratford in August 1974, directed by Peter Gill. The production displayed Nicol's gift for comedy – playing this conceited, deluded fool hoodwinked into believing he can win Olivia's heart. *Punch* magazine pithily hailed his 'excellent Malvolio … moving like a pensioner from the Ministry of Funny Walks, ambling from the hips down only, like a hobbled goblin'.

Gill remembers Nicol's skill in milking laughs:

> He was absolutely brilliant. He was just what the part called for. He was an extremely gifted comic actor. What Nicol captured was the self-righteous puritanism of the part. I vividly remember his very first line on the first night – 'Yes, and shall do till the pangs of death shake him. Infirmity, that decays the wise, doth ever make the better fool.' It was a little louder than normal, so totally in your ear and yet so natural and it got tremendous laughs.[16]

That said, Gill admits that he never particularly looked forward to working with Nicol. He compares him to Victor Henry, another talented but wayward (alcoholic) actor known for his aggression and self-destructiveness.[17] Gill says that some of the other actors in *Twelfth Night* – amiable, seasoned professionals such as Richard Griffiths and Ron Pember – had Nicol effectively 'sandbagged', made to look silly if he misbehaved.

Irving Wardle loved the interpretation:

Nicol Williamson's Malvolio towers over the production as its main comedian and main erotic victim … In his black steward's suit and chain he looks like some heavy piece of antique furniture and you can almost him hear creaking when he moves. He prefixes his early lines with sagacious power, and then the voice comes out – reedy, Welsh and ridiculous.

The Stage also singled out Nicol for special praise, 'We have a performance by Nicol Williamson that illuminates the character of the gulled steward, makes us weep for him as well as laughing at him.'

Roland Jaquarello thought that the role of Malvolio showed a different side to Nicol:

Nicol was a prissy and delightfully delusional Malvolio. He seemed to be using his 'feminine' side' in this part, in contrast to his 'angry young men' roles. The production had a fine, subtle air of melancholia without eschewing the play's humour. Nicol was at its heart and showed a wonderful sense of sad levity.

Theatregoer Patrick Salvadori wrote to Luke after Nicol's death about the same production:

I managed to see him as Malvolio at the RSC and I have always referred to that as the best performance of the character that I have ever seen. He captured the humour, the pathos and the vitriolic bitterness of the character magnificently and throughout the production I found his presence and 'absence' from the stage riveting. What an actor!

Gill did not see Malvolio as a small part, more as a star supporting role. Nevertheless Malvolio could be seen as a way of limbering up for the lead in what actors call 'the Scottish play'. It does seem odd that Nicol had never played a character to which he seemed well suited – the ambitious man of action haunted by dark forces.

When Roman Polanski had made his film version of *Macbeth*, his co-screenwriter Kenneth Tynan had recommended Nicol for the lead and Marianne Faithfull for Lady Macbeth. Polanski, however, rejected Faithfull because of her drug-taking and Nicol because, allegedly, he thought he lacked sex appeal. (Nicol and Faithfull did, however, co-star again, in a television production of James Leo Herlihy's one-act play, *Terrible Jim Fitch*, broadcast in 1971.)

Ironically, the actor who did eventually play Macbeth in the film, Jon Finch, had tried to persuade Polanski that Nicol would be a great fit when they had a chance encounter on a flight from Paris to London. 'He [Polanski] recognised me from photographs and introduced himself and I spent the entire journey telling him how marvellous I thought Nicol would be as Macbeth,' recalled Finch.

Yet Polanski apparently spurned Finch's advice, believing that 'Nicol Williamson should not play geniuses or kings or princes. He should play ordinary men who are extraordinary.' That was the official line anyway.

Trevor Nunn's *Macbeth* started at Stratford and then went to the Aldwych Theatre in London. Helen Mirren was Lady Macbeth. It was no secret that Nicol and Mirren feuded during this production – the reasons depending on whose version you believe. Nicol always claimed that Mirren had wanted to have an affair but he wasn't interested. Rumours floating around the internet that they *did* have a passionate affair appear to be just hearsay.

Mirren claimed it was just a case of personal friction and Nicol's bad behaviour:

> Days were spent waiting for Nicol to get going. He would argue terribly with Trevor and was just horrible to me. I think his plan, if there was such a thing, was to hold back until the first night and then just let it explode. This meant there was no organisation to the performance and it went too fast, leaving nowhere to go after the third scene … I was thrown right into the deep end of a pool where ego and self-centredness were paramount. It certainly had a kind of power, but it was a miserable experience.[18]

Yet – and this is by no means uncommon – through more than four decades' mists of time, recollections can vary. Trevor Nunn has a wholly different take. 'During *Macbeth*, I recollect lively discussion, animated debate, and sensing both my leading actors were feeling the pressure of expectation as they approached these great and demanding roles, seeking originality and revelation. But I don't remember animosity.' Luke relates that Nicol subsequently told him that Mirren 'couldn't access that deeply disturbing aspect to Lady Macbeth'.

Sheila Hancock tells an amusing story about Nicol during *Macbeth*. 'Trevor Nunn, who can go on a bit, was dithering about the most effective way to kill one of the Macduff children when from the stalls Nicol drawled. 'Why don't you take him into the wings and you can bore him to death?'[19]

Here, perhaps, we should be careful not to misconstrue. Trevor Nunn had become a close confidant. ('Nicol loved him', Jill told me.) Banter and ribbing, with a trusted friend and collaborator, can be misunderstood by outsiders. And Nunn remembers his time with Nicol as a wholly positive experience:

> Yes, Nicol was possessed of a caustic humour, and enjoyed making articulate, well chosen barbs about people or things that he didn't admire. But never during that

happy time was he violent, or aggressive or physically dangerous ... The stories of his 'anger and dissatisfaction' don't make much sense to me because, other than his laconic dry wit at the expense of other actors and directors, I didn't encounter this behaviour.

Couples and close friends sometimes develop a private language, with references and barbs only understood by the parties involved. Nunn recalls a funny story that he told Nicol which became a repeated laughter line:

I had got into a cab in London, with my friend and assistant Buzz Goodbody,[20] and said to the driver, 'It's to Kings Cross first, and then on up to Hampstead.' When Buzz got out at Kings Cross, the driver said he needed me to pay. 'But we have to go to Hampstead, like I said,' was my polite response. The driver insisted I had never mentioned Hampstead, told me he definitely wasn't going to take me there and shouted at me to pay and get out. I refused. The driver then said, 'Right, if you won't get out, you're going to London Airport.' He spun the cab round, and started a breakneck speed journey towards the M4. 'What are you doing?' I called out. 'You're going to London Airport,' was the only reply I got.

Several times in rehearsal, if I gave Nicol an acting note that he couldn't immediately accept, he would say to me, in front of the company, 'You're going to London Airport ... !' Nicol could drink heavily, but he was only what I would call drunk on one occasion in Stratford. I was asleep, and woke to hear a blundering and banging downstairs. I tried to go back to sleep ... I was aware of someone creeping into my room, and then, in my ear, a slightly slurred voice whispered, 'You're going to ... London ... Airport.'

A happy experience for Trevor Nunn, less so for Helen Mirren, but the critics raved about *Macbeth*. Of the original Stratford production Irving Wardle said, 'If you see Macbeth as a man of action with a tormenting imagination, this is the definitive reading.'

Roland Jaquarello recalls the Stratford production:

Nicol was a fervent Macbeth, egged on to power by a sexually powerful Lady Macbeth played by Helen Mirren. Both leading actors were strong but somehow the parts were better than the rather cumbersome whole. The production was later simplified, playing for just two hours without an interval in its London run.

Nunn concedes that the production underwent some major changes before its transfer to London:

> I had embarked on a search for originality. I felt that the theme of the play was 'faith', that in a deeply religious environment (saintly Duncan, Edward the Confessor in England), Macbeth was being urged to believe in the black arts, in witchcraft expressing the opposite of the Christian message. So very extremely, the production was set in an environment that looked like a ruined chapel, and in every sense, either Christian or Hellish imagery would be present. Some people in the company found these ideas very exciting, and some people were either confused or offended. So the production period was very much a time of questioning. I felt, although the production gripped audiences, that I should reduce the religious imagery when we took the work to the Aldwych. So I re-rehearsed, and made a substantially different version – in which Nicol and Helen were totally involved, and which fared much better than the Stratford attempt.

During the Stratford run Nicol delivered an onstage broadside to some noisy schoolchildren at a matinee. Gyles Brandreth noted the explosion in his diary entry for 4 December 1974:

> We were surrounded by ghastly schoolchildren, fidgeting, chattering, and making nuisances of themselves. Fifteen minutes into the performance, Nicol Williamson had had enough. Halfway through a speech, he grabbed the wooden stool on which he had been resting his foot and with terrifying violence flung it the length of the stage. He turned on the audience. 'Shut up! Shut up the lot of you! I have come to Stratford earning nothing a week to play Shakespeare when I could be in Hollywood making films and earning a fortune. There are people here today who have paid for their seats. And you kids had better shut up and let them hear the play. And if you won't shut up, get up and go now. Now!' Nobody moved. You could have heard a pin drop. He began the speech again and the play proceeded without further interruption.[21]

Trevor Nunn's account is slightly different – as recollections invariably are – but probably refers to the same incident:

> Nicol was particularly fearful that matinee performances attended by hosts of school-age youngsters could get out of control, with giggling, snickering and

talking at crucial moments of Macbeth's emotional journey. He was also rather proud of the fact, as the season progressed, he was managing to achieve rapt attention and silence at those school-dominated performances. Until, one day, provoked by what we will never know, he found himself with the giggling, chattering audience of his nightmares. He held firm, but the silliness didn't stop. Finally, as he approached the despair of 'Tomorrow and tomorrow and tomorrow', he could bear it no longer. But what he did was inimical only to Nicol Williamson. He stopped. He paused. He walked forward to the very front of the stage and said, 'Now look, any more of this, a colleague of mine will shortly pass amongst you … with a baseball bat' … and then very quietly and conversationally, 'OK?' There was pin drop silence. Macbeth continued his great speech.

Another theatregoer, Phil Ball – later an accomplished sportswriter – witnessed a similar outburst from Nicol:

> During the floating dagger scene, when all was hushed in anticipation of the soliloquy, someone belched. Though the audience controlled itself, Williamson didn't. Sitting down on a stool, he began to lecture the audience about how he was there to teach us Shakespeare, and how he was not going to be distracted from delivering one of the greatest speeches in English drama. It was a bizarre moment, because he'd broken the spell, making you want to pinch yourself, to check that it was really happening.[22]

By the time the show arrived in London in March 1975, however, the critics still raved, Nicol's outburst notwithstanding. Irving Wardle wrote, 'The reading stands as one of the most minutely studied and re-thought that we are ever likely to hear of an over-familiar text.'

Nicol crowned what had been a glorious year for him by directing and starring in a Stratford production of *Uncle Vanya* in which, as in New York, he played Vanya but with Jill as Elena, Jane Lapotaire as Sonya and Patrick Stewart as Astrov. This was staged at a small theatre Trevor Nunn had opened called The Other Place – which he describes as 'a theatre seating 150 people in a tin shed'.

Given Nicol's heavy involvement – acting in as well as directing *Uncle Vanya* – it was clear that commuting was impossible. As Artistic Director of the Company, Trevor Nunn had a pleasant detached house at his disposal in Stratford – with its own garden and overlooking fields on the edge of town. Nunn had one lodger in the house, his assistant on the Roman Plays and someone whose talent he was keen to promote. Her name was Buzz Goodbody – Nunn's taxi companion in his 'London Airport' story – an aspiring young director:

> Nicol and Buzz had enjoyed a good easy-going time on *Coriolanus*, so I knew they got on well. I proposed to Nicol that he should take the other guest room in my house during the Stratford season. He immediately agreed. So 'Nicol, Buzz and me' were a household, dining together, sometimes breakfasting together, late night talking together and yes, of course, drinking together. Buzz was politically very far to the left, and many times, the discussion moved into political areas, and indeed into feminist matters. They didn't always agree, but it was absolutely clear to me that their disagreements contained much affection.

Nicol's friendship with Buzz Goodbody has a sad postscript. Nunn recalls:

> The most constant and abiding memory I have of this extraordinary complex man and daring leading actor (Nicol) was not to do with our work in England. It so happened I was in Los Angeles, working on the final editing of a film, and Nicol had made his base there, I think at the house of his father-in-law. I was woken at eight in the morning in my hotel room by a phone call. I was told the unimaginable, indescribable, entirely unbelievable news that my dear young friend Buzz Goodbody had committed suicide.
>
> After many calls to colleagues, trying to discover how such an inconceivable thing could have come about, I rang Nicol and told him. He was overwhelmed. I agreed that I should go to join him where he was in Bel Air. He opened the door to me sobbing. I fell into his arms sobbing, and for several hours, we sat grieving, remembering, sharing, while repeatedly and tearfully agreeing that we couldn't understand how somebody so close to us could have done such a thing.
>
> We talked a lot on the phone over the next few days, as I caught a plane to London and began the appalling process of investigating the circumstances of this tragedy. I believe Nicol and I helped each other through.

Nicol, professionally at least, despite the tragedy of Goodbody's death, could not take a step wrong at this point. Irving Wardle wrote of his production of *Uncle Vanya*:

> If any evidence were still needed to disprove the old rule against actors directing themselves, Nicol Williamson supplies it in this production … this actor knows what he is doing and his Vanya is a superb counterpart to his emotionally starved Malvolio. Much of its power lies in its silences: sitting beside Elena and

allowing her languid phrases to peter out while he fixes her with an abject gaze of speechless hunger. Watching him at such moments you felt like an intruder.

This was the only time Nicol directed Jill but she remembered him as 'a wonderful director'.

Small screen acclaim followed stage triumph. 1974 was, of course, the year of Watergate and Nixon's resignation. Ironically, since Nicol had performed at the White House and won the President's everlasting gratitude, Nicol played Nixon in a television drama – *I Know What I Meant* – a reconstruction from audio tapes recorded in the White House after the Watergate break-in.

Jack Gold was at the helm again for what was certainly not an imitation, more a character study in, for Gold, who liked to shoot on location, a rare studio-bound film. 'David Edgar did a very good adaptation of the Watergate tapes,' Gold later recalled. 'We had a group of excellent actors and it wasn't easy. You can portray people who are dead, but when it is people you are seeing on the television screen every day, it's a different matter. You just have to gamble: the script is very important.'[23]

Perhaps Nicol always perceived himself to be a bit of a lone wolf much like Nixon, surrounded by enemies. Nicol could never quite live down his bad boy image and possibly, rather like Nixon, the sense that he was respected but not especially liked. Nicol, like Nixon, had a touch of paranoia.

Despite all the acclaim for his Coriolanus, for example, Nicol later reflected that he had felt uncomfortable. 'When I walked into the first rehearsal I felt them all giving me the eyeball. "Who the hell is this guy?" they were asking themselves. And I thought – "oh Christ, are they going to give me a hard time?" 'Perhaps he understood Nixon's 'black sheep' self-image, the man who Denis Healey described as 'sweating with anxiety … Nixon was more lacking in self-confidence than any world leader I have ever met'.[24]

Jill recalls having a few conversations with Nicol about Nixon around this time:

Watergate was my passion. I told him about a time when Nixon was vice-president and he came to our house, a little worse for wear after a luncheon hosted by someone else. He went into our basement, got on my brother's drum kit with a sombrero on his head, several sheets to the wind. I took a Polaroid and had that for a while before it went missing. Nicol loved that story. I don't think he actually *liked* Nixon any more than the rest of us.

Michael Ratcliffe in *The Times* judged Nicol's portrayal of the President as spot-on:

This was not a cartoon, although it was funny. Nicol Williamson occasionally permitted his upper lip to draw back over his teeth in an involuntary snark and used his hands as if trying to push down a volcano but he was not giving an impersonation of the president. It was a beautifully even performance of a bullet-eyed leader literally sweating it out.

Shane Rimmer, cast as Ronald Ziegler, thought Nicol was a total professional:

He had a fund of stories and anecdotes that could run well into the night and I can't recall any of them being malicious or discreditable to any of his co-artists in any way … which they could have been. He and Jack Gold had a longstanding admiration for each other which helped them bring off the difficult and sometimes questionable passage of Richard Nixon's career.[25]

Nicol, still not 40, seemed to have succeeded where many of his rivals had failed. He had now played three giant classical roles, Hamlet, Coriolanus and Macbeth, to wonderful reviews. O'Toole's and Finney's Macbeth would later be slammed by the critics; McKellen's, again for Trevor Nunn, would be hailed as the pinnacle of achievement. Yet, at this point anyway, McKellen was never as starry as Nicol and unlikely to be so.

Nicol was now, in many ways, the crown prince of the British theatre, having inherited the title from Richard Burton. Trevor Nunn says it is important to recognise not only Nicol's brilliant interpretations of the classics but also his insight. Not only had he been a good company man (at the RSC at least and flying in the face of conventional wisdom about his character), he was also something of a thwarted scholar:

He was interested in the careers and needs of young actors, he was part of the company work in big and small theatre environments and he was very articulate about theatre in general and Shakespeare in particular. Years later, I was employed to interview actors from around the world who had done defining performances of Hamlet. So, amazingly, I had many hours with Laurence Olivier, John Gielgud, Innokenti Smoktunovsky (the Russian film Hamlet), Jean Louis Barrault and Richard Burton   Nicol was one of my interviewees, discussing the startling and different Hamlet he had performed at the Roundhouse. He came to join me in the Roundhouse building, we had much talk together on camera, and then went off to dinner … I remember it like yesterday … to a restaurant called Keats in Keats Grove in Hampstead – where he tested my red wine knowledge as more than one bottle was consumed.

Nicol's reputation was riding at an all-time high. Yet, and this is important to remember, the classic stage roles may have earned critical esteem but – just as he had told the unruly schoolchildren – they didn't please his bank manager. One day, at Stratford, Trevor Nunn recalled Nicol saying, 'This has been great, I've loved my time with the RSC, but now, I have to earn some money. So it's farewell at the end of the season.'

It seemed that all he needed was a big film to bring him deserved international stardom.

9

BREAKING POINT

'Every single moment is like being taken home in an ambulance.'

Nicol Williamson on playing in the musical *Rex*

Was Nicol ever going to be a bona fide movie star? He was still waiting for a 'hit' film in the seventies. But it never really came. Instead it seemed that Nicol was to be a chameleon-like character star – which is totally different from being a box office attraction. Nicol had a strong, self-assured screen presence, exuding charisma and authority, but each performance was a unique construction.

Great stars – and I use the term 'great' in terms of cinematic durability – build an enduring screen persona. To examine just a sprinkling. John Wayne: forceful, genial, slow spoken, always on the side of right. Charles Bronson: rock-hard loner, dangerous when aroused. Clint Eastwood: super-tough, cynical, ultra-charismatic man of action, blowing his opponents apart with a twitch of a nostril. Robert Mitchum: laconic but never lacklustre, sleepy-eyed but watchful, deceptively casual. Burt Reynolds: cool, happy-go-lucky, offering a fun popcorn ride for his fans.

These were stars who became what George C. Scott once described as 'symbol' actors. Yet establishing an effective screen persona was also critical to the success of other Oscar-winning actors hailed for their 'great' performances. Jack Nicholson: sly, eccentric enigmatic outsider. Paul Newman: rebellious, sexy, charming in a thumb-on-nose rugged way. Jack Lemmon: decent middle-aged 'everyman' brought to the brink by injustice.

Jill notes that Nicol could get annoyed when certain other actors were over-lauded. Luke thinks that Nicol did not begrudge someone's success if he really thought it was justified but that, all too often, he thought it wasn't. 'He saw a lot of smoke being blown up people's arses for whatever reason,' Luke told me. He continued:

And this is the crux of it … he saw some very popular actors routinely hailed as 'great actors'. But Dad would have called them 'screen personalities'. People love them for whoever they are. They want to see that person be themselves in different roles on screen. The two actors that Dad mentioned in this context were Jack Nicholson and Michael Caine. Dad used to say, 'Don't laud them as tremendous actors on screen, that's not acting.' Dad was a different animal. The way he chose not to play the game prevented him from gaining what everyone considers success. And it could be irritating for him to see others acclaimed.

Nicol didn't want to just be a character actor. Neither did he always want to play villains, even though he acted them so well. One of his idols was Gregory Peck and perhaps Nicol fantasised about filling Peck's shoes. Jill believes that this inability to really break through with a hit film, his failure to be cast as the leading man, was a persistent bugbear for Nicol.

She claims that Nicol, who had a fragile ego under the devil-may-care surface, resented it when his associates, even friends like John Thaw, became leading men, albeit on TV. She remembers him saying, 'He's having the success that should be mine', and she would have to reassure him that just because his friends were doing well – and of course nothing rivals the power of TV – that this did not detract from his talent. A rather immature attribute perhaps but, in a reflection of Nicol's insecurity, he could get envious. 'And John's wonderful success, Nicol felt, was a "theft" from him,' recalled Jill:

Where was Nicol's success? If it was jealousy, it was mixed with fear … a lack of something within himself. And he wasn't 'gracious' really about anyone's success … even Olivier's. I would even use the word 'tormented' … I don't think Nicol was jealous of someone else's *fame*, it was *success*, and anything not directed toward him was felt as being taken away from him.

Nicol could also be suspicious of others. Jill recalls:

After we were married, I received a telegram from Tony Richardson declaring he wanted to see me for his next film. Nicol refused to let me answer it, saying that Tony was using me to hurt him … that he didn't really want me. Probably so. I don't know. I never met Tony, so I cannot say.

Jill says that Nicol never showed much interest when she appeared in the television series *The Golden Bowl* or in the movie *Sitting Target* opposite Oliver Reed. (She remembers Reed as 'a very kind person'.)

Sarah Miles had also noted in her memoirs that Nicol was frustrated and envious of others' success. 'Nicol wanted to be a movie star (what actor didn't?) although usually he kept this tucked well away. When I was on the phone with Robin Fox (her agent) sometimes I saw hints of dissatisfaction, which often ended with him openly begrudging me being one.'

Rand Bridges, a friend of Nicol's during his time in New York in the early eighties, always believed that Nicol *did* secretly pine to be a movie star. 'I used to say to him, "You really should do this role. You really should do that." And he'd say, "I'll do that when I'm earning a million dollars a picture."'

The director Peter Gill, who worked with Nicol several times, believes that ultimately Nicol simply lacked sex appeal, that indefinable 'turn-on' quality possessed by British stars such as O'Toole, Finney, Burton and Hopkins.[1]

Perhaps it was all made worse when he saw the praise showered on rivals. The two verifiable superstars of British cinema in the seventies were Michael Caine and Sean Connery. Nicol had little time for either of them as actors after working with them both back to back. 'Guys like Caine and Connery talk about acting as if they know what it's about,' he once said.

Caine's screen persona was discernible early on. He may have played an assortment of characters but he was still Michael Caine – blinking coldly behind spectacles, combining an unfluid acting style with an accent deliberately preserving his working-class origins. True, there's a big distinction between, say, *Get Carter* and *Educating Rita*, but there are also many films where he offers carbon copied portrayals, for example in *The Swarm*, *Ashanti*, *Beyond the Poseidon Adventure* or *The Hand*.

Likewise Connery – always tough, temperamental and dangerous. Of course, there's a difference between, for example, *The Offence* and *Finding Forrester* but also many films where he is similar – as in *Meteor*, *Cuba* and *Outland*.

It's a bit like ordering a McDonalds. You may seek a variation on your usual order but with Caine and Connery you knew what to expect. With Nicol, by contrast, you never knew what was coming.

The Wilby Conspiracy, filmed in Kenya in 1974 by Ralph Nelson, showed what Nicol could do with a villainous role – even if he didn't like playing them. He upstages the nominal stars, Sidney Poitier and Michael Caine, and makes a psychopath three-dimensional. And, of course, it was a well-written part. You want to find the nastiest character in movies? Always look for movies about Nazis or apartheid South Africa.

As a sadistic chief of security police (Major Horn), torturing and murdering all opponents, Nicol pursues escaped convict Poitier and his buddy Caine across country. It's Nicol who rivets you throughout, pale blue eyes burning, smoking endless ciggies, snarling sarcastically as he taunts white liberals. And repulsive though he is, he's no dope, which makes him more interesting. 'It hurts me to see an intelligent, educated white man so against his own people,' he says to Caine.

Nicol's opening scene opposite granite-jawed district commissioner (Patrick Allen) establishes the character instantly.

'You fanatics shout national security whenever you do anything immoral or illegal,' Allen barks at Nicol's Major Horn.

'And damn lucky for you we do,' replies Nicol as Horn. 'Three million whites surrounded by eighteen million blacks … listen, we built this country, every town, every factory, every farm, mine, and Christian church, and I protect it … no Zulu twenty years out a tree is gonna shove fifty cents in my hand and tell me there's a freighter in Cape Town harbour waiting to ship me out of the land I built   alrighty?'

Nicol's Horn casually inflicts brutalities, yet sometimes pulling back when going in too heavy would damage his interests. 'Two brutal insensitive officers from state security beat a lovely Bantu patriarch? No thank you very much, you'd be an overnight martyr.'

Nicol makes all this fascist fervour seem newly spun even though it's from the apartheid Bible of the country's then President, John Vorster, or even Eugene Terreblanche. It marked the start of filmmakers' interest in the injustices of South Africa, later seen in another of Nicol's films, *The Human Factor*, and, subsequently, Richard Attenborough's *Cry Freedom* and Chris Menges's *A World Apart*.

Luke cites his dad's performance in *The Wilby Conspiracy* as his personal favourite and probably his greatest on screen. And indeed Nicol towers over the silly banter between Caine and Poitier. William Hall, in his biography of Caine, noted the same. 'Nicol Williamson was highly effective as the bullish security chief stalking and taunting the two fugitives while enmeshing them in his own web of intrigue.'[2]

Overall, *The Wilby Conspiracy* turned out well, even winning praise from Leslie Halliwell. 'Reasonably exciting political chase thriller with a sufficiency of twists and action sequences; philosophy is present but secondary,' he judged.

In a sharp change of pace – from rabid racist to gentle giant – Nicol went to Spain to act opposite Sean Connery in *Robin and Marian*, director Richard Lester's account of the autumnal reunion between an aging Robin Hood and his sweetheart, played by Audrey Hepburn. Nicol was (eventually) cast as Little John. Also in the film were two other veteran hellraisers, Richard Harris and Robert Shaw. Writer James Goldman had originally envisaged Nicol as Richard the Lionheart and Harris as Little John, only to find the actors more interested in playing each other's role. Shaw was the Sheriff of Nottingham, a part also originally offered to Nicol but one he declined.

Nicol and Harris – and perhaps this will disappoint those who assume they would have been happy carousers – did not particularly gel. Maybe Nicol secretly envied Harris's international stardom, achieved despite the Irishman's (arguably) lesser talent as a singer and actor. We should remember that Harris had won the lead in *This Sporting Life*, a part that Nicol had prized. It's difficult to see what Harris had to offer over and above Nicol. By this I intend no disrespect to Harris – a talented actor but not quite in Nicol's league. If there was a difference between Nicol and Harris it was in their work rate. Harris, especially in the seventies, accepted any part that offered him a plane ticket and a fat cheque. He made twenty films during that decade, whereas Nicol made fewer than half that. Nicol was always far more discriminating, spurning big paydays if he felt the role or project did not suit him. Harris was also readier to grace the chat show circuit. He made serial appearances on programmes hosted by Michael Parkinson, Michael Aspel, Gloria Hunniford and Jonathan Ross in the UK, and their equivalent in the US. Harris might have decried his craft and the boredom of filmmaking but he was also, seemingly, a canny self-publicist, mindful of the old 'out of sight, out of mind' proverb.[3]

Harris was not the only person whom Nicol disliked on *Robin and Marian*. If Ronnie Barker is to be believed, then there was also no love lost between Nicol and Denholm Elliott (cast as Will Scarlett) who 'were at each other's throats often'.[4] Yet, according to Luke, it was actually Barker whom Nicol disliked. He does not remember his dad mentioning Elliott at all.

Nicol apparently thought highly of Robert Shaw, admiring his ability to combine a respected literary career with screen stardom.[5]

Several critics noted that Nicol was responsible for one of the film's most touching moments.

'You've never liked me, have you?' Marian asks Little John during a night-time scene.

'You're Rob's lady,' says Nicol as Little John, very softly, before adding, after some quiet reflection, 'If you'd been mine I'd never have left you.'

Richard Lester said the exchange was always one of his favourites in the film:

When we shot it, we had a problem with the film stock and in theory we should have gone back and shot it again. But I liked the original so much, I just said I don't care what it looks like. It played right the first time, and often when you do it again, it doesn't come up to the original frisson. So I said, to hell with it, we'll just have it as it is.[6]

Reviews for the film were mixed – Leslie Halliwell called it 'a kind of serious parody of medieval life, after the fashion of *The Lion in Winter* but much glummer'

– but many, just like Lester, thought the scene between Nicol and Hepburn was the film's best. Luke believes it reflected his dad's emotional vulnerability, a quality seldom noticed by observers. 'His scenes with Audrey Hepburn are so much rawer and more emotional than Connery's. I mentioned that to him one night and he pointed out that Sean can't do emotion.'

Perhaps Connery was simply too macho to express tenderness; he could project toughness, anger, determination, humour, belligerence and regret but profound feeling was beyond him. According to Luke, Nicol told him that Connery was also a notorious tightwad – at least when it came to gratuities – something that Nicol resented.

One day, during a break in filming, Nicol heard of a great restaurant just across the border into France and invited a couple of friends to join him for dinner. Connery got wind of it and offered to drive them all over to the restaurant. (Nicol thought this was just a way of Connery killing two birds with one stone because he needed to get his passport stamped.) Nicol subsequently told Luke that the service in the restaurant had been brilliant. 'After the main course the staff brought out this rare, very expensive complimentary bottle of green Armagnac (Nicol thought it cost about $300) to enjoy with dessert,' Luke told me:

Everyone split the bill when it arrived but, according to Nicol, Connery didn't want to contribute to a tip. He eventually slammed down the money on the table, saying 'I'll pay it but I don't have to like it'. But that was Sean. So Nicol didn't want to spend time with him again. My mom once said to him: 'Sean's a lovely guy, really. He's gone out of his way to help young Scottish actors.' But for my dad – the incident was enough. He didn't want to have dinner with Sean again.

Luke thinks the lunch revealed one of Nicol's most endearing characteristics. Yes, he could be rude about other actors, producers and directors – quite often famous people he believed were overrated – but he would *never* belittle or short-change the little guy:

He was extremely sensitive to anyone who suffered any kind of misfortune and had to rely on the kindness or charity of others. He felt an enormous empathy for them. He would never pass a homeless person on the street without giving them something. He would always stop to take time to talk to them, to ensure they weren't ignored or treated as unsightly. He was very much a champion of the underdog, perhaps because he felt he was *also* the underdog. And that feeling extended to everyone else in 'underdog' positions. He was an extremely generous person. He never let others pay for meals.

Luke says that Nicol had an innate bullshit detector and was an excellent judge of character. Perhaps it was that acute intelligence that placed him above most other actors. 'He wasn't formally educated, but he would meet university students and discuss philosophy and life and all the things they were learning. He knew a lot about a wide variety of things, but was always interested in learning more,' Luke recalled.

Tragically, Nicol's mother Mary died from cancer towards the end of shooting on *Robin and Marian*. Jill, who was then in London filming *Poldark* at the BBC, first heard the news by phone. She knew that Nicol, who was always close to his parents, would be devastated. Fretting that he would hear about it before she could tell him (there were no mobiles in those days) she instructed the production company that whoever broke the news to Nicol should immediately hand him a plane ticket home. Jill knew that he could not be alone.

Nicol's parents had been immensely proud of their son's success. But whenever he had returned home it was clear who was in charge. They were aware of his brilliance but also his foibles. They had always made a point of telling him when he got out of line. Trevor Nunn, who stayed with Nicol and his parents one weekend at their bungalow in East Stirling – probably about a year or two before Mary's death – noted a lot of tongue-in-cheek admonitions. Yet maybe that was a double bluff. The world's greatest Hamlet still needed a few lessons in etiquette. Nunn recalls:

Seeing him with mum and dad, everything made sense. He was adored by them, but they gave him repeated instructions – where to walk, where not to walk with me, what to buy at the local shop, what to say if we encountered a certain neighbour, and even a reprimand about putting his shoe-clad feet on the sofa! It was like a game. They knew their son was famous and successful, but they were play acting that they had to look after this wayward boy … Nicol took it all in good part, shrugging and gesturing to me … 'Do you see what I have to put up with?' I had a sense that, because he felt by sharing the house in Stratford, I had let him into my life, with this visit home, he was letting me into his. We did walk and talk a great deal and swapped opinions on pretty much everything, without putting up barriers and defences – about politics, religion and, of course, personal relationships. He made no secret of his impulsive delight in women and his urge (long before the days when such an utterance would be appallingly incorrect) to bed as many as possible.

Perhaps at this point, Nunn found Nicol happy because, on the stage at least, he was unequivocally the leading man. Other actors were aware of his stage charisma and seldom keen to compete for glory. In film it was different; Nicol had given two key supporting performances, but he was still waiting for a juicy leading role. It appeared that it might have arrived with Sherlock Holmes, Conan Doyle's Victorian super sleuth who still draws legions of tourists to London's 221b Baker Street – including some gullible souls who believe he was a real figure!

We're now in a golden age of Sherlocks, ever since Jeremy Brett's finely etched representation in the eighties. Recently, Guy Ritchie's fast-moving action spoofs starring Robert Downey Jr and, especially, Benedict Cumberbatch's hit TV series, have cemented the revival. Yet, for three postwar decades, nobody had come close to usurping Basil Rathbone as the quintessential Holmes, with Nigel Bruce as his bumbling sidekick. Television portrayals by Ronald Howard and Peter Cushing, and then Robert Stephens in a feature film, Billy Wilder's *The Private Life of Sherlock Holmes*, were tepid by comparison.

Back in the seventies, Nicholas Meyer's book *The Seven-Per-Cent Solution*, in which Watson lures a cocaine-befuddled Holmes to Vienna to be treated by Dr Sigmund Freud, sparked a major resurgence of interest. The novel debuted in July 1974, entering the *New York Times* top ten bestsellers' list that September. So much so that Meyer, later to rescue the *Star Trek* series with his direction of *The Wrath of Khan* in 1982 (after a disappointingly turgid first Trekkie feature film in 1979) was quickly hired to write a screenplay.

Reflecting on screen incarnations to date, Meyer thought Rathbone had been 'excellent' and Cushing had been 'good, if a little small'. He also admitted being 'rather partial' to Ronald Howard. For his film, however, Meyer needed a younger, more dynamic star. Meyer's first choice to play Holmes was Peter O'Toole. But O'Toole and the director, Herbert Ross, had clashed on the set of *Goodbye Mr. Chips*. Eventually Meyer and Ross settled on Nicol. Perhaps surprisingly, given his love of reading, Nicol was no Holmes aficionado, admitting to interviewer Rex Reed that he had never read any of the books or seen the films:

> I guess one of the reasons I'm playing Sherlock Holmes is a reaction against taking on so many classical roles in the past. I was offered the role in Billy Wilder's version a few years ago,[7] but the script was corny. This one has great excitement and colour and I'm playing him as a hopeless romantic. I'm playing him with a light touch but the movie is not a caper or a spoof. I'm sort of a quizzical Leslie Howard. It's something I've always wanted to play.

The casting of Dr Watson was certainly unusual. Meyer relates how Robert Duvall won the part:

Duvall came into the office to chat with Herb [Ross] and me about playing Dr Watson. It was the same day that he was 'meeting' someone to star as [folk singer] Woody Guthrie in *Bound for Glory*,[8] and so he came in, inexplicably, in the character of Guthrie! He had the full Okie accent, he was wearing a brown buckskin fringed jacket, and the entire time Herb and I were sitting there bewildered, staring at each other over his shoulder, and he was speaking with this outlandish twang. Finally, after fifteen or twenty minutes, he just got up and said, 'well, I'll be gittin' along now, and oh … by the way I brung this tape of me talkin' like Dr Watson' and then he puts this cassette tape down on the desk and walks out, leaving you sitting there thinking, 'what the hell was that?' Then we listened to the cassette and out comes this Oxbridge speech of this entirely different person! You could not believe it was the same person![9]

Yet doubts remained. Samantha Eggar, cast as Mrs Watson, listened to the tape and thought Duvall was 'trying too hard'. Eventually they phoned the English secretary of a Twentieth Century Fox executive who identified the accent, without being prompted about the actor's identity, as 'Oxbridge, BBC English'. So Duvall clinched it.

Interiors on *The Seven-Per-Cent Solution*, including 221b Baker Street, Professor Moriarty's flat and Freud's home, were shot at Pinewood. The second major location was Queen's Club, a private sporting venue in West Kensington, where the film's real tennis match was staged. Meyer was prepared to be ruthless and cut the contest between Freud (Alan Arkin) and Baron von Leinsdorf (Jeremy Kemp) from his screenplay but Ross objected, claiming – almost certainly correctly – that it was a celebrated event in the original novel.

Some exterior shots of Freud's home were shot on location in the Austrian capital. Nicol recalled that 'Alan Arkin, who has been in Freudian analysis for nine years, got claustrophobic and couldn't breathe when we were filming locations in Vienna'.

When filming began in October 1975 there were still concerns about Duvall. The American didn't seem to be doing anything, delivering his lines in a whispered monotone. Meyer recalls:

When we would watch the dailies, I couldn't see Duvall doing anything. I was getting kind of anxious and I said – 'can't we get him to emote? He's just delivering lines without doing anything'. So Herb talked to Duvall who became prickly and said 'what do you want me to do? Make faces?' So we sort of backed off, and then, when we stuck all the pieces of film together, Duvall walks away with the movie! That's real movie acting and he knew exactly what he was doing.

Duvall was your archetypal screen actor, the master of understatement. Opinion, however, was divided about his final performance. Luke Williamson disagrees with Meyer and believes Duvall was ultimately 'stultified' by the accent.

Nicol liked playing Holmes, exploiting his manic cerebral energy. Luke told me that the scene where they burst into a bordello and Nicol tells Duvall, 'Don't look, Watson, the Queen wouldn't like it', was Nicol ad-libbing. Meyer also believed that 'Nicol enjoyed the filming and viewed it, I think, as some sort of respite from "heavier" chores, although I had no doubt that he was able to plug himself easily into some of the issues that bedeviled the story's protagonist'.

Luke recalls that Nicol preferred Arkin's company and that he found Duvall 'quite boring'.

Jill had a small part in the film, playing Sherlock Holmes's mother. By this point in the shooting she intimates that Nicol was becoming moody:

I had worked with Robert Duvall before when he played a role in *Cimarron Strip* … so I was happy to see him again … But I just played the tiny part of Holmes's mother and the scene was a bed scene with Moriarty – played by Sir Laurence Olivier. I think Herb Ross thought it would be fun. But I could tell Nicol was coming into a 'difficult mood'. Sir Larry (as he was then) and I were in the bed getting ready for the 'canoodle' and Larry (who was very sweet) jokingly says to me: 'Do you think Nicol will be jealous?' I didn't know how to answer that … if I said 'no' would that insult Larry? If I said 'yes', would Larry tease Nicol? … We did the scene and were discovered by the young Holmes … and when it was over, and my role was completed, I slipped away. I don't know Herb's reason for asking me to do that one scene. Was it for fun? Maybe he thought I might be able to soften Nicol's moodiness. Anyway, I didn't hang around.

Overall, Herbert Ross believed that Nicol had succeeded in illuminating a 'new' Holmes. 'There isn't one single thing in it that will remind anyone of Basil Rathbone,' he said at the time, and other than a vague physical similarity – pronounced chin and angular features – that's true.

Meyer recalls he could find only two critical reviews out of more than 100. If there was a 'problem' it was that Nicol's performance jarred with filmgoers' conception of a meticulous, cerebral Holmes. He was offering us a manic crackpot instead.

Bruce McCabe in *The Boston Globe*, was an example, citing the surprise conception of Holmes. 'He's a user of cocaine and, as played by Nicol Williamson, a schizophrenic wreck. He's so at odds with the Sherlock Holmes we've come to know through our reading and our viewing of old Basil Rathbone movies that it throws us completely off stride.'

Most reviewers enjoyed it. Randy Sue Coburn of *The Washington Star* wrote that 'Nicol Williamson is a pleasure to watch exercising Holmes.' 'Holmes, Watson and a lot of class' was the headline over the review in the *San Francisco Examiner*.

Other Sherlockian devotees noted 'a brilliantly edgy performance by Nicol Williamson, whose wild eyes and rapid, almost gabbling speech give a real impression of narcotically-fuelled manic energy'.[10]

Meyer was particularly impressed that Pauline Kael, not a great fan of Nicol's, (as we will recall!), neither of Herbert Ross's work, loved the movie, describing it as 'a highly civilised light entertainment'. If Meyer faults the film, more than forty years down the line, it's not related to flaws in performances but, rather, his own screenplay:

> I'm embarrassed how wordy it is. Way too talky. I think I became a much better screenwriter after I started directing. I became much more aware of the relationship and the ratio of words to pictures when I did *Time After Time*. So I find, in retrospect, that *The Seven-Per-Cent Solution* is a fearfully talky movie. The only saving grave is that, by and large, it's good talk. I just wish there was less of it.

Meyer's observation of Nicol was strangely downbeat:

> My own impression was of one of the saddest people I have ever met, trapped in some hideous internal world of isolation and despair from which he was only intermittently able to escape. Acting and later singing provided some respite, but neither of these – as I'm sure the record bears out – were dependable in that regard.

Were cracks starting to show in Nicol and Jill's marriage? The previous year, Jill, apart from also appearing in Nicol's stage version of *Uncle Vanya*, had starred in a cheap, sexploitation follow-up to *Alfie* called *Alfie Darling*. Rumours swirled that Jill was having a relationship with Alan Price, but she says that this had nothing to do with her break-up from Nicol. Professionally, Jill would also enjoy her biggest success to date in the classic and very popular BBC series *Poldark*. Jill had practised her British accent on television before, for example in the very first episode of *The Sweeney*. She explains how she won her role in *Poldark*:

> One day, the director sat us down and explained how we all got our parts. He said he cast me as Elizabeth, the one-time fiancée of Poldark, because my upper-

class English accent was perfect. When I told him I was American, he froze. He thought he had made a terrible mistake and spent the rest of filming paying close attention to everything I said, terrified I would introduce an American accent. But I didn't – I'd trained at RADA.[11]

Superficially, everything seemed fine in their relationship. Nicol, in a contemporary interview, described how he had been 'trembling with excitement' at the thought of getting back into bed with Jill after a three-week separation. The same article described a reformed Nicol whom, it seemed, Jill had tamed. 'I no longer smoke or drink except I might have two or three glasses of wine and the odd glass of beer on the weekend. My wife won't believe me.' Jill, for her part, claimed to have taught him 'not to tackle every day like it's a title fight'. The profile tells us that even little Luke, then just 3, would remonstrate with his father – telling him, according to writer Fred Hauptfuhrer, 'to mind your manners' when he got over-excited at the dinner table![12]

The bliss did not last. Jill's success in *Poldark* did not draw them together. Jill claims that Nicol took little pride in her achievements:

To be honest, I don't think Nicol was very interested in what I was doing acting-wise. I would always play down what I was doing as not so important. I learnt to do this after the Tony Richardson telegram incident … then I was nominated as Best Newcomer at the Evening Standard Film Awards in November 1975. He got angry. I played down this nomination and didn't respond to the invitation to the awards ceremony, so as not to rile Nicol. Finally, they called Nicol to tell him I had won and could he make sure I got there. He went into one of his rages and I kept telling him that we didn't have to go … just forget it … it's not important. We went – I didn't know I had won and it was not what I wanted, being the focus of attention. And then he really laid into the alcohol that night. It just wasn't worth me getting excited about anything I did in the theatre world. If I accomplished anything in acting, it would be like taking something away from him.

By 1976 a very different Nicol began to emerge, no longer calm but on the precipice. And wounded. Jill and Nicol had now moved to a new house in Castelnau, Barnes, but she was finding him increasingly difficult. Luke occupied much of Jill's time and she observed that Nicol simply didn't know how to be around small children. Jill, whom we will remember had never been a drinker, also recalls that, by the time they had moved to Barnes, Nicol's boozing had worsened. If he didn't have an early morning call, Nicol would often sleep until the afternoon, waking up to a beer before moving on to wine and brandy in the evening.

Jill says that the word 'incompatibility' was an understatement to compare their lifestyles:

> My father was an alcoholic and I *so* dislike the taste of alcohol. When I was 18 my father said I *had* to find an alcoholic drink … it got reduced to vodka and orange juice … but I would leave out the vodka because it ruined the taste of the orange juice! No. The most I've ever had was a half glass of wine at Christmas. I didn't share Nicol's love of wines, brandies and ports. I wonder if it irritated him that I didn't drink … Nicol never physically hurt me. His rages were against probably what he saw as the unfairness of life. He could be verbally cruel about other people. This rage is what drove him to alcohol.

Ironically, it was Nicol's combination of vulnerability allied to his larger-than-life presence that won him the role in *Rex*, one of the most ill-fated musicals in Broadway's history, based on the life of Henry VIII.

It all began auspiciously enough. Richard Adler produced a show based on lyrics from the renowned Richard Rodgers, famed composer of more than 900 songs and forty-three Broadway musicals. Adler was keen to get Nicol on board, having seen and admired him in *Uncle Vanya*:

> For my money he was one of the greatest actors in the world and I was determined to cast him in the show. I discovered that he was presently living near Stratford, right next to a castle that had once been occupied by none other than Henry VIII. [Nicol and Jill, in between shows at Stratford, were renting the Gate Cottage at Warwick Castle and the Earl of Warwick would sometimes invite them for Sunday lunch.]
>
> Perhaps serendipity was on my side I thought as I flew to London, rented a car and drove out to keep a luncheon invitation offered to me by Nicol Williamson and his wife. The home was a comfortable British country retreat. I was let in by a butler and shown to the study which had a full view of a sumptuous staircase. Five minutes passed, and there was a stirring at the top of the stairs. I looked up and there, descending the staircase, was Henry VIII, red-headed, virile, and reining in regal energy and fire. It was as if the character I'd envisioned had suddenly, precisely come to life. We had a convivial, relaxed lunch. Nicol Williamson and his wife couldn't have been more charming. And to make it all perfect, as dessert neared, they both launched into the melody. Before I left he'd agreed to do the part. He was magnificent as Henry; few could have done it better. But

unfortunately for us, and unknown to me at the time, he was a load of trouble – incredible antics fuelled by copious amounts of wine mixed with brandy. It made for tumultuous times, in rehearsal, on the road and in New York.[13]

Nicol grew less comfortable in rehearsals. He said he could feel the audience's hostility towards Henry's character rolling all over him. Why was this nasty man killing these nice ladies? Director Edwin Sherin recalled that Nicol 'was extremely difficult, having a tough time with his marriage, his child and drinking … Nicol would participate somewhat languidly in the rehearsals, arriving late and leaving early. He also had some contempt for the writing, which was perhaps justified'.

Nicol, already tired even before the show opened, sometimes blew his lines, resulting in some amusing malapropisms. 'Madame, you diminish the throne that I shit on', was one that leaked out. (The whole cast collapsed in time-consuming laughter.) Another time, Nicol, leaving the script, suddenly said, 'I've had it with this kingdom. What I need is three brandies.' In the middle of one rehearsal Nicol apparently marched off to his hotel room and failed to show up for a scheduled interview.

Journalist Herbert Kretzmer recalls an encounter with an anguished Nicol during the try-out run in Washington. Nicol's mood was very different from the first time he had met Kretzmer. The combination of marital discord and the marathon part – he was in practically every scene and on stage for two hours forty minutes – had driven him over the edge. Kretzmer recalled that the sign on the door of Nicol's suite at the Watergate Hotel read 'do not disturb'.

He later took Nicol to lunch at the famous Jockey Club. 'I feel as though I'm dying,' Nicol told Kretzmer 'I'm absolutely beyond the point of no return.' Nicol went on to say he found musicals 'crushing' and 'diminishing', adding that 'every single moment is like being taken home in an ambulance'.[14]

It was a mistake one can only find out by doing it. There's no way of predicting these things. I will never do another musical. Never. Never. I'm smoking like a chimney again after months off it. I could wind up a 100 a day man here. I care for what I'm doing every minute of my life. I'm totally caught up in it. That's why people like me are not long for this planet. I simply can't keep pumping that energy into *Rex*. I do possess a sense of honour and fairness. I don't want to damage the show or its fine company … it's a grand piece of confectionery, a mammoth juggernaut, resplendent to look at. What's more, if I quit the show it will put me on the deck financially. I may not even be able to salvage my new home in England. But the prospect of doing the show for a year is killing.

Playwright Sherman Yellen observed Nicol's histrionics, perhaps in character for Henry VIII. Worse still, Yellen's indiscretion collided with Nicol's insecurity once the play arrived in New York for rehearsals:

> One day Nicol threw a crown he was wearing, a rather expensive piece of property, across the stage and Rodgers in his oesophageal voice [Rodgers had been stricken with throat cancer] turned to me and said 'he's every square inch a king'. And then, of course there was the trauma of my big mouth. I was sitting in Sardi's after having put up with what I thought was a lot, having a drink. It was the eve of Passover, right before we were supposed to open in New York, and I had just received the very troubling news that I had a polyp on my vocal chords – and Dick [Rodgers], remember, had started like that. I was very nervous about that, although fortunately it turned out to be nothing. So I was a little under the weather with the tension of the show and a reporter from one of the tabloids came by and recognised me. He said. 'What's a nice Jewish boy like you doing sitting in Sardi's tonight?' And I said, 'Well, when you're on the road with Nicol Williamson you no longer believe in God.' Would you know, the next day the paper prints that, right before we were supposed to go on … Nicol then said he would not go on and I was challenged to make some kind of apology … so I wrote out this apology, the kind you do, trying to get yourself off the hook without humbling myself too much. I couldn't really apologise for what I had said because, in truth, it was hellish, an awful experience and also for Dick as well.[15]

Rex opened in New York on 25 April 1976. Clive Barnes in the *New York Times* found that the show had almost everything *not* going for it. Rodgers's musical, he wrote, was a hodgepodge of 'airy fairy madrigals, lute songs jazzed up for a Broadway orchestra, a sort of mixture of Benjamin Britten and Irving Berlin … we appear to be hearing an anthology of songs from *Camelot* that were ditched on the road'.

Barnes went on pay Nicol a double-edged compliment:

> It is fantastic what authority, what strength this actor has on stage. His eyes command an audience and his voice is so unobtrusively musical that its hard brilliance is lost in the softer cadences of melody. But there's the rub. For while Nicol Williamson has a very good singing voice, when he sings his voice loses his character. It is most remarkable; suddenly the genius leaves him and he becomes just another singer.

The worst was yet to come. The cast had been stung by poor notices and the sense that the show still lacked cohesion. On the evening of 13 May 1976, Nicol slapped dancer Jim Litten at the curtain call. Nicol claims to have heard Litten say 'that was crap'. Litten says he actually said 'that's a wrap'.

Other cast members were stunned then, after a few seconds, raced into action, pulling Nicol into line. Barbara Andres, who played Catherine of Aragon, recalled:

> The wives tried to get Nicol offstage and away from Jimmy, who was on the floor. At first the audience thought it was all part of the curtain call, but soon they realised it was real. There was a terrible feeling in the company, against Nicol, the serfs against the king, as it were.

Penny Fuller, cast as Anne Boleyn and Princess Elizabeth, recalled that the incident happened just after her bow and curtsy. For a while she just stood there, agape, rooted to the spot. But she felt she had to intervene. Otherwise, she recently told a radio show, a trifle melodramatically (well, the interviewer happened to be a rabbi!) she would have felt like an onlooker at Nazi atrocities. 'Is this what the Germans did during the war? Just turned their backs and pretended it didn't happen? It was so terrible that I was turning away from it and running away.'

The press, needless to say, carried the story and ran with it. Some wondered if the coverage would extend the run, a mixed blessing because the cast was demoralised, almost looking for a reprieve. When Fuller saw the papers she was apoplectic. She charged into Nicol's dressing room and screamed at him. 'You SOB. Now we'll run for years.'[16] Needless to say, it didn't. A rare Richard Rodgers failure, *Rex* closed after just fifty performances.

Reflecting on the whole 'Nicol' experience, Fuller added:

> He was a wonderful actor but he was difficult. I'm not his psychiatrist ... it was a cover-up for some kind of vulnerability. But he was kind of tough and nasty and difficult to get along with. He was carrying this show. It was a complicated show and not quite right yet. It got a little better but it never got totally fixed. It was a great idea, I guess. He was cranky, 'not drinking anymore' – 'only white wine' if you get my drift! We opened on Broadway to not great reviews and we tried to do a commercial on the show. Nicol said he wouldn't do it. He was a really difficult and gnarly kind of guy but also extremely attractive. I found him attractive.[17]

Nicol had been under a tremendous strain. Nevertheless, Trevor Nunn was surprised when he heard about Nicol's violence. He said that throughout their collaborations he had never seen an inkling of it:

Many people said to me that Nicol was once again showing his true colours, and such stupidity and aggression were only to be expected from such a lunatic. Such reactions made no sense to me, at all. Throughout the time at the RSC, he had been jovial, mischievously funny, every inch a leading actor and a committed company member. We must remember in assessing Nicol that he was flourishing towards the end of the period when, by definition, great leading actors were wild men, heavy drinkers, bad boys … it was the age of Peter O'Toole, Richard Burton, Richard Harris, Hugh Griffith. The age when stardom was coupled with extreme behaviour, where to be drunk on stage was hilarious and entirely forgivable. I'm sure that Nicol was aware that very flamboyant behaviour would ultimately do him no harm. In my time with him, one would not have known that he was in that tradition.

Perhaps – to add to his woes – Nicol was miscast as Henry VIII. He was certainly the thinnest Henry there had ever been. Nicol was glad when it ended. A throwaway part as a 'cartoon kraut' in Neil Simon's misfire satire *The Cheap Detective* – which was dismissed, totally correctly in this case, by Leslie Halliwell as 'a lame spoof' – didn't help Nicol's career. Neither did an uncredited part in the same playwright's *The Goodbye Girl* – although his cameo as a slightly effete film director showed his ability to convey a character with the flutter of an eyelid.

A bad year for Nicol got worse. Much worse. He was originally cast as Peter Stockman in the film *Enemy of the People* starring Steve McQueen, based on Henrik Ibsen's classic play about a town doctor's crusade to warn its people about a contaminated water supply. Director George Schaefer said that Nicol was 'a nightmare'. Nicol apparently failed to show up at all. Author Christopher Sandford wrote that 'Williamson was fired when he called in, drunk, on the first day of rehearsals. From Hawaii.'[18] Charles Durning inherited his role.

Jill says the background was even more dramatic:

Nicol had signed a contract to do the Ibsen film with McQueen. I think I was doing *Poldark* at the time. The problem was that Nicol was not insurable because of his tendency to walk off the set/stage on a whim. So they made him sign an agreement that stipulated that, if he walked off this film, he'd lose his house and possessions. He signed the contract at the time that Luke was about to start nursery school. Nicol went out to California and then promptly disappeared. The accountant called me and told me that I was going to lose the house in Barnes I'd just bought. So I had to tell one of the guys over there, 'Just get a message to Nicol that we'll be on the street and they'll take everything.' My lawyer told me that the only way to stop this thing was to file for divorce in order to save the roof over our heads.

We do not have Nicol's version of his break-up from Jill. But Luke, who maintained a fantastic relationship with both his parents, said his dad told a rather different story. What is certain is that Nicol was enraged, ushering in a period that Jill still finds painful to describe, the words 'sad … sad … sad …' still being uttered with long sighs forty years later. Nicol became bitter and vengeful with threats along the lines of 'you'll never work again' to Jill. Nicol accused Jill of sleeping with various people and alleged that she had been living in a commune in Cornwall at one time and that Luke was a love child. Jill said she shunned the press, only contacting the *Daily Mail* to demand a correction to one particular story. 'I wanted a retraction but I certainly never sued the newspaper and neither did I sue Nicol.'

In April 1977 Nicol and Jill divorced. Feelings were strong on both sides but – as often happens – time healed them:

> I always told Luke – I will never *not* love your father. I'm so grateful to him for so many things. I got swept off my feet and I was taught so much. I'll never regret any of it although some of it was terrifying. I don't have anything against people who drink but he belonged to that group of actors – O'Toole, Burton, Harris – who did so to excess.

Jill is convinced that Nicol was an alcoholic who simply refused to be treated and that this was the source of his downfall – the repeated altercations with other performers and producers and perhaps the reason for Hollywood's reluctance to cement his status as a leading man. She doesn't think that Nicol was a manic depressive or bipolar. 'He certainly wasn't born with this condition. A lot of his problems stemmed from a traumatic childhood.'

Reflecting on their marriage, Jill described it as 'amazing, chaotic, confusing … he was so unlike me … I truly loved Nicol and thought we would be married forever. And I am so very saddened by his – not inability because he *had* the ability – readiness to toss things aside, 'never to be spoken of again'.

She describes him as 'a hard love'.

Over the years Nicol and Jill saw each other rarely but when they did Jill says it seemed like Nicol had just become a friend again. She saw him briefly when he was filming *The Exorcist III* in 1989 and also *Spawn* in 1996. She remembers Nicol telling her that she had been a wonderful mother to Luke. Of his parents' divorce, Luke told me, 'They didn't talk for a long time, but Dad didn't hold any bitterness after a few years, and I think he was quite OK with not having much of a relationship at all.'

Following their divorce, and a battle to win visitation rights to Luke, Nicol took some time off. Actress Carolyn Seymour remembers the recklessness of Nicol's (and her own) drinking from this period, in particular an incident from June 1977 when she was starring in a London play called *On Approval*:

I adored Nico but he was a difficult one. I drank with him which is why we got on so well, but we really used to drink to oblivion. We once emptied the Connaught's cellars of Gewürztraminer '73 and I had to perform that evening in the West End, a very shameful moment for me. I loved him for his vulnerabilities of which there were many, hidden beneath a cavalier surface. His drinking was a form of self-medication, as was mine, and that's what we really connected over. I would love to be more specific but if you understood the amount of alcohol that was consumed … you would understand why it's so difficult to remember specifics … Nicol and I also used to lose whole afternoons at the White Elephant, a lovely place on the river.[19]

Nicol would also go to Rhodes to recuperate, a place he had been visiting regularly since the late sixties.

A friend in Lindos, Martin Sandford, recalled:

It was a difficult time for him, I won't go into why, but my friends and I learnt how to arm wrestle and generally be thrown around the room (in Socrates Bar). To describe this place was simple, it was four walls, a wood plank bar with a hole in to slot drachmas through and Pink Floyd's *Dark Side of the Moon* playing over the stereo and two of the group sat playing backgammon in the corner. Weird, surreal and very memorable, something I will not forget. Being fairly ignorant of theatre and literature I suppose I was fairly easily impressed. Nicol did his best to organise either rugby or football matches to thrash us English but we never actually, really, played. One day I spent a considerable amount of time trying to 'pull' an American girl but having arranged to meet her in Socrates bar later, had to witness her being stolen by Nicol, sod![20]

Willard Manus, whose house Nicol subsequently bought on Lindos, recalls Nicol's fiery nature and also his sense of fun:

One rainy night in spring he came by and was delighted to discover that we had two Tom Lehrer records in our collection. He started singing them, doing Lehrer in an uncanny fashion … When the boy [Luke] flew out to Lindos to be with him, Nicol spent a whole morning sitting in our courtyard picking boarding school lice out of his hair. Nicol Williamson's temper was legendary … Being a Scot, he also enjoyed his glass and having an occasional punch-up as well. Thus you never knew whether a night on the town with him would end in fisticuffs. When that happened Nicol would come round in the morning to express his remorse – and to prepare breakfast for everyone. He'd make bacon and eggs and break open a bottle of 'retch', his name for retsina, which he slugged down as if it were iced tea.[21]

Luke's account of their time together on Lindos is altogether tenderer. 'He used to sing me to sleep, colour Jeremy Fisher books with me, read to me, introduce me to new foods, he taught me to swim, and, yes, he picked lice out of my hair daily for two weeks.' Luke recalls his dad being advised to shave his (Luke's) hair but Nicol refused point blank because he thought it would make it even harder for him to see his son than it already was.

Luke remembers the holidays as idyllic:

We used to drag a mattress out on to the roof and sleep outside. This was before there was aircon. We just used fans and mosquito nets. He would point out constellations to me in the sky, and sing 'would you like to swing on a star?' until I feel asleep under the sky.

Father and son would also bond during meetings in London. The usual weekend purgatory of the divorced father fortunately offered funny, even moving, memories to last a lifetime. Luke is still brought to tears when he recalls a visit he and his dad took to the Regents Park zoo in the late seventies:

When Nicol was in the hospice at the very end [when he was dying of cancer] I reminded him of this memory and he was really impressed that I could recall it. I was 4 or 5 years old. I had a wooden dog and was pulling it along behind me. We passed the orangutan enclosure and a young orangutan saw this wooden dog and made clear that he really wanted it. We tried to get it through the bars of the enclosure and it wouldn't fit. The orangutan even offered the only thing it possessed, its straw bedding, through the cage in exchange for this toy dog. It was just the most moving experience. It was heart-breaking.

The same day we went to the rhino enclosure that had a pool of water. We were looking at these rhinos, standing on a bridge overlooking the enclosure. Some of the rhinos were defecating, producing cannonball-size craps. Dad managed to pull me down behind the wall just as a large rhino produced a huge cannonball, fragmenting into tiny pieces. The rhino then back-heel kicked the ball of dung at the people on the bridge. All these people got sprayed by the crap. Those poor rhinos, it was probably the only entertainment they had!

On another occasion, dining at the George and Dragon restaurant near Hyde Park, Nicol was in the unusual position of having to chastise *Luke* for being tactless:

We were having lunch and there was only one other guy there. I apparently said to Dad, 'Dad, look at that great big fat man.' The guy in question started glowering at us. Dad said: 'You can't say things like that. You'll hurt people's feelings.' I replied, 'Not him!' I was pointing to a great green porcelain Buddha that decorated the restaurant. Now the guy is *really* upset – he has overheard the whole exchange!

Nicol had been destabilised by the divorce. After a difficult time, personally and professionally, what better than to return to the character who had ushered in his greatest success?

10

BATTLING OTTO THE OGRE

'I will tell you somezinc, Nicol. They used to call me Otto the monster.'

Otto Preminger to Nicol Williamson

Nicol had first played Bill Maitland when he was, as Osborne observed, but a cherub. By 1978, Nicol, at 41, was a smidgen older than the character. If Nicol had grown into Maitland, or at least now had the right jaded air, then Osborne was congealing into a Blimpish figure. It wasn't just simply moving from Left to Right, more deriving a perverse pleasure in railing against the tide. Osborne took pains to be on the illiberal side of every issue, ensuring maximum shock value.

So it seemed appropriate that Nicol and Osborne should collaborate on a revival of *Inadmissible Evidence* to be staged at its original home, the Royal Court. Osborne was determined to direct it himself, believing that the theatre now had 'a ghastly shop floor feel' about it. 'I told them all at the start of rehearsals that for the next five weeks democracy was dead. They all looked shocked at first but afterwards said they hadn't had so much fun for a long time. And that's what's missing there nowadays, apart from talent, fun!'[1]

Stuart Burge, the Royal Court's artistic director, was also keen for a revival. 'I thought it was John's best play. I wasn't going to direct it because Nicol Williamson was going to do what he liked anyway, and I thought it was best that John should direct it, who was desperate to do it.'[2]

Osborne was now living like a country squire at Edenbridge, in Kent, presiding over local fairs and pony-jumping. He invited the cast to his estate for a pre-rehearsals gathering. Nicol was virtually a permanent house guest in the summer of 1978. Helen Osborne, by now the writer's constant companion, later recalled Nicol as 'not the easiest of guests, recovering from a miserable love affair and preparing for an arduous stage role with many a butch session on his portable muscle-flexer'.

She went on:

> In those olden days, despite his macho sentimentality, faux paranoia, the lack of
> physical appeal which his sheer energy and danger on stage could overcome —
> much as Olivier could convince he was six foot tall — there was more than a
> fugitive hope that Williamson would substantiate his promise as unarguably the
> finest actor of his generation.[3]

Clive Swift, cast in the small but pivotal role as Hudson – chief clerk and
punch-bag for Maitland's diatribes – remembers they all gathered on a warm
August day. Osborne listened to Mozart's Don Giovanni champagne aria while
Nicol played frisbee in the garden. All the playwright's attention was on his star
player; Swift recalls that Osborne never engaged him or other cast members in
direct conversation:

> John Osborne was similarly distant in rehearsals, forbidding any queries about
> his play or characters and saying that it was a classic text to be spoken – 'like
> Chekhov or Shakespeare'. His concentration was almost wholly upon Nicol
> and he ordered me, on stage throughout the first act, to do nothing to distract
> from Mr Williamson. So I sat, listened and responded, though I felt that good
> old reliable Hudson would have been working, for sure as hell his boss wasn't;
> he was too busy spilling out his tortured soul. Perhaps it wasn't surprising then
> that, with three days to go before the first performance, Osborne asked why I
> was sitting there doing nothing. 'Because you told me to.' 'But can't you sign a
> few cheques or something?' I felt mild panic. Was he implying the integration
> of a whole act's business? Such choreography should have been incorporated
> much earlier. Improvisation now would be sure to distract from Nicol. 'You can
> do something!' hissed Osborne. 'Any cunt could do something.' 'Not this cunt,'
> I replied, stung by his epithet and sticking to my guns. In the end I remained
> sedentary, scanning a brief.[4]

Julie Peasgood, cast in the non-speaking role as Maitland's daughter, Jane,
remembers the whole experience as a happy one:

> Nicol was a consummate professional – dynamite on stage and kind and caring
> off. A special performer? Nicol gave me more support than anyone I have ever
> shared a stage with. I was hospitalised during the run and Nicol demanded I get
> back on stage sooner than advised (and although this went against my doctor's
> orders, it was very flattering for me in a non-speaking role!). So I went back

and whilst Nicol delivered a long monologue to me – a non-stop diatribe – he somehow managed to change his moves mid-speech and gently enfold me in his arms, whispering 'If you need to sit down that's fine'. I knew whatever happened on stage with him I always felt safe. It was a wonderful production to work on and it was a very healing time for me – I had been through a difficult time before being cast as Nicol's daughter Jane, and this production restored my confidence as an actress. I really enjoyed working with Nicol, and John Osborne was also delightful and made me feel so special. John always wore espadrilles and Culpepper's Stephanotis (bride's!) perfume and I loved that.[5]

She also remembers Nicol's intuition:

When I first met Nicol we had a chat in his dressing room and he said he could really imagine what I'd be like when I was a grandma! As I was only twenty-two at the time (and not even married – let alone being a parent!) I was a little surprised by his vision, but he reassured me that I'd be a fabulous granny! I am now sixty and became a grandma for the first time last year – and I just hope I can live up to Nicol's prediction!

Nicol and Burge pleaded for cuts to the play but Osborne insisted on an unabridged version. Swift recalled that 'audiences who at 10.45 p.m. were spell-bound, by 11.15 p.m. were stupefied' but Osborne was adamant, 'Let the bastards suffer!' he said.

Nicol's second coming as Maitland at the Royal Court was every bit as successful as the first, playing to packed houses and ecstatic critics; Osborne made sure that a bottle of champagne adorned Nicol's dressing room daily

Not that the length of the play was entirely welcome. *The Stage* commented, 'Running for just under three hours, this play still seems a bit overlong, particularly in the refrigerated interior of the Royal Court but wrap yourself up warmly and go to see Williamson's performance, for he makes it the focal point of a great evening of theatre.'

Irving Wardle thought it just right:

Nicol Williamson's original performance was a staggering tour de force for a young actor. He is now the right age for the part. I have not the memory to draw any detailed contrast but, taking the added emotional maturity for granted, the really astounding factor in the new production is its technical virtuosity. Some of Osborne's asides (often delivered in telephone conversations) are distinctly top-heavy but Williamson gets through them with amazingly articulated speed, passing from a moan to a snarl on a single vowel and abruptly changing from the hollow-eyed wreck into the master of the office.

The *Guardian*'s Michael Billington pointed out the flaws in the play, including the limited breathing space that confines its subsidiary characters. He nevertheless concluded that 'seeing the play again at the Court for the first time in fourteen years, I found it an overwhelming experience in which the sense of private pain, paranoia and anguish is deeply moving'.

Sheridan Morley said, 'If you see nothing else in the London theatre in 1978, see this.' Bernard Levin – always a perceptive critic – writing in the *Sunday Times*, thought that Osborne was:

> a moralist, searching constantly in the human condition for a clue to the nature of the fetters which hold and distort that condition and that it demonstrates Mr Osborne's conviction that in spite of hell and all its minions it is the search for the meaning of our existence that matters, and that that search is our highest duty and its own justification.

In other words, life can be a bitch but we owe it to ourselves to explore why!

Inadmissible's revival, successful though it was, did little for Nicol's bank account. He needed money following a High Court ruling in October that he pay £24,000 to Jill within six months. Ironically, TV, the medium Nicol despised more any other for its pay dirt and obsession with ratings hanging like a Sword of Damocles over every show, offered a couple of good paydays.[6]

He did an entertaining episode of *Columbo*, as a Californian doctor of psychology and perpetrator of a telephone murder by triggering a dog attack on the command of the keyword 'Rosebud'. Luke thinks his dad liked the script because he was a fan of Orson Welles and, in particular, *Citizen Kane* and *The Third Man*.

Nicol, with his hard stare and bellowing voice, seen most effectively at the outset when haranguing his audience from a stage, made a good foil for Peter Falk's dithering detective. The stage tirade was also revealing for its power; perhaps Nicol would have made a great motivational speaker.

Yet Luke said that Nicol rather regretted doing *Columbo*, claiming that he only did it for the money and could hardly remember it. Somehow, just occasionally, Nicol conveys a kind of forceful remoteness, a sense of going through it by rote. Such is the power of TV, however, that, when Nicol died, many 'fans' on forums noted his performance in *Columbo*.

If Nicol claimed not to recall *Columbo* it's likely he would have also conveniently 'forgotten' his part as a Dutch Protestant cleric in *The Word* – in which he undergoes an inexplicable road to Damascus conversion to accept the credibility of a so-called Fourth Gospel. An interminable, preposterous, trashy, ludicrous, thoroughly enjoyable TV miniseries of the type that Hollywood did in the late seventies, it featured David Janssen as a bed-hopping, capital city-flitting advertising executive commissioned to market the new gospel. (Actors like Janssen, in his mid-forties here, but looking at least fifteen years older, and sounding like he just *must* be carrying a case of Courvoisier around, simply *don't* exist nowadays.) As for Ron Moody – well, he virtually chews the Colosseum, indeed every antiquity in Rome, as a fraudster and ex-convict from Devil's Island.

The Word became compulsive kitschy entertainment over several nights in 1979, probably enjoyed by those who also savoured an evening in with an arctic roll and a bottle of R. Whites lemonade. 'I welcome this amazing American rubbish; the success of the director, Richard Lang, in securing so many feeble performances from so many good players is quite phenomenal', wrote Sean-Day Lewis (naughty boy!) in May 1979.

Around this time Nicol's bad-boy antics appeared to have scuppered his chances of a major role in William Peter Blatty's *The Ninth Configuration*. Ironically, the benefactor was Stacy Keach, long an admirer of Nicol's since he had been a student at LAMDA, seen him on stage and 'been blown away by his presence and intensity'. Keach describes the incident:

> William Peter Blatty had cast him as Killer Kane. The film was being shot in Budapest, Hungary. Nicol was staying at the Budapest Hilton, and was allegedly trying to make an international phone call when, presumably, something the operator did or said infuriated him, causing him to rip the phone out of the wall and toss it through the plate-glass window of his suite. Nicol was fired, and I was hired to play the role. It was a great part, and I often reflected on how Nicol would have played certain moments during the filming. I have no doubts that he would have been brilliant, as he always was. We became friends for a time, and I loved his company.

Blatty – who later cast Nicol as Father Morning in *The Exorcist III*, indicating that Nicol's allegedly bad behaviour had *not* triggered his departure or soured their relations – remembered the incident differently:

> I so desperately admired [Williamson] and wanted him in my picture that I persuaded myself that he could be an American Marine Corps Colonel. I realised during rehearsals that he was magnificent, but there was no way he could be an American colonel. He came to Budapest and we rehearsed for two weeks. And

we were coming up to the weekend before our first shoot on the following Monday, and then I remembered one of the people I'd strongly considered was Stacy Keach. And we found out that night that he was available and he was with us on Tuesday.

Yet Blatty has also, in his autobiography, corroborated the phone story. He adds that Nicol was overheard screaming, 'Wake up, you bloody aboriginals! Christ, we're living in the twentieth century in which telephones are actually expected to work.' According to Blatty, 'the Hungarian government declared Nicol persona non grata'.[7]

Luke has also heard the phone story (but not from his father) and says it could be true, or at least partly true. 'Dad did have a bit of a temper', he says with, perhaps, a touch of understatement.

Screen redemption seemed possible thanks to a Graham Greene classic. Nicol had first read *The Human Factor* – a study of how love can force even the most apolitical into becoming de facto Cold War players – during the revival of *Inadmissible Evidence*. The central character was Castle, a British intelligence officer forced into furnishing token information to the Russians in exchange for being smuggled out of apartheid-era South Africa with his black girlfriend.

Nicol was captivated by the book. He said:

It was so good I rationed myself to a few pages a day … it had such an incredible feeling of that sadness for England now which I absolutely share … Castle is not really involved in the secrets business … he has no political ideology, he had not been compromised sexually, he has no motive of financial gain.

Greene's story was compelling and so a film of the novel, with a Tom Stoppard screenplay, seemed promising. Except that it was being produced and directed by Otto Preminger, who made the likes of Henry Hathaway, Erich von Stroheim and Cecil B. DeMille seem saintly. Such was Preminger's reputation for sadistic abuse that many stars simply refused to work with him. Kirk Douglas, in his biography *The Ragman's Son*, has a nasty account of Preminger screaming at actor Tom Tryon on *The Cardinal*, amounting to psychological annihilation. 'I never liked Otto after that …' wrote Douglas, 'but he was a very interesting man …'. Yes, interesting in the way that war is more interesting than peace.

If you were a very big star like Sinatra, Wayne, or indeed Douglas, then Preminger usually treated you respectfully. (Yet even that was no guarantee. Robert Mitchum was fired from Preminger's movie *Rosebud*.) Others, like Anthony Hopkins, fell out even before a shot of film was in the can. 'I'd never work with Otto Preminger. I was offered a job with him once. He started on me at the interview. I said goodbye and got up and left.'[8]

Michael Caine recalled his unease about working with Preminger on *Harry Sundown*, telling him beforehand that he was a 'delicate flower' and that if he (Preminger) started screaming then Caine would just retreat to his dressing room. So it was perhaps small surprise that Caine, who wrote in his memoir that 'Otto's only happy when other people are miserable', turned down the chance of a rematch on *The Human Factor*. Richard Burton also declined the role. (At least he could have out-screamed Preminger!) A more eccentric candidate was Jeffrey Archer, Conservative MP and novelist, who apparently failed a screen test after he was found to be shorter than Iman, who was to play his wife, Sarah, in the film. And so the part went to Nicol.

Apart from liking the script, Nicol hadn't had a really good film role for some time. So in spite of Preminger's notorious reputation – or perhaps *because* of it in the sense that he always relished a challenge – and rumours of uncertain financial backing, Nicol accepted. He later revealed that he and Preminger sealed their deal over lunch:

> We never discussed one syllable of the film. Finally I asked him quietly if he thought I was right for the part. I thought I might hear something interesting about myself.
> 'Vot part? The lead? Don't you know?'
> 'Know what?'
> 'That you're perfect. Are you crazy?'

Nicol, never seemingly fazed, claimed to have few misgivings about Preminger's belligerent reputation:

> I don't mind it. It doesn't affect me the same way it affects others. It's necessary simply to sit on him once in a while. I admire his strength. He's so energised. Other directors will make a point intellectually. He makes his point through his stress mechanism – and he's nearly always right.

They joshed each other at the beginning.
'I will tell you somezinc, Nicol. They used to call me Otto the monster.'
'Did they? You mean, the moment is passed?'

Luke, who celebrated his sixth birthday on set, also recalls Preminger telling him that he was known as 'Otto the monster' but that it wasn't true. Meanwhile, Nicol, behind Preminger's back, mouthed the words, 'Oh yes, it is!'

It seemed like a veritable heavyweight contest. In one corner, martinet power-mad film director, known for bullying actors and terrorising the crew. In the other corner, temperamental perfectionist and fiercely independent star known for eating directors and producers between drinks. Fellow cast members must have taken bets on who was going to slug who first. Or at least who was going to walk off the set.

David Taylor, writing in *Punch*, observed some of the shooting and judged it to be an uneasy stand-off:

> Nicol Williamson is by no means shy. He shares with Otto Preminger an urge to speak his mind and the two of them don't half communicate on set. Preminger looks exactly the way people called Preminger are popularly supposed to look, which is totally bald, Teutonic, substantial and a bit sinister. He has an absorbing habit of whipping off and replacing a pair of black, juggernaut spectacles every ten seconds or so, compounding the effect, and of letting slip tart asides in a thick Viennese accent. Williamson can hand it out too, affecting a weary look of experienced disdain that stops just short of menace, as befits professional standards.[9]

The two *did* clash early on, shortly after shooting started in May 1979, when Preminger screamed at Nicol for blowing his lines. For Preminger, lateness or even momentary absent-mindedness – but not, apparently, a ridiculously stilted performance from Iman – were capital offences.

Luke recalls another key incident between his father and Preminger. 'Early on in the production Otto tried to keep Dad on set for eighteen hours or so, and Dad just told him, "I'm done, I'll continue tomorrow or not, up to you", and cabbed it back to the hotel. After that Otto was sweet as could be.'

Following Preminger's death there was an attempt to rehabilitate the director with several sympathetic biographies. Naturally, his immediate family were keen to downplay Otto's vicious reputation.

One biographer, Chris Fujiwara, quotes Hope Preminger, Otto's widow, to Nicol's detriment. She claims that Nicol 'behaved badly, was so sarcastic, had the crew all upset and was snarling at everybody'. She told Fujiwara that Nicol 'expected me to hand-wash all his Turnbull & Asser shirts. He warned me that his shorts were not to have a single wrinkle and he would not leave his hotel room until I sent in his shoes to be cleaned at the hotel barbershop.'[10]

Fujiwara also claimed that Preminger had a tough time handling Nicol. 'Preminger's main challenge was monitoring his temperamental star', he wrote – a loaded sentence and risible given the terror the director induced in those around him. For the consensus of cast and crew was that it was Preminger who regularly upset everyone. Derek Jacobi, for example, while acknowledging Nicol's impishness, recalled the bad atmosphere on the set as being Preminger's handiwork. 'Otto was a monster, disgraceful, dictatorial and vile with the crew. Nicol Williamson used to come up behind us unseen and boom out in Otto's voice to frighten the hell out of us.'[11]

Nicol's mischievous mimicry got him into trouble with Richard Attenborough who became Preminger's new target once it became clear Nicol wouldn't be bullied. Luke remembers that Preminger enjoyed belittling the veteran British actor/director, deliberately mispronouncing his name by calling him 'Attaboro' and, in particular, poking fun at the coat he wore in the film, 'Is zat your own coat?'

Luke recalls:

One time Nicol crept up on Attenborough and imitated Preminger's heavy Viennese drawl. Attenborough flew into a rage at Dad. He was spitting on him – he was so angry. And Dad just sat there and when he was done, Dad said: 'Why don't you say that to Otto, why do you let him treat you like that?' People were terrified of Otto.

Another of Preminger's victims was Robert Morley, cast as an MI6 Dr Death, who administers a lethal injection to an agent (wrongly) suspected of being a traitor. Preminger took to haranguing Morley so much that in one scene, which called for him to carry out a medical procedure alongside complicated dialogue, the veteran actor could not continue.

Filming proceeded with everyone counting the days to the wrap. By the time the final scenes were shot – in 'the Moscow flat' (although tangibly studio-bound) to which Castle had defected after abandoning his wife, Preminger's 'stress mechanisms' were even more visible.

Frank Williams (most famous as the vicar in *Dad's Army*) was cast in the film as a fellow defector, supposedly a British Council employee, and had a key cameo at the end. By then, Nicol, conscious of Preminger's regular explosions, especially with the humbler supporting players, was considerate enough to forewarn Williams of the importance of being letter-perfect and punctual.

Williams wrote in his autobiography:

I knew he [Preminger] had a reputation for being something of a bully. My fears were made even worse when I received my call for the day's filming. Having told me the time at which the car would arrive to take me to the studio, the assistant added a message from Nicol Williamson with whom I'd be playing the scene. He had asked the assistant to tell me that I must not arrive on set without knowing my lines perfectly, or Mr Preminger would go mad. I had learnt them, of course, but throughout the evening, I went over them again and again to make doubly sure. When I finally arrived on set, Mr P. was in a rage because of some technical problems that had occurred. To relieve his fury, he walked on to the set and kicked a cupboard door. The door broke and everything on top of the cupboard fell off. We all had to wait while the continuity people got the photographs out to match the position of the ornaments with the previous shot. It made the great man seem a little ridiculous and I found that I was not nearly as worried as I had been. I survived and completed the scene without incurring Mr P's wrath.[12]

By the end of filming, a crisis loomed over *The Human Factor*. A serious cash flow problem made Preminger rush complicated scenes to avoid the expense of another set-up. This made him even more impatient with any minor mistake. It seemed that anticipated funding had not materialised. Preminger claimed to have been 'the victim of three European bankers who promised to put up money for the film. The money never came'.

Screenwriter Tom Stoppard thought the final film betrayed the core problem:

You could see its bankruptcy all over the screen. One of the actors had warned me earlier that, as far as he could tell, the film was going to be awfully short of 'cutaways' and this proved to be the case. The editor was left nothing to edit with. The film seemed to me to be full of shots held for too long to save the expense of a new set-up. I thought that the lighting was primitive, presumably for the same reason, and one or two of the settings, especially the Moscow flat, were ludicrous.

Attenborough, himself a distinguished director – at this stage just pre-*Gandhi* – agreed that the overhasty shooting scarred the film, '*The Human Factor* ought to have been marvellous. There was a scene where I visit Nicol at his house and we had no time to cover a scene that ran three-and-half minutes. It was all done in a two-shot.' Understandably, Preminger shot quickly. 'We were nearly always ahead of schedule,' said Attenborough. 'I think we finished in England a week before we were scheduled to.'[13]

Preminger, perhaps to disguise his embarrassment at the breakneck shooting, pretended that his use of one tracking shot, without cuts or close-ups of Iman and Nicol, created a more seamless viewing experience. 'Let me tell you about filmmaking. Ven you cut you jar the audience, it interrupts the story.'[14]

When the film was released most barbs were directed at Iman. She had apparently offered to do it for free when she had met Preminger in New York. Somehow, Preminger, who liked her personally, believed he could get a performance out of her. 'Nicol will be very good with the girl,' the director told a reporter during the London shoot. 'She is very black. He is very white. Both are very tall. It is my choice, my intuition. It's the only way I can work.'[15]

Val Robins, Preminger's assistant, claimed that the director knew that Iman was 'giving a dreadful performance and indeed in rehearsals he had made the actress say one line twenty times. Even her English was not good'. Robins also said that 'Iman believes that Otto ruined her chances for an acting career'. Later, after the film's release, Preminger blamed his wife for selecting Iman.

Several actors remained out of pocket. Derek Jacobi recalled in his autobiography that he never got paid 'because the production money ran out, and Otto wouldn't dip into his huge personal fortune to pay his artists'. Nicol was never paid at the time either. Likewise Robert Morley, despite promises from Preminger late in 1979 to sell some paintings to pay salaries and other costs of the $2,500,000 production. Luke does recall, however, that on Preminger's death in 1986, his widow sent Nicol a cheque for part-payment of his salary. No hard feelings, obviously, despite their rumoured ruckus over the Turnbull & Asser shirts!

The cost-cutting and the on-set histrionics sadly distracted from Nicol's self-effacing, remarkably *un*dangerous performance as Castle – conveying just the right air of bland remoteness. Whether bantering good-naturedly with colleagues, or biking lackadaisically off to his quiet Berkhamsted home, Nicol offers a believable portrait of a political agnostic caught between two despicable ideologies. *The Human Factor* is definitely not a *bad* film as such, although not especially good either. It needed Hitchcock to make it more suspenseful and tauter. Reviews were generally unfavourable.

Most complimentary was David Ansen in *Newsweek* who praised it as 'a lucidly impressive return to form for the 73-year-old director … it's not really a thriller at all, but an understated, uncompromising dissection of an event, an anatomy of the murder of a soul'.

Leslie Halliwell, however, declared it had become 'risible' before the end while Rex Reed, known for his undying enmity towards Preminger, panned it: 'Under Otto Preminger's decrepit direction, it turns out to be not only the dullest espionage movie ever made, but the dullest movie ever made – period.'

Variety hit home when it alluded to the (over)-fast pace, 'Unfortunately Preminger stages it all as if he was just trying to get all the actors through their line readings in under two hours, allowing no breathing room or time for character nuance in a tale which resolutely calls for quiet moments.'

Greene himself said that Nicol had given a good performance which would have been magnificent if the direction had been better. He felt that Preminger had not given enough weight to what he called 'the conservative forces' – notably Castle's mother who threatens Sarah:

> One's presenting hells – Castle's hell in Moscow and his wife's hell at home. It's very important that Castle's mother, who's producing Sarah's hell, should have had a good part. In fact, she was given nothing to do in the film. So the point was thrown away. The hells should have balanced each other.[16]

The Times focused on the central casting weakness of Iman, 'Preminger has no success at all in making either actress or character out of the spectacularly beautiful Iman and since the point of Castle's tragedy is his relationship with his wife, this leaves a rather devastating lacuna in the middle of the story.'

The Human Factor was not the smash Nicol hoped for. He later reflected that it had been a 'dreadful' experience. His only real fun had been playing football with Luke. Ironically, Nicol had only accepted the part because he wanted to work with Preminger.

Luke, who was on set throughout, believes that, with hindsight, there were signs that Preminger was suffering from the early signs of dementia and that this may explain *some* of his misjudgements:

> They had moved to a hotel in the country which was a bungalow, a single floor hotel, as opposed to the multi-storey hotel in Knightsbridge where they had been staying. He accused a member of staff of not telling him where the lift was so he could go to his room. Of course there was no lift, they had moved hotels.

Perhaps momentarily forgetting which hotel they were staying in was excusable. But a further incident, also related by Luke, seems to confirm something was amiss with Preminger:

> All of a sudden there was a commotion in the lobby and they go out to see what's going on. Otto is virtually wrestling with the girl at the reception over a book. Otto's pulling the book away from the girl, demanding that she return his 'script'. Of course, it's not the script but the reception book. It's a funny story until you realised that he was starting to lose his marbles.

The seventies had not produced one hit film for Nicol. His private life was a mess; he no longer owned his own home and lived most of the time in a rented flat in London. David Taylor, interviewing Nicol for a *Punch* profile, noted how hard it was to live down a bad boy reputation, 'Labels, once attached, are devilishly difficult to shrug off. He might not be Bruce Forsyth[17] but, Christ, all it takes is one ill-considered rejoinder or a written-up raucous party and he's down on file as a volatile bruiser.'

Fortunately the new decade was to usher in a movie role that made an imprint on international audiences. It would also mark the beginning of Nicol's long exile from British shores.

INADMISSIBLE LOVE?

'He felt he was paddling for his life.'

Elaine Bromka

Perhaps peeved by the reaction to *The Human Factor* and hounded by the Inland Revenue, Nicol decided to leave Britain and the country's punitive tax regime. Ruling out California where Michael Caine had just emigrated ostensibly for the same reason, Nicol decided to base himself in Amsterdam. He didn't speak Dutch and never learnt it but he liked the people enormously.

Luke elaborates:

Also, Dad didn't drive, so a city like Amsterdam was just great for him. It's a terrific city for a pedestrian. Everyone speaks English, the people are friendly, the food is good, the options are endless and the public transportation is second to none. It feels like a town rather than a city. There are fabulous museums and weird little jazz clubs. Great food, friendly people. He loved Amsterdam for a long time. I think it just suited him, and he had a Dutch romantic interest for a number of years.

Nicol bought a seventeenth-century gabled home on the Singel, number 56, complete with a 'backhouse' – like the one Anne Frank hid in. The huge house had five storeys, each as big as a self-contained flat. Amsterdam would be Nicol's main base for the next twenty years although he still travelled a lot.

Luke loved the house and has many happy memories of it:

Dad sold that back in 2003 or 2004, somewhere around that time. I hadn't been there since 1999. I went back in 2006 to pick up some art he had left there in the basement. He had sold it to a Persian couple, nice people, but they had decorated the entire house red and gold. It was a bit strange to be somewhere so familiar and so different.

Leslie Megahey stayed there while he and Nicol were collaborating on their one-man show, *Jack*. He remembers it as:

a typical large merchant's house, overlooking the canal, tall and grand. It was not what you'd call showy inside, but low-key elegant, – indeed I'd expected it to be rather Spartan, but it was tastefully furnished with a traditional feel to it and a grand piano in the drawing room. The basement was a comfortable self-contained flat for guests – I remember very thick pile carpet throughout, and a horsehair mattress – I had never slept on one – very comfortable.

A good paycheque would have come in handy for Nicol at a time when he was buying a large property. When you mention Nicol's name to modern audiences it's generally for the role of Merlin in *Excalibur*. Although it certainly wasn't his favourite role, it proved to be one of his biggest hits. For director John Boorman, whose most memorable films were *Deliverance* and *Point Blank*, casting Nicol as Merlin was no easy feat:

For my account of the Arthurian legends I wanted Nicol Williamson to play Merlin. But Orion, the company financing the film, said they had made three movies with him and all of them had bombed – so I could use anyone except Nicol. Finally I worked up the courage to defy the financiers and told Nicol he would be my Merlin. He said, 'ok, but who's playing Morgana opposite me?' I said it would be Helen Mirren. 'No way,' he said 'we did *Macbeth* together and it was a disaster'. Then Helen said she was pulling out for the same reason. She said that Nicol Williamson hated her. But their characters in the story were enemies, so I cast them anyway. And it worked.

Mirren subsequently claimed that on her way to meet Boorman she had a chance encounter with Nicol:

My taxi was held up in traffic and I caught sight of Nicol in the back of a car in the next lane. Telling myself, oh well, let bygones be bygones, I might as well be sociable, I waved. And I got a dead-fish look in response. John sensibly ignored all signs of disaster and cast us both anyway. In fact, Nicol became a good friend to me on this film. I was just becoming entangled with Liam [Neeson] and was feeling miserable about it because of the age difference. One day, as the two of us sat alone in the make-up trailer, Nicol turned to me and in that distinctive nasal drawl asked –'so what's the matter with you, then?' He listened as I blurted out my predicament, then said, 'don't worry, it probably wouldn't work out if you were eight years younger than him either, so you may as well go for it.' ... Nicol is a difficult, brilliant, vulnerable person and on *Excalibur* I grew to care for him a lot.[1]

Recollections of bust-ups between two people are, by their very nature, subjective with each person remembering the cause and extent of the rancour differently.

Luke claims that his father didn't actually think the feud amounted to very much. 'For all the animosity Helen Mirren has for him, he really didn't seem to care much about her at all. I asked her what that was all about one time, after John Boorman had made some comments. It turns out she wanted a relationship and he wasn't much interested.'

As for the 'mending of fences' that Mirren sought, Luke doubts there was anything much to mend in the first place. Actor Paul Geoffrey, cast as Perceval, recalls little sign of friction. 'I never saw it when I was on set. When I wasn't there maybe they had an exchange or two, but generally speaking the entire cast was pretty friendly.'[2]

Both Nicol and Helen soon overcame any tension to give coolly combative performances. Luke felt that the movie lost a bit after his dad was ensorcelled. But Nicol liked playing Merlin. 'I tried to make him a cross between my old English master [Tom Reader] and a space traveller, with a bit of Grand Guignol thrown in.' Writer Alex Epstein, who subsequently interviewed John Boorman, claimed that the director told him 'that Williamson hadn't been able to make sense of his character until the costume designer made his odd little silver skullcap. Then the whole character came to him.'[3] It certainly was a canny prop.

The film was shot over the summer of 1980 in Ireland and Luke, just 7 years old, has vivid memories:

I used to wander around the set and see all these gold cardboard pillars and such. Later, I was amazed how real they looked in the film. I also remember going to Boorman's house and being terribly bored wanting to play football outside but it was raining and I wasn't allowed. He had a very interesting seventies-style house. I don't actually recall meeting Helen Mirren at all, though I suppose I might have done. I do remember thinking Cherie Lunghi was one of the most beautiful women I'd ever seen.

The rain continued falling throughout five months of shooting. Paul Geoffrey said the constant bad weather led to lengthy retreats into the pub with Nicol:

> We were getting this per diem that we couldn't spend because we were working six-day weeks. So every Saturday, we would go to this one pub and there was a private room upstairs, so we would go up there and start lunch about 11 a.m. and by the end of lunch – after a few coffees and brandies – Nicol Williamson and I would be arguing about whether it was raining or not.

Excalibur went down well with audiences and, of course, his Merlin became Nicol's most enduring screen incarnation. But Leslie Halliwell called it 'a curiously pointless retelling of a legend'.

Apart from Amsterdam, New York was another city Nicol had grown to love. Luke recalls that his dad liked it more than he did even though he (Luke) was born there. Nicol enjoyed the jazz clubs and for several years was a regular at a Monday night Shakespeare reading group, hosted by a cousin of Nicol's second wife, Andrea. So maybe that explains why Nicol did four plays there in the eighties but none in the UK. Perhaps also Nicol felt rejected by the British theatrical establishment and film industry. The move to Amsterdam and then spending so long Stateside was cutting him off a bit from British friends and associates.

In early 1981 Nicol was in New York for a revival of *Inadmissible Evidence*, directed by Anthony Page with whom he had made the film version. A (rather overformal) taped tribute to his old buddy John Thaw for Thaw's *This is Your Life* in March reveals a slight transatlantic tilt to Nicol's accent. 'This must be a great thrill for you,' said Nicol, 'and I, among many other people, am a great admirer of your work and naturally, of course, I value your friendship. I hope that the future holds as much and as many good things as the past.' Thaw squirmed a little in his seat.[4]

Nicol had only just opened at the off-Broadway Roundabout Theatre at the time of the taping. Anthony Heald, later memorable as Anthony Hopkins's pompous, smug, smiling psychiatrist in *Silence of the Lambs* ('the old friend' Hannibal is expecting for dinner) remembers sharing a dressing room with Nicol and the late Philip Bosco. He noted the ubiquitous bottle of champagne, a rarity in America but commonplace in the UK theatre. Heald spurned the bubbly, deterred by Nicol's overconsumption and experience of alcoholism in his family. Apparently, Nicol had it in his contract that a bottle of champagne should be in his dressing room nightly.

Several years later, when Heald appeared with Hopkins in *Silence of the Lambs*, he remembered Hopkins telling him that he had bumped into Nicol after the Welshman had joined Alcoholics Anonymous and forsworn the booze. 'I hear you're being a very good boy', he remembers Nicol saying to him rather disdainfully.

Nicol's self-destructiveness was tangible. 'There was a bad boy inside him,' says Heald who compares Nicol to George C. Scott and Tommy Lee Jones. He was, however, impressed that Nicol stayed on stage during rehearsals for Heald's small but pivotal role as the gay client. Anthony Page told Nicol he could leave the stage if he liked but Nicol insisted on staying, 'Of course, I have to be there.'[5]

Heald also describes a strained poetry reading attended by Nicol and Ian McKellen, which included some biting remarks from Nicol about his contemporary who was enjoying huge (Tony award-winning) Broadway success as Salieri in *Amadeus*. Actor Rand Bridges, later to appear with Nicol in *Macbeth*, also remembers that Nicol disliked McKellen, telling Bridges that he 'would dance on his [McKellen's] grave'. Bridges believed that Nicol despised what he called 'technical' actors and, also, viewed McKellen as (cough in anticipation of an unPC comment) something of a 'she actor'.[6] (Leslie Megahey, Nicol's director friend of later years, believes that Nicol had nothing against gay actors as such but that it was more that he liked 'actors who were strong of character'.)

Unusually, in a business where actors can be almost *over*-effusive about each other, Nicol never offered false flattery. He had firm views on which actors he rated highly and those he didn't. If an actor wasn't up to standard then, according to Luke, his dad would be open about it, 'And he wasn't particularly gracious about it, to be frank. He figured that was their job, and they needed to be damn good at it and, if they weren't, well, it wasn't really his fault. Dad had many flaws, but he owned most of them rather well.'

Heald remembers the speed of Nicol's performance, a motif in the recollections of other performers and directors. His acting kept pace with a brain that simply worked faster than most. 'I vividly remember his awareness of time,' he recalls. 'The first act would run to fifty-four minutes and then, the next night, it ran to fifty-three minutes. He was constantly trying to shorten it.'

Nicol loved doing plays at breakneck speed, gaining more and more intensity, almost exploding on stage before reaching a critical moment where he would pull back and linger. Luke thought his father's acting reflected his thinking. 'Dad was very quick mentally. You know how you're out somewhere and someone says something, and ten seconds too late you have the perfect reply or comeback or comment. That ten seconds didn't exist for Dad. He was so sharp.'

Elaine Bromka, cast as his wife in Page's revival, also noted Nicol's speed:

He was like a tornado on stage but with utter mental clarity. He deserved tremendous respect. He was always very smart. He spoke so quickly on stage because his brain was driving him on. The rapidity of his thoughts came to him through rhythm and nuance. He felt he was paddling for his life.[7]

Bromka believed that none of Nicol's volatility, the occasional need to ruffle feathers, stemmed from excessive ego. It was just his natural personality. He had a propensity for danger, a dislike of conformity and a conviction that you had to reveal all on stage, not just rely on technique:

> He was amazing but, most pointedly, I didn't find his ego large at all. He never did the prima donna thing. He really reached out to you on stage. In the play he always gave it to you. I've been with other stars who grabbed every second. He was doing all he did because he thought it was right for the play. It was as though he was reaching out from one lifeboat to another. He had a huge amount of energy. I always found him terrible earnest. He was a ticking time-bomb and you had to be careful. He had a quiver about him; he was always very polite but he was driven intellectually to show the torment he possessed. He always liked to go out after a show; he'd go out to a piano bar.

Bromka sensed that Nicol was truly tortured. The man who said he functioned best when contemplating his own death lived on the edge. Towards critics he showed at best sufferance, at worse open derision. She believes he also disliked his audiences. There's enough evidence to make the case: berating noisy schoolchildren, delivering lengthy curtain call diatribes. The implication was that audiences needed to be educated about the theatre. But perhaps 'dislike' would be a strong word. More likely he used them to vent his fury at his real targets – the critics and the 'suits'. Against that, however, is another anecdote from his friend, Peter Bowles, who claimed that Nicol 'would instruct his stage door keeper not to pass on but to destroy all letters that were addressed to him'.[8]

Nicol may also have had a slight contempt for 'the masses' in general. But that's far from unusual in great actors. George C. Scott used to threaten to walk off stage if any 'vulgar-looking lady with blue-rinsed hair' was in the audience. Sometimes he'd grab cameras off prurient theatregoers – as he did during *Uncle Vanya*. Olivier used to peer through the curtain before performances and mouth insults into the darkness, 'Fuck pigs – none of you is brave enough to do what I'm going to do.' Nicol probably used his audiences to psych himself up. When he was up there on stage he was a lone wolf fighting for survival.

It's no coincidence that Nicol was a fine tennis player. Tennis is a loner's game, one that engenders fierce competition. Luke remembers, 'He actually did some charity games with John McEnroe and Vitas Gerulaitis. And he entered a competition while we were in Ireland shooting *Excalibur* and lost in the final. I remember getting very angry with him for losing. Pretty sure I had a meltdown.'

In tennis terms Nicol was very like McEnroe, hating the crowd for being so damn comfortable and cosy, munching away happily at their cheese sandwiches,[9] while he is forced, gladiator-like, to fight for his life. 'First night audiences, I hate them,' Nicol once said, 'with their fur stoles and their boxes of chocolates, coming to the theatre because they think it's how the gentry behave.' Several friends commented that he didn't suffer fools gladly – or otherwise! Rand Bridges, who got to know Nicol quite well in the early eighties, believes that Nicol disliked 'weak or indecisive people'.

Anthony Page – who had come to know Nicol better than most – *did* feel that Nicol, Coriolanus-like, rather despised the masses. 'He was a very lonely man, and he had a great contempt for people.' Certainly Nicol always kept his audiences at bay and never depended on them to sustain his ego. Unlike Sammy Davis Junior, for example, who admitted that on some nights he had difficulty in dragging himself away from 'the love' on stage, Nicol was no applause junkie.

Staying true to the text was always more important to Nicol than priming laughs. He stressed he would never allow an audience, even if they were guffawing with laughter, to dictate pace. 'I will ride through laughs when I know the pace shouldn't slow down. If you pander to an audience and start pausing for effect – or to flirt with them – it becomes horribly self-indulgent and puts the play out of gear. The play comes first.'

Aware of the stamina such a role undertook, Nicol would try to keep himself fit. Away from the stage, Nicol had a kind of everyman quality to him, something Alistair Cooke also commented on several years later when he described him as looking like a 'lug'. Someone wrote to Luke with their impression of Nicol in the weightlifting room at the city's McBurney gym:

> Most of the off-duty cops and firemen and longshoremen that I worked out with there had no idea who he was. When we explained who he was they just shrugged non-plussed. He was tall and pale and looked like one of them. They could not buy that he was an actor. One guy I knew who was a local bus driver said that he thought Nicol looked like an out of work construction worker.

Nicol practised weightlifting from the mid-seventies onwards. 'It gives you tremendous stamina, the ability to last three times longer than other actors. When you become tired that's when your work becomes sloppy,' he would say.

Playing a character such as Maitland was no walk through Central Park. The stage actor's routine is bad for the health – conserving energy during the day, peaking at 10 p.m. and it's unlikely someone's going to drift off to bed after that.

After a show, Nicol would go to Jimmy Ryan's and drink and sing, sometimes by himself, until 4 a.m. and then he would sleep until the afternoon.

He once said:

> The theatre tends to be a mistress. It's an all-consuming job. You can't drink before a show. After you have done a tough physical show, you want to get something to eat, but most places you might want to go to are closed. You wind up going home at 3 a.m. with a club sandwich you have picked up from an all night deli. Try to get some woman to go along with that.[10]

Such a lifestyle undermined his mental wellbeing. Luke says that Nicol's demons were never far away. 'He suffered his whole life from depression but never treated it. He wasn't bipolar, but he definitely struggled with intense depression. I told him once that that was what he was describing to me but he wasn't the type to go to see a shrink.' Others, such as John Calder, hinted that Nicol had some kind of chemical imbalance. 'In person he was entertaining but often embarrassing company, carrying role-playing to extremes and needing to dominate every assembly at which he was present, especially in his manic moods. When depressive he was pitiable and usually stayed on his own.'[11]

Nicol's depressions could be savage. Luke recalls his dad conceding that there were periods when it was a wrench to get out of bed, to even do basic chores like the laundry. The discipline of doing live theatre would force him to overcome these lows but Luke says that there would be a sharp dip in his dad's moods – usually around the third night into a run – when the initial euphoria had subsided and reality had set in.

Jeanne Ruskin, playing Liz in *Inadmissible Evidence*, also noted Nicol's anguish:

> The deeper you go, the more pain you contact. It makes it very difficult to surface once the curtain comes down. An actor's instrument is himself. An actor can't put that away, as you can your cello or flute or guitar once the performance is done. And every role, if you are genuinely searching within yourself as you should, forces you to plumb new depths.[12]

Ruskin remembers that each of Nicol's performances as Maitland was different, 'For example, one night he suddenly chose to walk the perimeter of the carpet marking the centre of Maitland's office, as he pondered something. It was a brilliant touch.'

He was professional and never missed cues. But:

It was never the same twice. He was masterful at being in the moment and so each performance felt like an improvisation: fresh and new. I never knew how the scene would be played. Exhilarating. An acting lesson each night. It's no secret that he was a notorious drinker. It never interfered with the control of his performance, although I think it may have contributed to a certain unpredictability which I found exhilarating and challenging.

Ruskin felt supported by Nicol throughout, even though he could always surprise her with an unexpected move. She recalls an example of Nicol's mischievousness:

As soon as I made my entrance onstage and before the dialogue actually began, Nicol would let out a powerful sneeze. It happened at exactly the same moment each performance. After it occurred a few times I began to wonder if he'd planned it as an acting/character choice and I began to wait for it. (But I don't know if I added 'God bless you' as my opening line!)

She compares Nicol to another Maitland, Ian McShane, with whom she acted several years later:

Consummate actors both, but very, very different. I learnt a great deal from each. Nicol's performance was definitely unpredictable and risky. Ian's was more controlled, carefully shaped and honed, and dramatically crafted so it grew from the beginning to the end of the run. It was truly a gift for me to have been able to work with both of them.

And history was about to repeat itself. Just as Nicol had fallen for Jill Townsend, the young actress who played his daughter in the first production of *Inadmissible Evidence*, so the same thing was happening fifteen years later. Andrea Weber, playing his daughter in this revival, was a fresh-faced muscular girl of 20, twenty-five years younger than Nicol. Born in 1961, Weber had decided at the age of 10 that she wanted to become an actress.

She started out in a ballet company before turning to track and field events, even training with the Mexican national hurdling team. By the time she met Nicol on *Inadmissible Evidence* she was fresh out of Hunter College. In many ways, rather like Jill fifteen years before, she was putty in Nicol's hands.

One cast member reflects on their relationship:

When I realised that Nicol and Andrea were interested in each other beyond the reality of the play I was a little puzzled, mostly because of the considerable age/experience difference: Nicol was clearly old enough to be her dad in real life as well as onstage. But it became apparent during the run that they were in a relationship and devoted to one another. At one point he had to be away for a brief time and she expressed openly 'I miss his bones', which stuck with me because I hadn't heard the phrase before. Of course they were both very attractive people; he because of his charismatic emotional vulnerability (and celeb status?) and she because she was quite simply young and beautiful … I see that she has gone on to triumph in her own right, reinventing herself and having a separate career in showbiz, seemingly without mention of their years together, at least in the bio I read. Good for her. Seems she took Maitland's advice to his daughter from the play, something about (I paraphrase) 'taking the world and making it your own', to heart. I must conclude that they were good for each other.

During the run Nicol gave an extensive interview in which he said that he had grown into the role of Maitland. Referring to his original 1965 performance he said – modestly but incorrectly – that he couldn't have been all that good:

> I had to work and push to construct the character from a lot of people I knew. It was a sort of composite. I've experienced a lot since then. Your life just happens to you. Over the years you experience a few high points and quite a lot of disappointment. So it's become easier for me to relate to Bill Maitland … the play is much more human this time. It's less strident and more chilling. Bill Maitland is a little smaller, a man more easily seen from the standpoint of human frailty. He's a man to sympathise with. He doesn't ask for sympathy but he gets it because the audience recognises in him the human condition. The audience itself is different this time. People are terribly quiet. You know they are disturbed by the play.[13]

Referring to his image, Nicol said, 'I don't love commotion. There have been only three explosions in fifteen years, so one every five years isn't bad. But I've always been the odd man out, the black sheep.'

Nicol also repeated his belief that actors shouldn't overwork. 'Too much acting can make you a bad actor. Actors who do play after play tend to rely on bad habits or technique and do shoddy work. Film pays for my theatre work. I've never made any money in theatre, except the first time I did *Inadmissible Evidence*.'

The New York run was Nicol's final outing as Maitland, the part that had become so indelibly associated with him that future productions always seemed odd without him. The critics still loved Nicol's portrayal. Frank Rich, the so-called butcher of Broadway, who subsequently savaged Nicol in *Macbeth* and *The Entertainer*, dissected Nicol's acting in a review cited by many as a model of theatrical criticism:

As delivered by Nicol Williamson, Bill's lengthy diatribe is not the teary wallow in self-pity or self-hatred that one might expect. It's a lawyer's tallying of the facts of his own bankrupt life. By thinking through every specific gesture of his character the actor gives a performance that is beyond pity and far too complex to devolve into a sentimental archetype. He shows us Bill clearly for what he is; the case is presented without prejudice. Nicol Williamson is something to see, standing tall in a pin-striped three-piece suit, he enters the stage in darkness, then stands weaving in a blinding spotlight … his voice splutters and whinnies as words tumble out in babbling incoherence. He searches his vest pockets for his pills and then sends his long arms flying up his temples – as if he were trying to push his spilling brains back into his skull. Nicol Williamson sits behind his desk and hurls verbal darts at all comers … He explodes with a withering insult – only to turn ashen a second later and beg like a child for forgiveness.[14]

Still looking for lucrative films to fund his plays, Nicol flew to London to accept a thankless role as a detective (you can tell he's a detective because he smokes all the time) in Piers Haggard's biting(!) kidnapping story, *Venom*. Luke believes that Nicol only accepted because he wanted to appear with Sterling Hayden.

Venom could have referred to the poisonous on-set atmosphere. Klaus Kinksi, chief villain, should have been in a straightjacket. He was ferociously ill-tempered and occasionally violent without provocation (a documentary by Werner Herzog called *My Best Fiend* about the making of a movie called *Aguirre, the Wrath of God* should convince any doubters). Kinski was also known for a one-man show in which he impersonated Hitler (too) convincingly.

Kinski had turned down a part in *Raiders of the Lost Ark* on the basis – unbelievable but true – that *Venom* paid more. Also appearing in *Venom* was Britain's 'hellraiser par excellence' (as Garry Bushell once referred to him), Oliver Reed, cast as chauffeur, Dave. Nicol's reputation for roistering might make it seem they were a compatible duo but they seldom socialised. Nicol's drinking was rather more convivial than Reed's, not just a case of getting 'bombed'. Luke says, 'Dad drank out of boredom and pain if one or the other got too bad or both. And it was part of his social life, gatherings with good food, good drink, music, conversation, he loved that.'

Leslie Megahey, a close collaborator of Nicol's later in his career, said that he and Reed were totally different. 'Nicol had no gimmicks, his behaviour was genuine and natural to him, and it was never employed as a trademark. There was no resemblance at all to Reed's drunken escapades. Nicol never appeared in public blind drunk, and certainly not on TV.'

Curiously, Megahey adds that he never thought of Nicol as an alcoholic and draws a further comparison with Ian Hendry, the subject of a previous biography of mine:

Alcoholics tend to keep up a certain level of alcohol in order to get through the day. Nicol could drink quite a bit but he didn't behave like a drunk like, for example, Ian Hendry. I worked with Ian once and he had a bottle of spirits on him when he did a voice-over at 9 a.m. The first thing we heard through the microphone from the boot was the glug-glug of drink being poured from the bottle into the water glass. That's what I'd call a serious alcohol problem.

Not that Nicol didn't have problems with booze; he clearly did. Luke, who knew him best, believes that his dad probably was an untreated depressive who self-medicated with drink.

Another key difference with Reed was that Nicol, although ambitious, loved acting for what it offered in its own right. Reed, on the other hand, was in love with stardom. So Nicol and Oliver stalked each other warily. Reed had a constant minder, Reg Prince, who later suffered a serious back injury when drunken horseplay got out of hand on the set of *Castaway* in 1986.

According to Luke:

Ollie liked to act the tough guy and Dad would tease him about him being so tough he needed a minder. One time Ollie said to Dad at lunch, 'I'm much stronger than you, you know.' And Dad said, 'Well that's as may be, but I am certifiable,' and he said he got no trouble after that.

Reed and Nicol soon united against the actor who really *was* certifiable – Kinski. Nicol was soon referring to him as 'a cunt'.[15] Reed took to shaking his caravan and screaming at him 'you Nazi bastard!' Kinksi would emerge from the caravan, apoplectic. Yet accounts differed as to how confrontational Reed could be. One biography of Reed cited Sarah Miles's memoirs (reunited with Nicol here despite the episode in Cornwall many years before). She described it as baffling 'why Oliver and Nicol Williamson – smiling sweetly on tippy toes', according to Miles, should ignore Kinski's arm-waving high pitched rantings. At the end of one obnoxious outburst she asked Nicol, 'Why don't you give him one? The actor turned physically pale and shuffled off.' She asked Reed the same thing. 'Why do you stand for it? You're big enough to sort him out.' 'Because,' whispered Oliver, 'I'm no bloody fool.'

According to Sarah Miles, 'Neither Sterling nor Nicol was as incorrigible as old Ollie Reed.'[16] Luke says one thing is sure, 'Dad had a reputation for being disruptive on set but on *that* movie he was *not* the one causing the problems.'

Venom opened to little fanfare, although thirty-five years later it's become something of a voyeuristic pleasure, watching its eccentric band of boozy brothers and a venomous monster trade blows. And that's not to forget the snake. Geoff Brown in *The Times* said, 'The cast is starry but the snake easily out-acts them. Still, they come in useful for camouflage: at heart *Venom* is just a pot boiling British thriller.' Leslie Halliwell called it a 'hoary melodrama which veers between dullness, artificial suspense and unpleasant detail'.

After *Venom* it was back to New York where Nicol decided to star in, and direct, another production of *Macbeth*. It was to usher in one of the most explosive periods in his professional life.

12

VAULTING AMBITION

'Show, show, show!'

Nicol Williamson directing the witches in *Macbeth*

Overseeing, and starring, in *Macbeth* was always going to be a stretch and this was actually Nicol's first stint directing Shakespeare. In the words of Elaine Bromka, 'you couldn't do both', but Nicol relished a challenge. And *Macbeth*, or 'MacB' as Nicol called it to save the theatrical superstition of saying its name, was the most challenging of all. Yet even Nicol couldn't have imagined at the outset that he would be effectively toying between *four* Lady Macbeths.

The *New York Times*, on 8 December 1981, announced that rehearsals would shortly begin. Sigourney Weaver would play Lady Macbeth and J. T. Walsh would be Macduff. The Circle in the Square on West 50th Street was a large thrust stage and Nicol's idea was to do the play with very little scenery.

From the beginning it was clear that Nicol had total control over the production. Actor Rand Bridges says that Nicol ordered Theodore Mann, producer and artistic director, out of the auditorium, 'If you're not gone in five minutes, I'll be gone in 10!', Bridges recalls Nicol telling him.[1]

According to Ray Dooley, cast as Malcolm, 'The principal idea was that as Macbeth became more and more isolated, the furniture was piled higher and higher and he, Nicol, was perched on it alone. Nicol cut the script to less than two hours without an intermission.'[2]

Casting Weaver, fresh from her explosive performance as Ripley in *Alien*, seemed an inspired choice. But by 5 January 1982 the *New York Times* announced that Weaver had 'left' the cast, reportedly to start filming on *The Year of Living Dangerously*.

What had happened? Certainly Sigourney Weaver had been due to leave the production a month after opening. But this was altogether different. She had been fired. Rand Bridges, cast as the porter in *Macbeth*, said that 'she didn't have the pipes or the equipment or the vocal range necessary and I could see the frustration on Nicol's face during rehearsals'.

Actress Tara Hugo – then known as Tara Loewenstern – had been hired to play one of the witches and to understudy Weaver. She offers her account of Weaver's departure, bearing in mind that Nicol had also fired Jon DeVries who played Banquo, after just a week of rehearsals:

> Nicol had hired me to play a witch, to understudy and to take over Lady Macbeth from Sigourney Weaver, who had a film job and would leave a month after opening. A huge break, he insisted I attend all rehearsals and help Sigourney with the text. (Unusual to offer up the understudy as coach, so no surprise she never asked me.) Sigourney was finding her way and given time would have been stellar. One day I shared a taxi with the two of them. Nicol remarked to silence, that when I played Lady Macbeth, he was going to have the press attend all over again. He got out at his stop, and after a pause, Sigourney, who kept her distance with most of the cast, asked if I'd ever understudied before. She empathised, as she'd once been an understudy. I smiled. I empathised with her too.

Gradually Nicol began to confide in Tara. He started to share his grievances regarding Weaver. According to Tara:

> I was flattered (and fearful) at being a confidante. I also suspected Jon DeVries was gone because he was *too* good! One night the phone rang and a voice asked 'Are you ready?' It was Nicol. (I *was* ready and knew all the lines for Lady Macbeth and had the passion and the technique to play it.) He told me he wanted to fire Sigourney and if the producers didn't like it, he'd quit. I told him his Macbeth was brilliant (it was) and begged him not to quit. (Inner dialogue: 'Forget the takeover – I just got my first Broadway job!') He fired her, rehired her, fired her again. One day Sigourney was alone on the stage tossing the *I Ching* and the next day she was gone. The *New York Times* reported she quit due to artistic differences. Years later, I saw Sigourney when my husband Steven Crossley and I visited Alan Rickman on the set of *Galaxy Quest*. The four of us had lunch. I'd changed my name to Hugo, was blonde, and she didn't recognise me. I told her I'd understudied her Lady Macbeth. Without hesitation she said, 'Nicol Williamson fired me and I didn't get over it for two years.'[3]

Tara thought this would be her big break. But her Lady Macbeth would never be seen:

> The actor J.T.Walsh, who played MacDuff, ran lines with me and I continued to be ready. But, over a drink, stage manager Michael Ritchie and Nicol told me I was all washed up. I was hired as takeover, not opening night star. Laurie Kennedy, a name back then, would play the role for the duration. Nicol wasn't happy with Laurie, but we were on course to open. Andrea Weber, his 20-year-old girlfriend, was at every rehearsal, ran errands for Nicol and on occasion, entertained us at his command with back flips.

One Monday morning close to opening, the cast was assembled in the house and seated as audience members when Nicol suddenly announced that Kennedy too had 'departed' and that Andrea Weber would play Lady Macbeth. Over the weekend, Nicol had apparently been preparing Andrea.

Tara Hugo was aghast:

> A group of highly professional actors sat there with mouths open like in *The Producers*. I felt the insane injustice that is showbiz. Andrea's only professional experience was a small part in *Inadmissible Evidence* with Nicol. However, she gave a good drama student performance and one admired her courage for getting through it with sporadic Svengali commands from Nicol of 'Think, Think, Think!' He now envisioned Lady M. as a child woman. She *was* that. We closed a month into the run. Circle in the Square did limited engagements. This was the first time a show closed early.[4]

Rand Bridges believes that Kennedy, although very capable, was too slow to get moving and simply lacked the sex appeal required. 'I really loved Laurie but Lady Macbeth needed that quality, that lust to keep people interested and to explain why Macbeth felt so compelled to do what he did.' Bridges believes that Nicol could be 'a little capricious' in his appraisal of actresses. 'Does she have a good body?' was one of his key criteria.

So Nicol had, unbelievably, effectively fired – or 'got through' – three actresses, Sigourney Weaver, Laurie Kennedy and Tara Hugo. To paraphrase Lady Bracknell, getting rid of one Lady Macbeth looks like bad luck, two looks like carelessness, three calamitous.

Elaine Bromka, cast as one of the witches, believes the rapid succession of leading ladies was a reflection more on Nicol's state of mind than the quality of their contributions, 'All three gave smart, engaging interpretations of Lady Macbeth. Starring in the show while directing was clearly a strain.'

The omens were not good after such a tempestuous beginning. (Well, perhaps the omens are never good in *Macbeth*!) The play got a mauling when it opened in January. Walter Kerr wrote:

> Naturally, no actor who also stages the play in which he is appearing can ever hope to see himself in the part. He's got to guess and he's got to gamble. I am sorry to say that Mr Williamson loses just about every gamble he takes in this two-hour intermission-less *Macbeth*. The fundamental wrongness at Circle in the Square is his responsibility. As an actor, he has not yet been willing to train himself beyond a nasal, naturalistic, markedly provincial use of his voice. Certainly he makes no effort here (as he did so when he tried Hamlet) to avail himself of Shakespeare's cadences or Shakespeare's music. When he approaches his lady through the dark of the castle to say 'I have done the deed' it is as though he were saying 'I put the cat out'. As Lady Macbeth, Andrea Weber is simply inexperienced. But as Macbeth says at a particularly calamitous point, 'twas a rough night'. And I don't think Shakespeare meant the line to get the laugh it's getting at Circle in the Square.

Frank Rich was also critical:

> The resulting star performance is not in control. If this play is to gather its tragic power – if we are to see our own frightening potential for evil within its hero – we must believe that Macbeth at some point was a man of nobility and grandeur, while Nicol Williamson's Macbeth isn't just a monster from the outset, he is a quivering wreck – and excessive ambition seems the least of his ailments.[5]

Time magazine slayed Weber, 'Andrea Weber may be a gifted young actress but she is definitely not – or not yet – Lady Macbeth.' Jay Sharbutt in *The Hour* wrote that Nicol had failed as actor and director, 'As Macbeth he's oddly unmoving. As the director, well, it's hard to figure out what he has in mind here.'

Perhaps most damning of all was *New York Magazine*, which wrote that 'Nicol Williamson has turned *Macbeth* – all of it – into a tale told by an idiot. Not one scene is allowed to work, not one line of poetry to survive as poetry'.

The magazine also noted the poor acoustics, adding that many of the actors could not be understood at all, and described Andrea Weber as 'a flaky teenybopper (say 15, going on 5) given to jumping up and down and delivering some of her speeches not only on but also to the floor'.

Ray Dooley remembers that the damning *Times* notice, in particular (probably because it held the most sway) drove Nicol mad:

> Nicol was very angry and, I think, hurt by the critical response to the show. He asked the producers to have the *Times* review posted in the lobby. His strategy was to give a speech after the performance (this started after the review was published) in which he said to the audience, basically, you've seen the play and you've read the review. If you think the review is wrong, please tell your friends to come see the show, etc. He would start the speech 'now that you've had your nickel's worth, I'll have mine', obviously punning on his name.

Rand Bridges also remembers Nicol's fury at the critics, believing that the opinion of one or two 'experts' should not be able to close a play.

Nicol also had a special instruction for his cast, in light of the poor reviews. Perhaps in a bid to rebut the critics and reconnect to the public, he asked his actors to come out at the half hour before every performance to mill about silently onstage while acknowledging the audience. Elaine Bromka said, 'It was never clear if we were to be ourselves or our characters. He just wanted all of us, cast and audience, to be together. It was a bit daunting, but he wanted to reclaim the experience.'

According to Tara Hugo, Nicol's behaviour became more careless as he fumed over the reviews:

> One night, Nicol put alcohol in the chalice we passed around in the banquet scene. The sobriety of an alcoholic cast member was compromised. And so it went. I was relieved not to be in the firing line-up of Lady Macbeths. I watched Nicol rehearse and I played scenes with him as a witch. His effortless power and command were riveting, electric, and a lesson from a master.

Once a show opens to bad notices then morale tends to sag. Little things go awry. Ray Dooley remembers Nicol fluffing a line. 'Nicol came on in Act V and started the wrong scene. It sounded something like this, "Doctor, the Thanes fly from me … That's the wrong scene. Michael Ritchie, line please!" Michael, our SM, gave the line over the God microphone and on the scene went.'

Nicol's temper was severely frayed. According to Dooley, Nicol, always a quick performer, wanted to go even faster:

> Once the reviews came out and (if memory serves) the show was not doing well in attendance, a game was started in which we drew running times for the show

out of a hat, I think in thirty-second increments. When the performance was over, the one closest to the time won the prize (perhaps just bragging rights, as I don't remember any actual prizes). This didn't have much effect on the quality of the show as the show played well at pace, and few of us had enough lines to substantially alter the running time. The show ran about 1hr 45mins–1hr 50mins as we played it, and we might have cut some time off that if Nicol was moving particularly fast. Again, in my view this was something of a device to keep spirits up in the face of disappointing reviews. I believe we closed at least one week earlier than planned.

Rand Bridges remembers that the same 'game' became known as 'the great Dunsinane betting pool' with prizes awarded to the person who came closest to the running time. He remembers some of the 'witches' were bewildered by the whole thing. 'We shouldn't be thinking about this. We should be thinking about our roles', they would say. Yet Nicol, as the lead and director, could control the tempo. 'I used to watch him from the wings and marvel at his ingenuity,' recalls Bridges.

It seemed like the curse of *Macbeth* had returned. As Frank Rich commented in 1994, 'Every production of this play I covered, whether with Philip Anglim, Nicol Williamson or Christopher Plummer, was a fiasco.' *Broadway Plays and Musicals* said that Nicol's direction of *Macbeth* turned the play into 'a superficial farrago'.

Tara Hugo stayed friendly with Nicol in subsequent years and, although she's no sentimentalist about his faults, believed he was a great teacher on *Macbeth*. 'One of the directions he gave in *Macbeth* when the witches reveal the future, was to repeat the words "Show, show, show"… He showed.'

Rand Bridges recalls a lot of laughs during the run, notwithstanding the poor notices. 'He used to call for notes after rehearsals. One time we heard this very authoritative voice over the speaker "Now hear this! Now hear this! Shortly punishment will be meted out".' He cites Nicol as one of the three or four greatest actors he has worked with – the others being Victor Buono, Jon Voight and Peter Donat (Robert's son).

Ray Dooley believes that Nicol was impressive despite the critical carping. 'Nicol was a brilliant speaker of Shakespeare's language. He had a gift for making the language clear and immediate. Nicol's performance, the clarity and forcefulness of the language, was a principal virtue of the production. The late J. T. Walsh was effective as Macduff and the cast was, generally, quite capable.'

All productions of *Macbeth* carry the possibility of a curse and critics can be especially vitriolic. Perhaps it's because what we witness seems repellently unnatural – a woman, Lady Macbeth, inciting her husband to murder an old man in his bed, talking of 'dashing' her baby's brains out if she must. If the play somehow doesn't succeed in horrifying, it becomes risible instead. Another obvious problem was that Nicol was overpromoting Andrea's talents. Casting a 20-year-old as Lady Macbeth was a huge gamble.

Nicol's production, which only ran for twenty-one performances, bears some similarity to another panned *Macbeth*, Bryan Forbes's 1980 staging at the Old Vic with Peter O'Toole. However, O'Toole's was the subject of such vitriol that it became a box office smash. It's unlikely that Nicol would have seen O'Toole's performance – he was never one to notice competition. Coincidentally, the critics mentioned similar flaws in both: an off-centre Macbeth, a misconceived set and unintentionally funny emphases – for example, a dull rendition of the line 'I have done the deed'.

The BBC version of *Macbeth*, which Nicol made later that year, and became a touchstone for students everywhere, made no casting concessions. Instead Jane Lapotaire played Lady Macbeth and the director was Nicol's trusted collaborator Jack Gold. The BBC production was certainly slower paced than the Broadway one. It is also the only film of Nicol's Macbeth. It shows the same approach to Shakespeare that characterised all his performances – saying each line as if it were freshly minted without exaggerating the cadences, the rhythm, the ebb and flow of the verse. Lapotaire's acting, by contrast, is rather more emphatic.

Nicol gives an arresting performance in the BBC version and yet something is not quite right; somehow he is slightly out of kilter. Peter Gill, who had directed Nicol in *Twelfth Night*, thought that Nicol spoke the verse 'brilliantly' but was so caught up in the intensity of the part that his body had become somehow uncoordinated.

Doubtless, just as with his *Hamlet*, the same tendency not to genuflect to the verse would have antagonised the purists. Yet it became Nicol's standard methodology – show by thought, not overemphasis. Leslie Megahey noted it too. 'Look at his performances on film or TV, especially in Shakespeare – no savouring of the words, no long pauses for effect, fast fast fast!'

Nicol and Andrea were together during the New York run of *Macbeth* and during the BBC production in the UK. A cast member remembers it was always clear who was boss:

Andrea was a young 'yes man' to Nicol. Always smiling, polite, quiet, with a deep voice. She seemed star struck, ambitious and maybe not very bright, though that could've been youth and naivety. All-American girl puppy dog, and not terribly genuine. Nicol took her for expensive dinners, dressed her in cashmere. He treated her with respect in public, but then again, she never said boo. She was a disciplined hard worker with an athletic body.

Another remembers her as 'young, bright, and a tireless worker – perhaps borrowing from her training as a gymnast'.

A twenty-five-year age difference was bound to tell. Now, thirty-five years later, Andrea feels she was naïve during her relationship with Nicol:

> When I think back on the time I knew Nicol, I am struck by many things, but mostly, how young I was and how little I was able to comprehend the depth of his torment. His talent was still easily available to him but the demons that undid him were always close by. He could be generous and thoughtful but he was also an extreme drinker whose cruelty and violence could be horrifying.[6]

Nicol had always had a reputation as a heavy drinker, as many explosive British actors of that generation did. Tara Hugo – many years later – remembers Nicol retching in the toilet when he visited to see her in a play. She thinks he was taking antabuse, a substance to combat alcoholism.

Luke, however, always remembers Nicol's vehement denial of alcoholism:

> Dad drank to escape boredom when he wasn't working. Certainly in his earlier career, when he was in his forties, he would be in very good shape physically and not drink much, if at all, when working. After Andrea, he drank to kill that pain, he drank to escape thinking about death and the void. Earlier on, he really could take it or leave it, but in the mid noughties he chose to take it more than leave it, I'd say.

Nicol once admitted to David Frost that he needed drink to relax him but said he seldom got really drunk. But that was back in 1968.

Rand Bridges doesn't recall Nicol's drinking ever interfering with his acting. At that stage it was just fun. Bridges says that Nicol was a regular at a jazz club on 52nd Street called George's Club:

> He always loved music and used to give a demonstration of a highland fling – whether it was accurate or not I don't know. He always preferred male company – didn't like the girls coming along – perhaps because he felt he could more easily let his hair down or just be more flamboyant and honest.

Leslie Megahey, who worked with him later on, agrees that Nicol was essentially a man's man:

He was an old style male in the sense that he could be very courteous to women (though not always, according to Ken Tynan), but I think was more at ease in the company of men. He was very respectful of my partner Jana, and she liked him. She has a soft spot for highly individual people who seem a touch mad, bad and dangerous to know but I sensed he didn't totally relax in female company.

Another friend, Louise Penn, agreed. 'I never felt he particularly liked women, and he could be misogynistic at times, but for a man born in the mid-thirties, he could have just been old-fashioned.'[7]

Nicol probably relished drinking sessions where he could get merry without too much female tut-tutting. Luke believes that somewhere along the line booze became a prop for his father and that it may have even exacerbated his depression:

He loved good wine and good food. He always refused to eat fast food and he taught me to eat many things I'd never have tried. It was part of his enjoyment of life. But alcohol is also a depressant and when you're already depressed and unhappy and you're over-drinking it won't lead to a good place.

But Luke stresses that drugs were an absolute 'no-no' for Nicol. On one occasion back in the sixties someone had laced his drink with LSD and Nicol had summoned a doctor. 'Ultimately, he liked to be in control.'

Attitudes to addiction have changed drastically over the last thirty or forty years. Perhaps that's why the movie *I'm Dancing as Fast as I Can*, in which Jill Clayburgh played a television producer, Barbara Gordon, hooked on valium and Nicol was her controlling and abusive husband, Derek, now seems dated.

David Rabe, who wrote the screenplay, was thrilled to have Nicol for such a challenging role:

I don't recall casting Nicol as a risk. I remember being thrilled by the idea, believing him a superb actor capable of all that the part required. We weren't overly concerned with his bankability as much as his talent, which seemed very right for the part. He and Jill worked very well together. The shooting schedule was short and demanding … I was very pleased and impressed with his performance. Both Jill and Nicol had to go into some extreme places, each in a particular and personal degree of madness, hers drug and withdrawal driven, and his – the slow revelation of a raw dependent personality, deeply invested in control and fear of loss of control.[8]

Halliwell was unimpressed with the final result. 'Unabsorbing case history more suitable as a TV movie except that the acting for TV would not have been so far over the top.'

David Denby in *New York Magazine* said, 'Speaking in a nervous high voice, Nicol Williamson makes Derek into a harmless, vaguely dislikeable twit – or so it seems at first', before noting his descent into 'a screaming lunatic who loathes Barbara's success so much he wants to do her in'.

Excalibur apart, Nicol never seemed to have much luck with films. And at this stage in his career they were just a side-line for his real love – the theatre. Opinions are divided about whether Nicol favoured theatre or film work. Luke thinks that Nicol probably preferred theatre but found film work less draining and a different kind of challenge.

As international screen stardom had eluded him, Nicol simply knew there were more avenues of creativity open to him in theatre. To his credit, Nicol kept testing himself in major classical roles. Another Osborne play would shore up his reputation as an individualist who always blazed his own trail.

13

BANISHING OLIVIER

'He was tremendous looking out into the audience, drained and broken, a wild spirit that had given up.'

Keith Reddin on Nicol Williamson's final scene as Archie Rice in *The Entertainer*

Nicol once said he never noticed competition. He was a centre forward. He was determined to make every part his own. Osborne's *Inadmissible Evidence* was certainly Nicol's crowning achievement, so much so that it was always difficult to see anyone else as Maitland. That perhaps is the ultimate arbiter of success, that someone owns a character so totally.

Since Nicol had enjoyed so much success with Maitland it was natural he'd want to attempt another Osborne classic – as Archie Rice in *The Entertainer*, another in Osborne's canon of self-loathing, self-pitying failures. Just as any actor attempting *A Streetcar Named Desire* would be aware of Brando's shadow, so a new Archie Rice would have been aware of Olivier's. Yet here's the catch. Sacrilegious though it may be to say so, Nicol did not rate Olivier's Shakespearean performances highly. Nicol also believed that certain other actors – Hopkins, Caine, Connery and McKellen – were also overrated.

Leslie Megahey, a great friend of Nicol's in later years, director of *The Hour of the Pig* and his collaborator on the musical *Jack*, remembers his attitude to actors:

His greatest accolade for a performer was two simple words, said after their names, in parenthesis but with conviction, thus – 'Joe Schmokin ... Good Actor'. He said this most often of female actors he had worked with – Francesca Annis was one such. He mostly admired great Hollywood stars of yesteryear – Tracy, Stewart, Gregory Peck (Nicol did the most brilliant imitation of Peck on his answering machine), John Barrymore of course, and so forth. Less so with British actors, but he respected Olivier and, I think, Ralph Richardson (he was a great mimic, and when you mentioned one of these guys you'd get a perfect imitation of them right back). He loved great character actors like Wilfrid Lawson, who appears to have put away more alcohol in his career than anybody else of the time, including Nicol. The actors he really admired seemed to me to be those who were strong of character, not necessarily physically tough or especially macho, but with their own kind of power. You wouldn't call Ralph Richardson a notably macho actor, but Nic thought he was great – there was a strength, resilience, physical power to him that, you could argue, came less naturally to Gielgud. Olivier was probably the most butch of that group, and I know Nic had much respect for him as a force of nature on stage.

Nicol rated Olivier's non-Shakespearean roles more highly but there was simply no way he would have been daunted at the prospect of reprising Archie Rice. Not only would he *not* be intimidated, he certainly wouldn't imitate. He could take off Olivier, Richardson, and even John Osborne, to a tee, but that was not how he created a character.

A further problem in staging *The Entertainer* in America was that it is a quintessentially British play with its allusions to the decline of empire, the music hall tradition and the Suez crisis. Even in 1983, it would have seemed dated because it was, in part, a reaction to the hail-fellow-well-met plays of the forties and fifties.

The team at the Roundabout Theatre was very auspicious. Esteemed director William Gaskill was at the helm and Frances Cuka played Archie's wife. *The Entertainer*, however, was very different from *Inadmissible Evidence*. Maitland was like a torrent on stage, spewing out his self-disgust, a man at least full of feeling, even if it was entirely negative. Archie Rice was a vacuous washout, not even affected by the death of his son, 'dead behind the eyes' as he says in the final act. Like Maitland, a mediocrity yet, unlike him, emotionally shallow. So Nicol had to downsize to play this downtrodden, beaten figure. Nicol, who had a wonderful singing voice, even had to play down his singing ability to do justice to Archie's limited talent – which, of course, is difficult to do.

Shortly before the opening in January 1983, John Osborne unleashed a pre-emptive strike. He sent a vitriolic letter to critics telling them they wouldn't understand the play and how stupid and biased they were and that, naturally, they would fall into the mistake of comparing Nicol to Olivier. According to Keith Reddin, who played his son in the play, Nicol read the letter to the entire cast. Nicol apparently thought it was hilarious, and perhaps it was, but Reddin remembers he and the other actors were aghast.

Reddin had enormous respect for Nicol – he had seen him in the acclaimed 1973 production of *Uncle Vanya* – but he found him in a naughty mood. Reddin claims that Nicol sometimes made his disdain for certain supporting players all too clear:

> He was clearly a raw talent. I enjoyed his slyness, his danger. But anyone who crossed him could be mercilessly punished. I witnessed him being quite cruel to other actors. True, he didn't suffer fools or laziness, but sometimes he would talk over them in performance, turn his back on them, actually walk off stage one performance – but certainly *not* with Frances Cuka whom he greatly respected – because he didn't feel they were truthful or connecting with him.[1]

Reddin noticed Nicol's contempt not only for some of the other actors but even the audiences. Was this deep insecurity or anger, or self-loathing, like Archie? Perhaps again, that was what attracted him to the role. He shared Archie's bile, disgust, violence, and sadness. 'I went out drinking with him after performances, and he was a wonderful storyteller and shared terrific insights into the profession,' recalled Reddin. 'Sometimes we ran across the street to a nearby bar and he would down a gin and tonic or a beer before running across traffic to get into the dressing room before the curtain rose for Act Two! Of course this was dangerous, probably illegal, but he didn't care.'

Downing drinks between acts is highly unprofessional – he might also have missed his cue. Theatregoers who had also ventured across the road for a little lubrication would have been shocked to find Archie Rice guzzling spirits at their side! It seemed Nicol went as close to the edge as he could. Throughout his career Nicol never took bullshit from anyone. Yet he also seemed intent on making clear not only that he was his own man but that he would set the ground rules.

Luke says his dad believed that rules were there to be broken:

> Let's say you're forbidden from doing something. Even if he didn't want to do what he had been forbidden from doing, on some level he would feel like he was allowing someone to control him. So he would do whatever it was, irrespective of the cost, to say 'I'm not your lackey'. But, in a way, he could be manipulated. If you wanted to get him to behave badly, all you had to do was tell him that, under no circumstances, would he be allowed to do something. If he was given leeway, and allowed to just give his performance, you probably wouldn't have too much trouble. But then you still have the depression to cope with and I think the fear of death, the void that was always a looming concern.

Keith Reddin spent a lot of time with Nicol outside the theatre, acting as his unofficial minder. He remembers a host of funny stories. A particular favourite of Nicol's concerned Wilfrid Lawson. According to Reddin:

> One Lawson story he told was about an actor locking himself in his dressing room before a performance. The actor was terrified of going on, had started drinking and wouldn't come out. Lawson knocked on the door, and said, 'Please come out dear boy, you don't want to end up like me.' In retrospect, it seems so ironic that Nicol told that story because he was immensely talented and could be amazing on stage and film but, yes, often self-destructed through drinking (on and off stage), bad behaviour and rudeness. It was sad to see that greatness wasted.

Yet it was Nicol's acting that made the most impression on Keith. 'I will never in my lifetime forget him in that final speech in *The Entertainer*. He was tremendous looking out into the audience, drained and broken, a wild spirit that had given up. Despite his bad behaviour he was an important performer who, when he connected, couldn't be matched.'

Nevertheless when the play opened, just as Osborne had predicted, it was panned. Frank Rich was again dismissive:

> Only an actor of rare courage would ever dream of following a legend into the flickering centre spotlight of Osborne's bitter elegy for a dying England … and if this star is brave he also deserves credit for refusing to give an Olivier impression. Nicol Williamson has chosen his own distinctive approach to the role – to such an extent that he does partially obliterate our mental image of his predecessor. But, in the end, the play is obliterated too. Nicol Williamson's characterisation proves wrongheaded and so does the mostly slack production that surrounds him … Williamson arouses no strong feelings of any sort, with his sagging shoulders, mild voice and vacant, almost cherubic face, he seems defeated before the play begins – more a Willy Loman than Archie Rice.

John Beaufort wrote in *The Christian Science Monitor* that 'although he handles the music-hall routines and John Addison tunes with a breezy finesse, there is in this performance an insufficiently sharp distinction between Archie's stage persona and his offstage personality'.

Glenn Currie said:

It's inevitable, if unfair, that Williamson's performance will be compared with Laurence Olivier's, so let's get that out of the way first. Olivier works on his roles from outside in, and his Archie Rice – one of the great performances of the era – was a dime-store Pagliacci crumbling behind his stage make-up and props: red nose, gap teeth and shaggy eyebrows, a bowler hat and cane. Williamson is one British actor who adopts the American method of internalising the character and letting it shine through the cracks. He uses no extra make-up, no hat, no cane. But his Archie Rice seldom appears through the cracks. He also is unable to play off the other actors, and William Gaskill's low-key direction makes it difficult for Williamson to make the most of the high points.

You can't win with critics. Currie seemed to be saying that Nicol was too self-effacing. Perhaps that was on purpose to illustrate Archie's mediocrity, Nicol could still steal any show off the nominal leads if he wanted to. In March, along with Michael York, Sam Wanamaker and Cleo Laine, Nicol appeared at a Pittsburgh memorial concert honouring Princess Grace of Monaco, who had died the previous September. The programme was sponsored by the city's Pittsburgh-based International Poetry Forum in association with the Shakespeare Globe Centre of London. Princess Caroline, still in mourning for her mother, attended the evening at Carnegie Music Hall.

By all accounts it was Nicol who gave the most impressive reading. Giving the only performance without a script, he offered a dramatic whispered rendition of Macbeth's soliloquy before he murders Duncan. Later, he transformed the mood by singing *Dunsinane Blues*. The local Pittsburgh press hailed Nicol's performance as 'the most striking stunt' of the evening.

Nicol was next invited to direct – and star as The Inquisitor/Robert De Beaudricourt – in a production of *The Lark* at the Citadel Theatre in Edmonton. Maybe the clincher was that Andrea Weber would play Joan of Arc. Nicol was trying to boost her career at the time. The producer was Joe Shoctor,[2] a big name in Canadian theatre. (He was Jewish and was adamant that, under no circumstances, would *Merchant of Venice* ever be staged at his theatre.)

Nicol was allowed to take two actors with him – and he chose Ray Dooley,[3] whom he much admired from *Macbeth*, and his then wife, Diana Stagner. Ray and Diana often went to Nicol and Andrea's luxury suite in Edmonton to play bridge, drink white wine and eat snacks that Nicol had prepared in advance – spicy lobster pate and crepes suzette, according to Dooley who remembers that, at this stage, Nicol was very caring and protective of Andrea.

From the beginning of rehearsals at the Citadel it was clear that Nicol was not getting on with Shoctor. Luciano Iogna, the assistant director on *The Lark*,

remembers that the set resembled a huge slate-coloured rake but at some cost
– $20,000.[4] A few days before opening, Nicol demanded changes to the set and
confronted Shoctor.

Throughout his career Nicol seemed compelled to feud with producers. Perhaps
it was his artistic commitment but he reserved a special disdain for producers.

Luke said, 'He hated that the decision men were not artists in any way and had
no idea what they were interfering in … Dad didn't like inequality, he didn't like
financial meanness. He was also a strongly empathetic character who identified
with the underdog and against authority almost without fail.'

Leslie Megahey believed Nicol did himself no favours with his hatred of 'the
suits'. It's worth noting that Nicol was seldom – if ever – hired by producers,
only directors:

> He didn't make it easy for executives and producers. Largely he disliked intensely
> anyone who made piles of money out of the talents of others. This seems to me
> how he saw most producers and entrepreneurs. He viewed them as a necessary
> evil, as they got the money for the shows, but he kept as far away from them as
> possible. He had an allergy to offices. He refused to see even the most grand of
> movie moguls in their offices, no matter how powerful they were, or what was at
> stake. He said he would happily meet them on neutral ground, like a bar.
>
> Harvey Weinstein once asked him to come in for a meeting in the Miramax
> offices in Tribeca before we shot *The Hour of the Pig*, just to say hello (Harvey was
> buying the distribution rights for the USA). Nicol was in New York at the time
> but refused to come to Harvey's office. He said he'd be delighted to meet Harvey
> for a drink in the Tribeca grill downstairs. Not surprisingly, no meeting took
> place. I remember saying perhaps he should try to quell this allergy to powerful
> people and their offices, and he said with a bit of a smile that Steven Spielberg
> hadn't liked it much either.

And so it was with Shoctor. Nicol abruptly walked out and went to a restaurant at
11 a.m. with Iogna and started drinking wine. Iogna tried to reason with Nicol –
the set was expensive and with only a few days to go it was unlikely to be changed.
Nicol told him not to worry. 'He wanted to state his position. He wanted power
play of some kind. Later that afternoon everything was fine. He just wanted a little
push back from his perspective.'

Iogna said he learnt a lot from Nicol during rehearsals. 'He was both the actor
and director. Everyone respected him and his vision of the play. There was perhaps
a certain fear and awe but there was certainly also strong respect – "this guy knows
what he's doing, I'm going to take what I can".'

Nicol quickly fired an American actor, James Naismith, two days in, but showed exemplary patience towards a British actor called Peter Curtis who would blank at least once every performance, often foreshadowed by fidgeting with his ring finger. Perhaps because he was British, and his voice suited Nicol's ear, Nicol tolerated his idiosyncrasies. Iogna noticed that Nicol could be tough but never used the old directorial trick of exposing people's vulnerabilities to extract a better performance. 'Other than the manipulative moments (with Shoctor) I saw him in his best light. He never abused someone in order to get their soul on stage, as I have seen others do.'

Iogna also remembers the speed of Nicol's performance. He noted how Nicol, rather like Peter O'Toole, would rattle through banal lines and then linger over the more telling dialogue – an old actor's trick. He was struck by Nicol's magnetism. 'He had a charismatic aura about him that rather reminded me of Ray Davies from the Kinks.' Yet his torment was tangible, 'I sensed a deep disappointment in him – there was a huge potential in this man but he wasn't getting the right work.'

Dooley has fond memories of Nicol despite witnessing his mercurial temperament:

[He was] the life of the party and sometimes morose for lack of a better word. I had the great luxury of knowing him during those weeks in Edmonton when things were, dare I say it, normal and quite happy. Games of bridge and all that sort of thing. He always treated me well, even warmly, and was unfailingly generous.

Actor Brian Knox McGugan, who had a bit part in *The Lark*, also recalled Nicol's generosity:

I had just one line near the end of the play (the soldier with the cross), and I'll never forget the end of the week's rehearsal when we finally got to my part. At the end of that scene, with full cast onstage, Nicol said 'good work, good night, and we'll see you all next week'. I tentatively raised my hand and said 'Uh … excuse me, please can we do that one more time … please?' Nicol swept around grandly, and in front of the entire cast and said to me with his best theatrical voice, 'is it heavy on your heart?' After a moment, I replied very shakily 'yes, actually, it is'. And so, we did the scene again.'[5]

The Lark, which ran for a month – 24 September until 22 October – was quickly forgotten. Nicol moved on to a small role in *Sakharov*, the story of the influential Russian dissident, played by Jason Robards. Glenda Jackson played Yelena Bonner but it was hardly a reunion – Jackson didn't even know that Nicol was in it! He had a larger part as the king in *Christopher Columbus*. Murray Melvin remembers the latter production as scattered, cast members all over the place. Nicol might have had misgivings at being cast opposite notorious prima donna Faye Dunaway but, if he did, there were no obvious tantrums. 'Nicol Williamson is an odd, rather lopsided King Ferdinand. His face keeps falling from attention. He may be thinking about Henry VIII or Hamlet, although Ferdinand was less thrilling', said *New York* magazine.

Nicol's next movie *Return to Oz*, a sequel to *The Wizard of Oz*, did little for his career. Playing both Dr Worley and the Nome King in a film that somehow lacked the necessary charm – and in some places was even too scary for children – was perhaps not the kind of work Nicol should have been doing at this stage in his life, in many ways the prime ones for an actor. A dark, intermittently powerful, attempt to capitalise on the original, it gave Jean Marsh, who was still being pursued by young fans of the film at memorabilia events until recently, a memorable role.

Director Walter Murch recalled the poor reception:

> The film was ambitious and expensive, and then turned out to be neither a critical nor a commercial success, which is a heavy hit for someone's first directing job. There were a few reviewers who liked it – Mike Clark from *USA Today* – but most compared it unfavourably to The Wizard of Oz. The climate of the times just wasn't receptive to anything other than the MGM Land of Oz.[6]

'Children are sure to be startled by the film's bleakness', said the *New York Times*'s Janet Maslin in an opinion probably echoed by many. 'He did *Return to Oz* because he thought it was truer to the original book, as opposed to the original movie,' Luke told me. 'The book is much darker than the movie, and I think he felt it rang true. Unfortunately it was too dark for the young audience and suffered for that.'

The part did, however, usher in a lot of fan mail from children, continuing right up to the end of his life.

Just when it seemed that Nicol might be fading from view he won a major part on television playing a senior member of Britain's aristocracy. Yet again, Nicol would reveal his dark side to colleagues and go to war with the establishment.

14

MOUNTBATMAN

'I think you do rather grow up as you realise what an idiot you were.'
Nicol Williamson during an interview to publicise *The Last Viceroy*

By far the biggest role Nicol had in 1984 was as Mountbatten, the last viceroy of India, who was tragically murdered by the IRA in 1979. A huge juggernaut of a miniseries – filming in Delhi for ten weeks, and then two weeks in Sri Lanka – it cast Nicol against type as the lantern-jawed royal with clipped speech. Nicol was definitely not first choice – as with Sherlock, Christopher Plummer was in line but he was unavailable. It was a difficult role for Nicol who decided against a flat-out impersonation, attempting instead to convey Lord Louis's personality and charisma, albeit in a serious situation – the threat of civil war in India.

Lord Snowdon had visited Nicol on the set of *Return to Oz*. According to Nicol:

> He told me that he couldn't really say very much but that one of the things that really struck him were his [Mountbatten's] manners – he had the best manners of anyone he had ever known, in the way that he talked to and dealt with people. He was very strong and definite and a very imposing personality.

'Imposing' certainly was an apt word to describe Nicol's bearing but manners depended on the moment. Filming began in the summer of 1984 with Luton Hoo standing in for Broadlands, the Mountbattens' seat. Shooting got off to a bad start when Nicol slapped a cameraman who, he thought, was laughing at his appearance. 'I got that lip injury playing rugger', the crew remembered Nicol as saying.

The incident plagued the rest of filming. Sam Dastor, cast as Mahatma Gandhi, remembers that it caused a terrible commotion. Janet Suzman (Lady Mountbatten), though absent on the day it happened, recalled that 'a feeling of some scandalous behaviour ran through the set for a day or so, but in true English fashion nothing was said. He must have been under some stress to do that, but taking it out on a techie seems like really bad judgment.'[1]

Luke remembers his father referring to the role a bit disparagingly as 'Mountbatman'. Nicol was in a 'moody'. The rest of the cast stayed at the Taj Palace hotel but Nicol insisted on staying at the Sheraton. Nicol also kicked up a fuss about the military uniforms hired from Bermans, insisting that he should be allowed to keep them. What he was going to do with them exactly was anyone's guess (set them alight?) because Sam Dastor believed that Nicol hated anything that smacked of elitism. 'I had a feeling that he regarded the role of Mountbatten as a challenge precisely because he hated the upper classes. I think he was his own worst enemy and he had an enormous chip on his shoulder.' Dastor remembers that Nicol seemed to view Ian Richardson, cast as Nehru, as the enemy camp. He saw him as a 'toff', indulging in some show of temperament by staying in his caravan and deliberately making Richardson wait for important scenes.[2]

Janet Suzman, putting it tactfully, remembers that Nicol was simply uncomfortable. 'I had the feeling that Nicol was not completely at home with the character, and this made him a little withdrawn. Most of my scenes were with Ian Richardson, so Nicol and I did not see much of each other. However, I admired Nicol's acting abilities very much.'

Nevertheless, as always, when Nicol felt like it, he was a joy. Dastor remembers he was always pleasant to him and delightfully entertaining, doing spot-on impersonations of Vladek Sheybal, the incisive character actor with a deadpan, deadly drawl, and producer Judith de Paul with whom, predictably, he did not get on. 'Nicol was quite the best mimic I have ever known in my fifty years in the business. When you heard Nicol mimicking either of them you would swear that you were actually listening to them. He was uncanny,' recalls Dastor.

Nicol gelled with Tom Clegg – an underrated, professional journeyman director who had delivered some excellent episodes of *The Sweeney* and *Van der Valk* as well as *McVicar*, an entertaining gangster biopic. Was it class again?

'I can work very well with Tom,' said Nicol. 'He's very down to earth, rational and sees things very quickly. He's the essence of the north countryman – phlegmatic, stubborn, can dig his heels in, but he has that wry humour. He doesn't elaborate – he has an easy and good talent for quickly getting down to the heart of the matter.'

Andrea accompanied Nicol and had a small, recurring part as Mountbatten's daughter, Pamela. Dastor thinks she was a good influence on Nicol:

She had a very likeable personality and was extremely friendly to me and indeed to other members of the cast. I also remember that if I wanted to approach Nicol about anything, I always thought it safer to consult Andrea first. She was always very helpful and knew just how to put things to Nicol in a way that he would respond to well. She was a very sweet girl and we all used to wonder how she could ever put up with someone as moody as Nicol. Nicol was always very kind and helpful to me … but nevertheless one was always conscious of being on the edge of a volcano and he was at his best when in Andrea's company.

Dastor also recalls that, though American, Andrea's Received Pronunciation English 'was virtually perfect both on and off screen'.

By the time filming reached Delhi, tragedy struck. Prime Minister Indira Gandhi, with whom Nicol and other cast members had been photographed just a few days earlier, was assassinated on 31 October 1984. Nicol and Janet immediately returned to the UK while Richardson and Dastor went to Sri Lanka to film further scenes.

In publicity interviews, perhaps wary of his reputation, Nicol was well behaved and professional. A profile in *Photoplay* magazine in 1984 carried a rather ironic comment from Nicol – given what had transpired on the set, 'I think you do rather grow up as you realise what an idiot you were'.

In other interviews Nicol was self-deprecating, admitting he found his way into the role tentatively:

I'm not someone who is tremendously bright in getting hold of text quickly. I'm a very, very slow learner. I cannot learn parrot fashion. There has to be something spiritual about it. I must fully understand the sense and how it is presented. The language, syntax and everything else has got to work. I more or less locked myself in the bedroom for five days in my house in Amsterdam. Everyone else had a wonderful time while I forced myself to get the shape of the story into my head. And when we were at Luton Hoo, I worked all the time, in the car getting there, over lunch. I didn't really have lunch – I just ate, drank, slept and thought the script through and concentrated hard on the changes that were made.

Nicol explained his interpretation:

One of the things about Mountbatten is that you have to humanise the man. Very little is known of his personal life, a lot about the public one. There are, of course, salacious insinuations. I'm not interested in that – you know – Edwina and Nehru and all that nonsense. If you are going to examine that then it becomes a different story from the one that we are actually doing … here I thought was a man with a munificent personality, a modern hero in every sense. A past master at making people feel relaxed and important. Not only did he epitomise the statesmanlike qualities of tact and diplomacy but he was possessed of genuine charm, not a coating. He was very good at asking questions, had a high intelligence and an absorbent mind and filmic looks. I had to play him!

Nicol, sounding slightly paranoid, predicted some misgivings in royal circles about his portrayal:

I should think that there is apprehension that someone like me is playing the part. Within the Mountbatten clan it will be regarded as a great misfortune. By and large, there will be people looking, lurking, waiting for me to fall over, which makes it even more of a challenge for me. In his family and at Buckingham Palace there will be great discontent that some rather more society figure of an actor hasn't done it. But I don't think that that kind of guy could have pulled it off. Obviously the reaction of the royals, the Queen, Prince Philip, Prince Charles, will be the most interesting because they are the people who will know. If they can say 'that's Uncle Dickey' then I will have succeeded.[3]

The view of the Queen is not known but Mountbatten's daughter, Lady Pamela Hicks, speaking in 2016, thought the portrayal was not quite right:

As the Shakespearean actor that he was – Nicol Williamson's diction, of course, was excellent. But the impression he gave was of a crumpled figure in a crumpled uniform. He had very little scope for acting because he was the whole time confined to a chair round a committee table. Whereas, of course, my mother, played by Janet Suzman, was so brilliant and was always coming and leaving, flying off to refugee camps and leading an astonishing life while the poor Viceroy was doomed to a conference table and had no possibility of showing his acting abilities. He just had words to say across a table – it's very difficult to act when you are only projecting your voice – and the vision, which struck everybody, was not of my father's very, very crisp white naval uniform, of which, even sitting down, the whole top would be still very crisp. I suppose by the end of a day's work it might have got a bit creased, but you never thought of him as creased because he bore himself so well. The impression poor Nicol Williamson gave was of a very crumpled man.[4]

Reviews for Nicol's performance were not flattering. *India Today* judged that 'the pivotal flaw of the series was the choice of Scottish-born actor Nicol Williamson to portray the charismatic, autocratic but much-loved Lord Louis. A woeful piece of miscasting, his performance was deservedly savaged.'

The view that Nicol was miscast was reinforced when Alistair Cooke, most famous for his *Letter from America* on Radio 4 but also the compere of Masterpiece Theatre, made a great *faux pas* when *The Last Viceroy* aired in 1986. Cooke was forced to apologise for an unguarded remark to an interviewer. Thinking the formal part of the discussion was over, he offered his opinion of Nicol's performance. Cooke, while praising Nicol as 'a very good actor', described him as 'a lug' who looked like a London School of Economics professor who never wore a suit.[5]

When the remark leaked out Cooke was forced to write a letter of apology to Nicol. For Nicol, who was hoping that the Mountbatten series would relaunch his career and reintroduce him to American audiences, the comments were most unwelcome. For once he was the victim of someone else's indiscretion. 'It's like saying I have this product, fish, and I'm selling stinking fish in the marketplace … when one plays a public figure one is always subject to criticism,' Nicol said at the time. Yet he played down the rift:

> The whole matter is simply forgotten. I never flaunt these things and I have no intention of doing it now … everyone has his own opinions in life. I think it was an unfortunate situation that may or may not have been taken advantage of. The whole thing is best dropped. It was unfortunate that his confidence was betrayed. I have no intention of exploiting it.

Nicol added it was important only to be believable, citing the diminutive Martin Sheen's brilliant portrayal of the six-footer Jack Kennedy in the miniseries *Kennedy*, and, ironically, echoing another remark of Cooke that Nicol playing Mountbatten was like casting then House Speaker, Tip O'Neill, as Kennedy.

Others noted the bleakness of *The Last Viceroy*. Nicol commented:

> This was a very serious situation. One could inject some humour and lighthearted moments into it when the script permitted. But for an actor committed to a script and a director there's very little one can do. It's like changing a huge Broadway musical or trying to rearrange the deckchairs on the Titanic. You can make suggestions and try to improve it as you go along but once it's underway you're committed like everyone else.

By the time *The Last Viceroy* was screened Nicol appeared to be considering a more permanent move to the USA. He admitted his agent thought it would be beneficial. But, then again, agents *would*. 'In this large, convoluted country, while some people are familiar with my work, the vast majority don't know me … I'm not being rediscovered. I haven't been seen by the majority of Americans,' he conceded.

It seemed that Nicol was definitely happier in the US than in the UK. In early 1985, Nicol replaced Jeremy Irons as Henry Boot in *The Real Thing*, Tom Stoppard's play about theatrical infidelities, at New York's Plymouth Theatre. 'I thought it was a great play,' Nicol said in an interview the following year, 'I like Mike Nichols and I love Stoppard. I didn't agree with people who say "it was a bad career move". For me it was a wonderful career move. It gave me the opportunity to perform in something light, intelligent and comedic. I loved it.'

Nicol's co-star Laila Robins found him to be mainly 'delightful' for the three-month run but he was railing against a short rehearsal period that left him under-prepared. Nicol, as usual, vented his anger at producers from the stage post-performance, although on this occasion he had at least forewarned Robins. 'I knew what it was like to be shot out of a cannon and on to a stage,' she commented.[6]

Nicol seemed to need an enemy. His incessant feuding, although some of it may have been justified, revealed a troubled mind. Around this time an executive at a public relations firm, Sharlene Springer, knew Williamson as a neighbour at Chelsea's London Terrace building in New York. 'I would see him at the grocery store, meditating over the meat counter,' she wrote, 'He was clearly a very depressed man and obviously medicating that condition with alcohol'.

Luke remembers that his father was reluctant to 'see someone' as the saying goes. 'He wasn't the type to go see a shrink. It's possible he thought it would remove his empathetic angst and he may have been right, I don't know.'

Laila Robins also remembers Nicol's resistance to therapy. Several years later, when she was appearing with James Earl Jones in a TV show called *Gabriel's Fire*, she saw Nicol in a matinee during his run of *I Hate Hamlet* in 1991. They then went to the Landmark Tavern on West Side where staff kept a bottle permanently on ice for Nicol. Laila was undergoing therapy sessions. She told Nicol she was finding it helpful and asked him if he had ever considered it. Nicol almost choked on his wine, 'Oh no, Laila, that would take away my magic'.

And 'magic' was the word that Laila used to describe Nicol's charismatic presence. 'It was like watching children or wild animals but never to the point of making me feel uncomfortable.' As for actress Anne Bobby, then just 17, she reportedly found Nicol to be 'a sweet, kind man' who walked her back to the port authority every evening.[7]

Alfred Lynch as Estragon and Nicol as Vladimir in *Waiting for Godot*, December 1964.
Nicol established a warm friendship with playwright Samuel Beckett. (Rex Features)

Nicol and Anna Karina in Tony Richardson's *Laughter in the Dark* (1969). Nicol was a last minute replacement for Richard Burton. (Rex Features)

Nicol and Rachel Roberts in *The Reckoning* (1969), Jack Gold's powerful film about class and revenge. (Alamy)

Nicol and Jill Townsend on their wedding day at Kensington and Chelsea Registry Office on 17 July 1971. (Rex Features)

Family photograph at the wedding of Nicol and Jill. Left to right: Nicol's father, Hugh; Jill's mother, Joan; Jill; Nicol; Jill's grandmother, Helen; Jill's father, Robert; and Nicol's mother, Mary. (Jill Townsend)

Nicol and Jill cutting
their wedding cake.
(Jill Townsend)

Nicol and Michael
Caine in *The Wilby
Conspiracy* (1974).
Luke believed this
was one of his father's
best screen roles
but Nicol resented
playing villains.
(Rex Features)

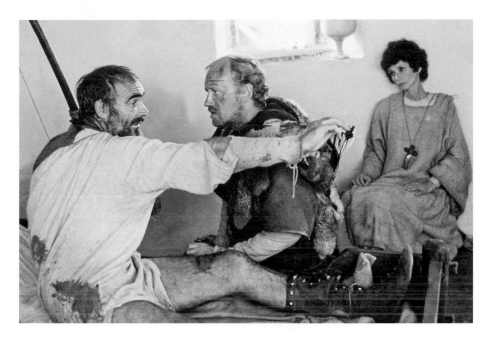

Sean Connery, Nicol and Audrey Hepburn in *Robin and Marian* (1976). Nicol was praised by director Richard Lester for a key scene with Hepburn. (Rex Features)

Nicol with his son Luke. (Lord Tony Snowdon)

Inadmissible Evidence, 1978
Royal Court revival.
Clockwise: Nicol, Rowena
Roberts, Marjorie Yates,
Deborah Norton, Elizabeth
Bell and Julie Peasgood.
(Rex Features)

Peter Falk and Nicol in
the *Columbo* episode 'How
to Dial a Murder' (1978).
Nicol, who hated TV,
claimed he could not recall
making it. (Alamy)

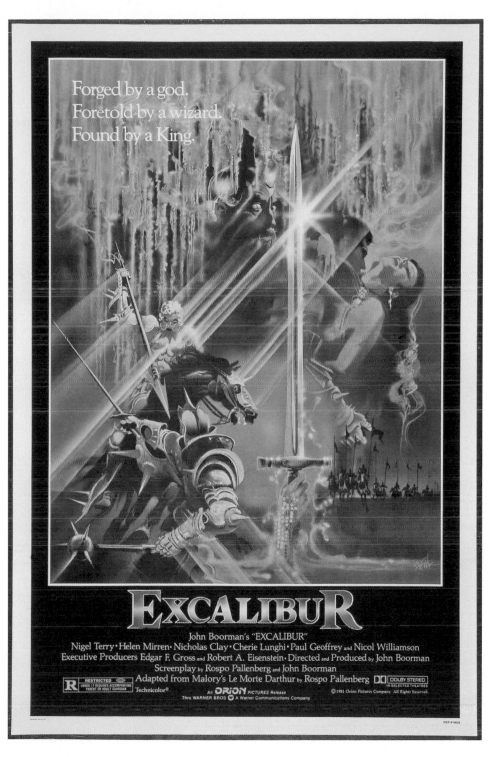

The poster for *Excalibur* (1981), which starred Nicol as Merlin.

Nicol and Theresa Russell in Black Widow (1987) in which he played a lonely museum director. (Rex Features)

Nicol as Jack Barrymore on the London stage in his one-man show, May 1994. Veteran critic Bernard Levin cited it as one of the half-dozen greatest theatrical performances he had ever seen. (Rex Features)

A couple of juicy supporting roles gave hope for better screen roles. In *Passion Flower*, one of those melodramatic, overheated movies that so suited the eighties, Nicol was a shady, short-tempered Singapore-based businessman. In Bruce Boxleitner's words, Nicol, cast as Barbara Hershey's father, even though he was only twelve years older, was a 'modern-day pirate' – involved in various nefarious activities.

Boxleitner played Barbara's suitor. He enjoyed the role because he admitted having had a crush on Hershey ever since her TV series *The Monroes*. Cue intense, longing gazes at the sweat dripping off Barbara's breasts, frenzied lovemaking surrounded by mosquito nets and all against the backdrop of Nicol's stern and disapproving father. Hershey arrived on set fresh from her great, relaunching role in *Hannah and Her Sisters*. This must have seemed like a silly, school-boyish yarn by comparison.

Boxleitner had admired Nicol ever since *Hamlet* days and especially in *Excalibur* He found Nicol enjoying the role but with a wink and nod to the audience, a no-nonsense attitude that Boxleitner shared. Take the work seriously but let's not pretend we're curing cancer or on the Oscar trail – perhaps to the chagrin of director Joseph Sargent. 'Nicol really liked the character, a shadowy character but nobody plays a bad guy as a bad guy,' recalled Boxleitner. 'By the time Nicol arrived Barbara and I had already started working. He got on particularly well with John Waters – playing Barbara Hershey's husband. They were like peas in the same pod.'[8]

Bruce enjoyed shooting 'on the fly', often in the Chinatown area of Singapore. He particularly remembers the fight scene with Nicol. Boxleitner, a big guy, then fourteen years Nicol's junior, was supposed to succumb to a blow from Nicol. Boxleitner, pricked by vanity as he cheerfully admits, tried to change the scene. Sargent, however, was having none of it – it was to be as scripted. The only concession was that Boxleitner would be felled by a karate chop that blindsided him. 'That's the only way I was going to go down,' recalled Bruce who says (light-heartedly!) he felt quite 'cocky' back then.

Boxleitner remembered the speed of Nicol's reactions. He cites an old analogy but one worth repeating, 'He hits it immediately back at you. It's like when you're playing tennis. You raise your game when you're playing with someone better than you.'

Passion Flower was agreeable hokum, if a bit too obviously forensically crafted, with Nicol giving a sinister but unsurprising squinty-eyed performance that did little for his career.

Nicol's next role, however, should have done. Bob Rafelson's *Black Widow*, filmed in early 1986, was a nearly great film about a female predator (Theresa

Russell) marrying and then killing off a succession of rich men. A simmering sub-text – at least that was the idea – centres on federal investigator Debra Winger's pursuit of her quarry, perhaps with a frisson of envy for the lifestyle Russell enjoys, as well as lesbian lust. At the time Winger said, 'These two women find something in the other that complements what each of them has and they begin to exchange identities'.[9]

The best part of this tense thriller comes when the almost over-beautiful Russell reinvents herself as a dowdy 'spinsterish' philanthropist librarian to capture the heart of a lonely numismatist, played to perfection by Nicol.

Rafelson was thrilled to get Nicol on board and found him extremely helpful:

> I was a huge fan. I'd seen Tony Richardson's version of *Hamlet*, with the next 'great voice', Anthony Hopkins. I'd seen all the working-class movies of the fifties. I knew Marianne Faithfull, she told me he struggled for perfection (with a wink towards other things). During my interview with him I talked about Osborne and the Angry Young Men. And I was identified somewhat with Beatniks here in the USA. I told him that BBS [Rafelson's production company] was inspired much by Woodfall productions [Tony Richardson et al.]. I feared his role in *Black Widow* would be dashed off by Nicol, because it was so small. But he made quiet and brilliant suggestions. I remember one conversation (since he was to be murdered in the movie) that we had in which Nicol remarked there were no curtain calls for dead actors.'[10]

It is the mark of a skilled actor to convey a lot about a character with a few gestures and Nicol – whom we remember was criticised by Pauline Kael for his overintensity, 'trying to reach out of the screen and grab you and strong-arm you' – is wonderfully understated here. It's a beautifully modulated, subtle portrayal of a successful but disconnected and sexually thwarted middle-aged man. Rafelson says that Nicol quickly got a hold of the character. 'We had a talk about his being patrician in the movie – in American terms. Shy, reserved, wealthy, the director and chief financial officer of a museum but nervous in relationships.'

Catch the scene where he and Russell first have a long talk, 'I don't know why I never got married. I take out my reasons and polish them every once in a while. I kept on growing into these peculiar, idiosyncratic directions,' he says, fiddling with his watch along with wistful, watery-eyed gazes.

Rafelson recalls, 'I thought it might be distracting for the audience if he fiddled with his watch. But Nicol persisted. And even covered it up with his free hand. He was right to do it.'[11]

If the character had been fleshed out a little more, it might have netted him an Oscar nod for best supporting actor. Instead, it is effectively an extended cameo, over much too quickly after Nico, with endearing shyness, takes Russell to his rambling Seattle spread. Rafelson recalled that Nicol improvised a little skip as they entered the house. He noticed on the dailies what a charming touch it was. When he and Russell had to make love, Nicol asked Rafelson, 'Bob, how do patricians make love – shyly?' Rafelson replied, 'Not necessarily'. Instead, according to Rafelson, Nicol made love 'ravenously'. A great shot was accomplished in one take.

With a few flourishes Nicol had succeeded in making audiences care for this rather nerdy, vulnerable character who, we cannot help but feel, should have known better and perhaps almost does. 'You seem almost too good to be true', he tells her at one point.

Luke Williamson remembers Nicol – who he found to be 'very sweet' in the movie – liked working with Rafelson. 'He detested Winger but adored Theresa Russell, absolutely adored her. I remember Dad mentioning that Winger had a bad habit of chewing with her mouth open.'

The director remembers what could be taken as a typical 'Nicolish', waspish ending to his role in the film:

> When the part was over, and he left, there was a bit of a ruckus in the office. Something about his hotel bill or some other absurdity. I tried to get off the stage to embrace him, say goodbye and thanks. His agent said 'don't worry, Bob, he ends all his jobs with an argument'.

Rafelson – most famous, of course, for his classic collaborations with Jack Nicholson, including *Five Easy Pieces* – directs skilfully but there's a bit too much of Winger's office antics at the beginning. Leslie Halliwell thought it insubstantial, 'Watchable but overlong cop show with nothing very surprising about it once the plot is clear. TV movies have done just as well.'

Nicol's career should have been taking off again but instead it seemed to be spluttering after *Black Widow*. His second marriage had failed and Nicol had made too many enemies in the industry.

15

ANATOMY OF A MARRIAGE

'Matter itself will know itself no longer.'

From *Ming's Kingdom* by Nicol Williamson

Fifty is normally a good age for an actor and it should have been in Nicol's case. Yet a perfect storm of matrimonial trouble, bad luck and botched projects ushered in one of the most difficult and depressive periods in his life. By 1985 Nicol's relationship with Andrea was in trouble. Tony Croft recalls that Nicol had been extremely generous in inviting several members of Andrea's family to Amsterdam, all at his own expense. She and Nicol married briefly for their last six months of their relationship, yet it was hardly a wedding on the crest of a wave. Rather, a last ditch attempt to solve their problems. Luke didn't even know that Nicol had married Andrea until after their divorce.

Tony Croft remembers, 'I thought they were an odd match and remember telling Nicol just that – after she had left! We agreed that maybe his problem was that he had a lot of love to give.'

Luke added that the relationship's failure 'killed a lot of light' in his father's life. 'He always had ups and downs but after that there weren't many ups. He could slide into long depressions that were hard for him to get out of.' Nicol nursed a lot of anger, not only towards Andrea but also her whole family. In his essay on Nicol, *I Hate Hamlet*, writer Paul Rudnick noted that Nicol had taken to composing various ditties, each venting his fury:

In our second week, Nicol invited me to his small, bare Hell's Kitchen pied-à-terre, where he hunched over a Hohner organ and played and bleated a song cycle that he'd composed, based on his divorce. Each number was devoted to a militant, obscene hatred of his ex-wife and assorted female members of her family. After each ditty excoriating another ungrateful bitch, Nicol would turn to me eagerly for an opinion. 'Wow,' I kept repeating. 'She sounds awful.' 'Yes!' Nicol thundered each time. 'That's exactly right!'[1]

Perhaps in a further bid to exorcise the relationship for good (at least in Luke's view) Nicol wrote a novel, *Ming's Kingdom*, which, according to Nicol's friends, seemed to be at least partly based on his marriage to Andrea. Some of it, although not qualifying as revenge porn in the current graphic internet-era meaning, is a remarkably explicit and intimate account.

The usual description for such a book – in which someone is clearly referring to a real life event – would be 'a thinly veiled autobiographical novel'. In this case it scarcely applies. It isn't 'veiled' at all. And here we do jump ahead several years when the book was published to get Nicol's take on events.

The title *Ming's Kingdom* is deceptive. When, in 1996, I saw the book I assumed it was a King Lear type of story about relatives feuding over the spoils of an inheritance. Ming was actually the term Nicol invented for his mother-in-law – coined from the comic strip Flash Gordon – who was the focus of much of his derision.

The book features a fictional actor, Rick, based mostly in America, who marries a younger woman and aspiring actress, Adrienne. Rick is obviously Nicol and Adrienne would appear to be loosely based on Andrea, although, of course, it is technically a work of fiction and, we should emphasise, exclusively Nicol's subjective take on the relationship. He describes Adrienne thus, 'She was a fledgling actress, a stunning honey blonde with mud-green eyes, glove breasts, tight flat belly over slate grey pubes and smooth as marble little bottom'.

Full of kinky sexual obsessions and intensely scatological humour, containing a graphic account of defecation and even urination in a crypt, it's a kind of Last Tango in Paris – and New York. Rick relishes making love to a much younger woman. We are spared no details, 'In thrilling seconds he would put his milk in that sweet, pink tea-rose, laying open for him, lippy as a wet baby'. Or:

> He had taught her to shag him like one of those tight-arsed young fillies astride her show-jump mount – in the saddle in control and loving it, the dewy fur-burger pounding joyously upon her buckaroo. She had learned quickly, eagerly exploring him, thoroughly excited by each carnal sip and snippet, squirreling them away to hoard in secret for some magic spring.

There's a lot about sex, mentoring a young girl on how to satisfy him, less about Adrienne's character. Rick comes across as a sex-obsessed middle-aged man, excited even when Adrienne has to take an authorised toilet stop in a church on the way back from a party, 'As she spoke, the jet stuttered into long spurts, like a huge ejaculation ... it was one of the most erotic sights he had ever witnessed and it had prompted a giant erection he was fighting to conceal, hand within his left pants pocket'.

Pornographic sexual encounters aside, Nicol conveys little of what drew Rick and Adrienne to each other beyond his enjoyment of her as a sexual plaything and her perception of him as a kind of Svengali figure. It's clear that when the sex started to wane that Nicol, or rather, Rick, began to tire of the relationship. Gradually the encounters became less *Nine and a Half Weeks* and more *Gone in 60 Seconds*. 'She masturbated him at speed like a maid in a hurry polishing a brass bed knob, his climax greeted with a smile, and a lightning "I love you" before she ran to the bathroom, as she did this morning, to wash the jet of sperm from hand and arm.'

Much of the book is about Rick's 'odious' mother-in-law, Alice. British readers of a certain age will be familiar with the late Les Dawson whose mother-in-law jokes provided fodder for his stand-up material. He paints her as a risible figure, trying to pass herself as a young actress, even auditioning for ingénue roles. 'At one audition they told her. "Sorry there's been some mistake. We're seeing people for the role of the mother in the afternoon."' She even bridles at the word 'mum' whenever it's uttered. '[This] was taboo, a guarantee that she would suffer a broken-winded vapour, then an instant mild stroke. The title precluded her from being offered 30-year-old leading lady roles. She was 55 or thereabouts.'

None of this, of course, would really have mattered were it not for her relentless envy and all encroaching presence, inviting herself for extended stays in their home. 'Rick felt that she hung around in fear that she would miss out on anything exciting that might happen professionally with himself and Adrienne.' Another time Alice is quoted as saying, 'Whenever he and Adrienne talk about being in the theatre and movies, I can't bear it because I want it so much'.

The book ends with weird, and not very involving, family feuding and Rick concluding that his wife and mother-in-law are an insoluble problem. 'He'd put a stop to Ming's shenanigans, only to find his own wife an instant foe. His situation with her family had always been hopeless, like trying to tackle the hydra with a steak knife.'

Ming's Kingdom, written, in the mid-nineties, in other words several years after the marriage's failure, contains themes that had always obsessed Nicol and would do so even more as he passed 50. One was the black dog of depression (perhaps this biography should have been called *Black Dog* rather than *Black Sheep*) – the brevity of the sparrow's flight through the light.

Nicol's book is the nearest thing to some kind of self-analysis and self-appraisal – remembering that Nicol never agreed to any therapy – and there's every reason to think he is writing of his own feelings when he ponders extinction. 'Matter itself will know itself no longer. Imperishable moments and immortal deeds, death itself and love, stronger than death, will be as though they had never been … black dog … booze needed now.'

At the end there's a fretting fear familiar to everyone whose relationship breaks down in middle-age. Does that spell the end of love? He is shaken when he sees a homeless man on the streets. The tatterdemalion derelict had opened the floodgates of his own anger and misery, his fear of being alone.

Anxiety attacks also afflicted Nicol. According to Luke:

> They would almost certainly be connected to death and the void. Anything he feared he tended to confront. He hated flying and heights so he joined the paras and threw himself out of airplanes for several years. He still never liked flying but he dealt with it. He believed in facing everything head on.

Nothing unusual about anxiety and depression, of course, except that in Nicol's case – as well as his strange premonition, ultimately fulfilled, that a terrible cancer death awaited him – you have to add in the strange circumstances of an actor's career. You really *are* only as good as your last role. By 1986 Nicol was no longer being considered for substantial parts.

Nicol had always been entranced by the beauty of language. Yet to know that his employment depended on someone else deploying beautiful (or sometimes dreadful!) lines must have rankled. In *Ming's Kingdom*, Rick confides the actor's eternal dilemma to a friend, 'I can't work without being given the chance to do so. I'm not a painter or composer'.

Leslie Megahey tells a similar story from frequent phone calls with Nicol in the nineties:

> He used to call me from abroad and say how lucky I was to be able to keep on working even in down times – I was writing screenplays and working on film ideas, but as he rightly pointed out, an actor simply can't work until somebody gives them a job. That, above all, was what he hated – being idle and reliant on other people to give him work. You have to set against this that he was very selective and self-willed about what he would do and what he turned down.

Ming's Kingdom is the nearest we've ever come to an autobiography or at least a full account of what ultimately seemed like a doomed May to December love story between a middle-aged actor and young actress. If Nicol – and again here we are jumping forward a bit in time – had hoped that the novel would be a springboard to some kind of literary success, he was to be disappointed.

Even the manner of its delivery was, as ever with Nicol, eccentric. The late publisher Paul Sidey recounts its inception – beginning in a restaurant meeting around the time Nicol was doing *Jack*:

> He [Nicol] was not interested, at that stage in doing a memoir, although he had an evocative store of stories about Beckett and Osborne (and could do murderously accurate impressions of their voices), but, apparently had more or less finished an autobiographical novel. After I had paid the bill, he invited me to return to his dressing room, where he had a tape recorder with a couple of excerpts I could listen to.
>
> Once back at the theatre, he opened a couple of beers, and settled down to watch how I responded. It was hard not to be self-conscious. I liked what I heard, though. The Williamson voice was deep and mellifluous, there was a rhythm to the prose, and the situation – an oversensitive man betrayed by his wife – had clear dramatic potential. Perhaps the hero's hatred, though, was reserved more especially for his mother-in-law … She was going to be in the title – *Ming's Kingdom*.
>
> The second extract made me laugh out loud. One of the characters was caught short with terrible diarrhoea. The whole scene was a scatological tour de force.
>
> A contract was signed. Producing the text, however, was a far from straightforward process. Nicol would handwrite or tape sections, and I had to find a patient typist. Then I would edit the new material, he would check it through, and, afterwards, we would sit down together to make the pages the best we could. More retyping after that. It may be that he had knocked the Broadway producer David Merrick to the floor and had also struck a fellow actor with his sword during a performance of *I Hate Hamlet*, but Nicol remained the model of cooperation during the long working sessions on his manuscript.
>
> One Sunday, as the last rays of the sun seeped into a deconsecrated church in Notting Hill – an artist friend had lent their place to Nicol for the week – I wondered what on earth I was doing with this project. After a protracted session in a vast, high-ceilinged hall, the kitchen area concealed by an ornate, wooden ecclesiastical screen, Nicol sat down at the piano and sang *Nessun Dorma*. He had a pretty good voice and did a week's gig at Pizza on the Park with a band to coincide with publication of his novel, but Pavarotti this wasn't.

Marianne Velmans, Paul's wife, also remembers them both visiting Nicol's house on the Singel:

> I remember that after showing us round, he wanted us to come to his favourite bar for a drink and we walked through a street in the Red Light District to get there, Paul and I trying to shield our young kids' eyes from the sex shops on either side of the street while Nicol strode ahead. Paul liked Nicol in spite of what a difficult man he was … And I always thought Nicol was a tragic figure in the Shakespearean sense.[2]

Sidey remembers Nicol saying, 'No one will buy this book. Everybody hates me.' He was right about the book.[3]

It was sad that Nicol thought everyone hated him. All the actors I interviewed spoke highly of Nicol's ability. Yet he never courted favours. Nicol's screen presence was usually slightly acerbic. Affability did not come easily to him on screen or stage – more smoldering intensity. Nicol once described his own 'chemistry':

> I think the only valuable thing you can do as an actor is to make people recognise in themselves what is also there in you, and what you see in them. Then they'll hate you because they don't want you to do that to them. That's why I'm hated a lot of the time. They don't want you to show these things in you because it makes them uncomfortable. It makes them frightened. But I think you must show these things in order to be true to yourself.

Ming's Kingdom did not do well and perhaps didn't deserve to, written in a machine gun, scattered style. Helen Osborne, John Osborne's (by then) widow, called it 'quite dreadful' when she reviewed it in *The Spectator*.[4]

Luke told me:

> I think he needed to exorcise that relationship [with Andrea], all the shit he was put through, and the games that were played. He changed after that. He was never the same light-hearted person he was so often before that. As for the commercial side, I'm sure he would have been happy if it had been a best-seller. But he never complained about it.[5]

The late eighties was not an easy time for Nicol. Perhaps he had too much free time. According to Leslie Megahey:

I'm sure he felt under-regarded and under-employed in later years, and he was. But he wasn't a moaner, he didn't whine about anything, and he didn't just act tough and resilient, he really was tough. He felt that was the way the hand had been dealt and the cards played, and why moan about it. He knew full well that he could have done a great deal more in acting if he'd had the right offers and maybe sometimes a more considered attitude to those offers that did come. And he knew, in his heart, the main reason – i.e. that many directors and producers were afraid of him, not just as a person but as a 'difficult' personality. A reputation like that is hard to shift. When he was offered work, he didn't grab it with both hands even if he needed the money. It depended on the role. He was adamant about which parts he wanted to play and which not, and he would never have done a role just to get the billing or to 'keep his hand in'. He preferred to be unemployed rather than accept something that didn't measure up.

In Amsterdam, Nicol would spend time with Luke, playing games in the basement of their large house:

> We had a ping pong table. And he would beat me, but I got better and better. I used to practise at school a lot. I remember being about 10 and almost winning, but losing in the end, and getting quite angry about it, and Andrea telling Dad to 'let him win, Nicol'. But Dad was adamant that I had to legitimately beat him. And when, finally, I did beat him a couple years later, it was our last game. We never played again. He played to win so I'm pretty sure I earned that win.

Nicol also liked to have visitors. Sally Dietzler and her husband Tony Croft, an old school friend of Nicol's, would stay. 'He was always the entertainer, playing the piano and singing,' recalled Sally. 'He had a magnificent wine cellar and we enjoyed some nice dinners. He had wonderful paintings and an old gramophone which we could play and just have fun.'

Croft also recalls Nicol's love of food and wine:

> When I stayed with him we would often walk for miles across Amsterdam, this being his main daily exercise, to some restaurant he would frequent on a regular basis for lunch where they would provide his preferred fish dish and favourite Gewürztraminer Alsace wine. Nicol had an extensive cellar and to say he enjoyed a drink would be an understatement. I would often tell him that the sugar content of his various drinks had to be his main form of nourishment. At home I recall that Nicol enjoyed displaying his skill at making a very commendable curry.

Nicol's father, Hugh, would often stay with them and he'd get up early to make his porridge.

As good acting offers dried up, Nicol embraced music and poetry. In August 1986 Nicol made his stage debut at the Hollywood Playhouse in *An Evening with A Man and his Band*. This was a one-man show in which Nicol read and sang from, among others, Beckett, Betjeman, Hoagy Carmichael, E.E. Cummings, Walter de la Mare, T.S. Eliot, Jerome Kern, Rudyard Kipling, Tom Lehrer, Shakespeare and Stevie Wonder. Each evening the show varied.

Nicol explained his motivation:

> The supreme irony of my life is my metier is light comedy. People like to pigeonhole you. One of my first major roles was *Diary of a Madman*. After that, people thought that's what I am. When you play a part, you always mask yourself. If you want to know my motive for doing this, it's that it's a pleasure for me to give pleasure. Something has gone out of the theatre today, when people putting together a production are mainly concerned about finance and success. Theatre to me means first and foremost that you must entertain. What I want to do is to allow people to sit back and loosen their ties and shoes and enjoy.

Dan Sullivan in the *Los Angeles Times* damned Nicol with faint praise:

> Williamson can sing. Sometimes he sounds like Hoagy Carmichael (as in Carmichael's *Old Music Master*). Sometimes he sounds like Bing Crosby (as in an up-tempo *Old Man River*). Never does he sound like Johnny Cash, Little Richard or the Big Bopper, but that's fine. Each man to his own fantasy … The poems tend to bring more out of him than the songs, reminding us what an incisive actor he can be when he's challenged. But he needs a director to keep him concentrated and to the point.

In early 1987, Nicol did accept a role that looked impressive. He played a Nazi war criminal in a film adaptation of Stephen King's novella *Apt Pupil*. Ricky Schroder, the former child actor, played the boy who blackmails an old Nazi he finds living in his town. Several weeks' footage was shot. Schroder claimed there was one week of filming left under the stewardship of tried hand Alan Bridges. Sadly, the production ran out of money. The whole project was aborted, much to Nicol's disappointment who told Luke he believed he had been doing some of his finest work.

By the time another producer was found Schroder had matured so much that the original film was unusable. The film was eventually made with Ian McKellen and the late Brad Renfro. Schroder remembers what was shot felt very dark and intense. And Stephen King allegedly saw the footage and thought highly of it. Yet, since an actor's work is only really valid if seen, there seems little point in chewing it over. To 'lose' several weeks' work must have been devastating, like a novelist losing the bulk of his book. You couldn't blame Nicol for feeling jaded. Later that same year, 1987, Nicol also walked out of a movie called *Berlin Blues*.[6]

And there was an ever so slight air of London blues when, in the summer of 1988, I saw Nicol dining in a French restaurant in Lower Sloane Street, not far from the Royal Court Theatre, the scene of his greatest triumph in *Inadmissible Evidence*. It can hardly be called a 'meeting' as such because we did not actually speak. But I'll never forget it. Great actors dominate a room. Somehow they take ownership of it. So it was with Nicol.

I was more than a little starstruck, just a callow kid of 21, but I'd already began to acquire an impressive budding stalker's CV. I'd followed Jack Lemmon back from the Haymarket Theatre to the Savoy Hotel, traipsed alongside Anthony Hopkins through Foyle's back to his car, handed coins to Malcolm McDowell for the parking meter when he arrived for a matinee at the Old Vic, chatted to Topol as he sauntered down Finchley Road. In the flesh they seemed mere mortals, earthbound. But Nicol Williamson was different. Suddenly in that restaurant Nicol was the centre of attention. People were looking at him, not necessarily because they knew who he was, but because his presence, energy and voice filled the room.

I kept casting furtive glances his way. Nicol, then 51, was holding court at the table, a man and woman on either side of him. Nicol's ruddy complexion betrayed the years of hard-living and there was perhaps a hint of solitariness to him. My staring was become conspicuous. Nicol's companion looked over at our table and encouraged me to speak. I still didn't know what to say, 'Oh, let him stare', Nicol eventually said.

Nicol finally got up to leave, a little uneasily. I watched him go, a light jacket draped over his shoulder. He sucked the energy with him. On the table were drained wine and brandy glasses. The restaurant felt empty without him. Now, of course, almost thirty years down the line, I wish I had spoken to him. At least I might have stood a better chance of a conversation than Mick Jagger!

By the time Nicol did resurface as an actor it was in a TV series called *Chillers*, filmed in 1989. By then it was several years since he'd acted. The television series *Mistress of Suspense* (also known as *Chillers*) was an international co-production based on stories by the eccentric American crime writer Patricia Highsmith, best known for the Hitchcock classic *Strangers On A Train*. Director Robert Bierman, offered the chance to oversee one episode, along with a shortlist of actors, chose a script entitled *A Curious Suicide*. Bierman had happy memories of

Nicol from his time as a film preservationist in *Inadmissible Evidence*. He also loved *Black Widow*.

A producer put a call through to Amsterdam and the elusive Nicol was soon on board and, in a line that was to become familiar, Nicol claimed that he had stopped drinking and was on his best behaviour.

Nicol played an American doctor who plots the murder of one of the friends of his wife (Jane Lapotaire) who had stolen his recently deceased true love. All went well until Bierman asked writer Evan Jones to craft a monologue for Nicol to give his character more 'hinterland'. Yet, according to Bierman, the additional lines proved too much for Nicol. On the morning of his big speech Bierman found that Nicol had raided the prop drink before moving on to the real stuff:

> Nicol turned up on the set. He hadn't been drinking at all (until then), but obviously this particularly long speech had made him quite nervous and he'd taken to drink. And he was bright red, like a stop light! We sent him off to make up to try and powder him down and ply him with coffee. This continued for several hours! And Barry Foster, the other guy who he had this big speech with, was so fabulous with him. We kept bringing Nicol back and he could only do two lines of this speech and then he'd forget it. Then I'd have to send him back for more coffee and powder. This went on for most of the day. I cursed myself for giving him this fabulous speech because it was exactly what he didn't want.[7]

Nicol apologised profusely, accompanied by the usual middle of the night phone calls, but he was now back on the booze. The wrap-up party in Cardiff ended in carnage. Bierman gives a sad account of a sozzled Nicol trying to goad a diminutive but powerfully built bouncer. When Nicol started to – rather like Ollie Reed – debase proceedings to the point of probing the bouncer about whose 'cock' was bigger, Bierman panicked and whisked him away:

> I thought, 'Oh my God!' so I grabbed Nicol and pulled him out of the club before this bouncer had smashed him one. It was closing time, so I was dragging him down the street as all the people were coming out on to the street. Nicol was bumping into them and trying to pick a fight with anybody. I prevented him from having at least three or four fights on the streets of Cardiff at 11 p.m. and took him back to the hotel.
>
> The next morning we had breakfast together and he regretted everything … he had a warm disposition but the evil drink turned him into a raging person. We parted on good terms. On the whole we had worked well together but I

never saw him again and I didn't want to be on the other side of his neediness and his childish self-obsession.

Luke, then 16 and at boarding school, does not recall Nicol ever mentioning either the role or the meltdown. Nicol omitting to mention that he had been paralytic on the streets of Cardiff was no surprise. Perhaps Nicol was ashamed of the whole episode, in both senses of the word.

Bierman also relates that Jane Lapotaire who had acted with Nicol in circumstances of professionalism and sobriety – on *Macbeth* and *Uncle Vanya* – now found a different Nicol, obsessional and still railing against his ex-mother-in-law. So much so that she took to circumventing the bar, in the hotel foyer, where Nicol would invariably buttonhole her with his latest jottings – diatribes that, subsequently, formed part of *Ming's Kingdom* when it was eventually published. A 52-year-old man sharing tales of his mother-in-law with a colleague is strange, to say the least!

If you combine everything going on in Nicol's life – the painful divorce, aborted movie projects, his protracted unemployment, hitting the big 50, perhaps the debasement (as he saw it) of taking a supporting role in a TV series then, cumulatively, they could explain his fall from grace.

By 1990 Nicol's career was in the dumps and financial necessity had become paramount. Hence he agreed to take the role of Father Morning in the *The Exorcist III*. Luke remembers:

> That was also my fault in a way, although it's not a terrible movie, but I had school fees due, and that was Dad's responsibility to pay for. That was a period where he was starting to have to work again after taking years off after Andrea. Dad didn't often share financial reasons with me. These are my observations.

Apart from *The Exorcist III*, Nicol still refused parts he thought were completely beneath him. Leslie Megahey remembers Nicol's attitude from slightly down the line but it applies equally to all periods in his life:

> You couldn't help but be impressed by his strength of conviction – it was splendidly bold, and he was unshakeable once he'd made up his mind to say 'no'. Which doesn't mean I think he was always right. I argued often with him that taking a smaller part in a movie than the ones he'd been used to could be the start of a return to the screen. Then he'd be able to be choosier. But Nicol was always true to his lights, even when it scuppered his chances of a real comeback.

His Father Morning was a stern piece of work but didn't make much of an impression in a movie that reunited him with George C. Scott, his co-star from *Uncle Vanya*. The film was directed by William Peter Blatty who had directed *The Ninth Configuration*, the film Nicol had been fired from after the phone-throwing incident. *The Exorcist III* quickly came and went and Nicol was off again. Luke remembers that Blatty wrote him a nice letter after Nicol's death but the film did little for Nicol's career.

When Nicol eventually resurfaced he made headlines for all the wrong reasons. He was to play Jack Barrymore – the original bad boy of Hollywood's golden era – in what could be seen as a bout of 'method' acting. With a little madness throw in for good measure.

16

MADNESS ON BROADWAY

'Give it more life!'

Nicol Williamson's impromptu command to Evan Handler in *I Hate Hamlet*

Nicol's Hyde made it happen, but thanks to the press, his name became irrevocably associated with a bout of buttock bashing during a performance of a new play called *I Hate Hamlet*.

By 1991 we see a different Nicol, no longer in total control of stagecraft but venting his spleen to the press and also to fellow actors. Nicol had now been away from the stage for six years, an eternity for a middle-aged actor. Sadly, when Nicol died twenty years later, the incident was recounted over and above his great Hamlet, Macbeth or Coriolanus.

It all began auspiciously enough. Writer Paul Rudnick had spent some time in the New York home of John Barrymore, the most famous of the illustrious Barrymores, the first family of the New York stage. Barrymore was known for his brilliant talent, chiselled good looks ('the Great Profile'), also his wayward, eccentric personality and carousing. Rudnick fashioned a comedy around a young actor, Andrew, playing Hamlet (Evan Handler) who is advised by Barrymore's ghost.

Finding an actor charismatic enough to play Barrymore was not easy. The playwright was also new and the director Michael Engler a novice. Rudnick relates that they finally homed in on Nicol, despite the casting director's misgivings and his warning that Nicol would be hired 'only over my dead body'. Given the nature of ensuing events, finding a corpse somewhere in the Walter Kerr Theatre would not have been surprising. In the end, despite their reservations, Nicol *was* hired.

Casting Nicol as Jack Barrymore was always a risk because Barrymore was a notorious drinker and something of a parody, maybe too much of an open goal for Nicol's exhibitionism. Perhaps Peter O'Toole would have been a better fit, an actor whose drink problem was in abeyance and who had memorably portrayed debauched bohemian hack Jeffrey Bernard on the London stage two years earlier.

At this stage, before Nicol decided to 'go' the whole hog with the Barrymore character, playing someone rather like himself might have unsettled him. Maybe he noted a whiff of condescension in being chosen for such a role – a passed-it roué playing the father of all hellraisers.

So a gamble it certainly was. And when, subsequently, Nicol accused the producers of mounting a 'gutless' production – of failing to open up a promising premise – the producer James B. Freydberg, perhaps justifiably, bridled:

> Any group of producers who had the guts to hire this man, with his renowned, unbelievably wild reputation as an actor, could never be called gutless. Stupid maybe but not gutless. If I had the choice of Nicol playing this role or Barrymore himself, I'd choose Nicol. But the only person I found to be scared was Nicol Williamson himself.

A lunchtime meeting was arranged with Nicol, then 54, in which he formally accepted the part. Rather ludicrously, he claimed he was on the wagon, despite, in Rudnick's account, a wine bottle, brandy glass and beer bottle littering the lunch table.

Early rehearsals went reasonably well. Nicol liked veteran actress Celeste Holm, then 73, who has a fling with Barrymore's ghost in the play. But he resented appearing on stage with other people when his Barrymore character had nothing to do, just 'ghosting'. In particular, he disliked Handler, cast as Andrew Rally, the would-be modern Hamlet. Rudnick became the latest victim of Nicol's middle of the night calls:

> He took to calling me at 3 a.m. always opening with a solicitous 'I didn't wake you, did I?' He'd had a brainstorm: what would I think if Evan left the show and Nicol played the parts of both Andrew and Barrymore simultaneously? I couldn't even begin to formulate a response, since not only was Evan first-rate but the characters had many scenes together, including a rip-snorting duel that climaxed the first act. As I sputtered, Nicol jumped in: 'Oh, I know just what you're thinking. Of course I could play both parts easily, but Andrew is intended to be what, twenty-six years old? And you're wondering, will the audience accept

me as twenty-six? It might be a concern, but it's not a film – from the stage, there'd be no problem at all!' Nicol was then fifty-two [sic].[1]

Rudnick noted that Nicol was fine in previews. Clad in a luxuriant wig and sculpted black tunic and tights, he made an impressive Barrymore:

> He commanded the stage, and seemed to be having the time of his life. He was possessed by Barrymore, both in the play's more burlesque moments and in his speeches from *Hamlet*, which he delivered with eloquence and simplicity, as a lesson for Andrew and the rest of us. It was too good to last. After the first few shows, Nicol embarked on a self-destructive binge. He repeatedly propositioned the stage manager, and when she resisted his groping advances he called the management and demanded that she be fired. This didn't happen, but the atmosphere backstage became poisonous. The cast posed for a raft of promotional photographs, and Nicol tried to block the release of any pictures in which he appeared with another actor. Then he began murmuring directions, while onstage, to other cast members: 'Is *that* what you're doing?' 'God, that's awful,' and worse. During scenes in which the script called for him to hover, as a ghost, and eavesdrop on the action, he would leave the stage. He gradually and deliberately alienated almost everyone, until the production became a war zone. One night, I stopped by his dressing room to make a final attempt to repair our relationship. When I entered, he took a wobbly swing at me, aimed at my head and connected with my shoulder. I was more surprised than hurt; it was like being assaulted by a sleeping bag. Further revisions to the script became impossible.

Tara Hugo, the would-be Lady Macbeth from Nicol's 1982 production, was invited by Evan Handler to a dress rehearsal of *I Hate Hamlet*. 'Afterwards we joined Evan and Nicol for a drink. When Nicol left the table for the toilet, Evan said Nicol was a nightmare. And when Evan went to the toilet, Nicol said Evan had an ego.'[2]

At Nicol's invitation, Tara also attended the opening night and the after party at Tavern on the Green. She remembered it as 'a truly brilliant, funny, original show', but Rudnick was appalled by what he saw as Nicol's growing recklessness:

> Everyone's friends and family were in attendance, and Nicol ruled the night. He still wasn't speaking to many of the others, but there he was, in a white dinner jacket, grabbing the microphone and forcing the band to back him on assorted Tom Jones hits. It was like attending the coronation of a sadistic, self-proclaimed

emperor, with toasts encouraged by armed guards. I longed for Nicol to be a caddish yet magnetic rogue and to win everyone back. But he couldn't. Owing to drink and bitterness and rage, he needed to be loathed by friends and adored by strangers.

Ironically, the production received favourable reviews. Frank Rich in the *New York Times* wrote:

> Do be cheered by the news that the ghost is played by Nicol Williamson, a first class Hamlet in his own right once upon a time, and on occasion as flamboyant an offstage figure as Barrymore was, Nicol Williamson offers a riotous incarnation of a legendary actor, lecher, and lush (not necessarily in that order) whom even death has failed to slow down. Nicol Williamson gets the audience laughing from the moment he enters in full Hamlet regalia and makes a beeline, as if yanked by a magnet, to the nearest uncorked champagne bottle … his woozy swoons, bombastic braggadocio and … swashbuckling sexual antics are so eerily reminiscent of Jack Barrymore himself in his self-paradostic decline that Nicol Williamson creates the illusion of bearing much more of a physical resemblance to his celebrated prototype than he actually does.

Yet Nicol was proving destructive. At certain points in the play, he told the producers and director he would exit, stage right or left, because at these times 'the central character has nothing to say and nothing to do except be set-dressing'.

On the second night Nicol also summoned Adam Arkin to his dressing room and told him he would be 'rewriting the play and wouldn't be onstage very much'. Arkin later recalled that he and a fellow actor had ten minutes before the curtain went up to figure out what to do:

> We had to make up a play that we'd just opened in the night before. It was a scary, insecure environment, for you never knew what would happen … I had a lock on this character, and I knew how to play him. I wasn't going to let anything sabotage it. The whole experience was like being in a madhouse.[3]

Then, a week into the run, Nicol gave an (overly honest) account of how he believed the play could be improved to Mervyn Rothstein. Nicol effectively did what he had accused Alistair Cooke of doing to *The Last Viceroy* – 'I'm selling fish and they stink'. Except that Nicol seemed to be accusing the writer and director of a sin even greater – mediocrity born out of cowardice:

I will give you only direct answers. I am not somebody who wishes to create an illusion except onstage. This play could have been sensational. They think they've written the be all and end all. And while I think it is a very effective piece, if they had wanted to take it one stage further and expanded it, they could have had something extraordinary, they really could have let it take off to the moon. There should have been a nice, wide open scene for Barrymore at the end. But there has been a little bit of intransigence. They haven't used all the juices that are there. They didn't have the sight. They are terrified. They don't want to get their butts kicked on Broadway. The play is silly. But it's good silly. It's farce and what you do with farce is you never let anyone in to look at the weave. You must keep the internal energy going. You must never leave a gap, you must never ever let it stop for a second, and you must never let the audience pause to look at the play. Because once you give them a chance to consider what's there, they'll just tear it apart. They'll say: this is really nonsense. [4]

Nicol then offered his take on why they had hired him, an account which may have been truthful but sounded slightly arrogant:

They don't like me. And that's fine with me. But I think it was too much for them not to go for it. Barrymore was the Hamlet of his generation. So it was kind of: wouldn't it be great to have this guy who's done all this, and we think he can look like Barrymore, and he too has been a bit of a rouser in his time and thrown some people around and stopped some shows … I don't do that anymore. These are isolated things that people pick out. They say – when you meet him, you will find him the rudest man you've ever met. But I don't give people problems … I have a problem on this show with someone. And I say … 'You're not to comment on me. You're my slave. As I am slave to the audience. You serve me and I serve them.'

The interview finished with Nicol lying about his age, telling Rothstein that he was about to turn 50 – when, in fact, he was 54. For an actor like Nicol, who didn't seem over-concerned with image, it was a strange deception, more practised by ageing Lolitas. (Comments Luke, 'He also probably didn't want to get old. Who does? But 1936 is his actual birth year. Even the papers wouldn't believe me after he died and printed 1938.')[5]

For Nicol to broadcast his differences with the producers and cast members so openly seemed self-defeating. Perhaps he was intent on bringing his problems with Evan Handler to the fore. Yet … some performances continued seamlessly. Actor Tony Osoba and his wife, in New York at that time, remember seeing him in a matinee in April. 'He gave a riveting performance … and we met up with him after the performance. He was extremely friendly and genial, though not effusive about the production,' Osoba recalled.[6]

On the evening of 2 May 1991, just a few weeks after the first Gulf War had ended, World War Three broke out. In the middle of a duelling scene towards the end of the first act, Nicol ignored the choreography and struck Handler on the back with the flat part of his sword. According to Freydberg, Nicol began coaching Handler and Jane Adams, who played his girlfriend, while all three were on stage. Freydberg recalled:

> In the middle of the scene Nicol suddenly said to Handler and Adams, 'Put some life into it! Use your head! Give it more life!' The act continued uninterrupted until the final scene in which the two actors duel. In the first movement of the fight, when the swords are supposed to hit, this time they missed. Nicol later said he thought that Evan was pulling something on him and Evan felt that Nicol was pulling something on him. It's a very intricate choreography and the truth is, it really may have been an innocent miss on both their parts. The rest of the duel was thrown off and when it came to the part where Nicol Williamson is supposed to nick Handler from behind, he actually hit him with the sword.

Handler immediately stormed out of the theatre and headed for home. Nicol turned to the audience and offered a joke, 'Should I sing?' He then sought to blame Handler. 'It seems someone who has missed a few parries has elected to leave the stage which unless one is very, very sick, is an unprofessional thing to do. Please excuse us. We'll begin the second act as soon as possible.'

Elaine Stritch – the doyenne of Broadway – and Gregory Peck, who happened to be one of Nicol's idols, were in the audience that night. Stritch was appalled:

> That was the most frightening thing I ever saw onstage in my life. My whole profession went in the sewer. Anyway, there's this woman sitting near me and at intermission she's really mad. And she looks over at me as if this is all my fault. And says, 'What's going on up there? You should know.' And I said, 'Well, I think there's something rotten in Denmark.'[7]

Handler was furious:

> I removed myself from the production because from the first day of rehearsals I have endured the show's producers condoning Nicol Williamson's persistent abusiveness to other cast members. When it came to the fight onstage, Nicol Williamson never learnt it adequately. Actors' equity requires he know the

choreography but he wouldn't go to fight rehearsals. I think he got embarrassed at not knowing the fight, then became angry and struck me, which was when I left the stage.[8]

Luke Williamson says Nicol was never one to rue his actions. Clearly, he had little time for Handler:

I think he did what he did for very specific reasons that he understood. It was pretty in line with his intent. And he wasn't the sort to voice regret. What's done was done. That was how he was. You have to understand there's always a salacious aspect to the retelling of these stories. The understudy got better reviews than Handler. He had told Handler to 'put some life in it'. Handler didn't take it too well. He then abandoned the choreography so Nicol slapped him on the arse. Dad wasn't the type of person to create trouble with somebody for no reason. He didn't think Handler was a very good actor.

Luke adds that Nicol told him – a trifle cattily – that he thought Handler was extremely well cast (in the play) as a 'TV actor who was out of his depth on stage'.

It seems extraordinary that Nicol was not immediately fired after the Handler incident. But in a strange corroboration of the old adage that there's no such thing as bad publicity – the incident was even plastered on the front cover of the *New York Times* – Nicol's antics became the talk of the town.

According to Freydberg:

Evan Handler wanted to bring Nicol and the production up on charges. A meeting was called, and the producers and I tried to determine a course of action. Should we fire Nicol? We realised that he had been brilliantly, maliciously sly: because of all the publicity, he now *was* the show, and no other star in his right mind would step into his role. The situation was impossible. At an earlier meeting, two of our producers, the gentlest and most well-intentioned men, became so frustrated that a fistfight broke out. The brawl ended within seconds, with instant apologies all around. Even when he wasn't in the room, Nicol was winning.

Jane Adams recalled the atmosphere. 'That morning I went to get coffee and was surprised to see the cover of the *Post* and the *Times*. It was pretty tense backstage – like a dysfunctional family with Nicol as the alcoholic father.'[9]

Handler's understudy took over, and the show staggered on for a few more weeks. Nicol was happy that Handler had departed and regularly praised his understudy, Andrew Mutnick. Two days after Handler walked, Williamson gave an impromptu speech to the audience, 'You've heard we've been through difficult times and Andrew's done wonders.' Mutnick returned the compliment, 'Nicol has been really quite incredible and supportive and encouraging.'

Nicol still liked to address his audiences at the curtain call, telling them – in a good mood – to 'head home and enjoy a nice juicy slice of sexual intercourse!' and, in less jovial moments, berating the nominating committee of the Tony Award nominations when co-star Adam Arkin received a nod and he did not. The cast had to endure more unprofessionalism from Nicol when, a week or so before closing, he missed a performance. Apparently he had turned off his telephone at 4 p.m. to take a nap and woken up fifteen minutes before the show ended. Nicol's understudy, Richard Davidson, had gone on. After the performance Celeste Holm made a curtain speech in which she intended to thank Davidson but ... promptly forgot his name. Sometimes shows are just cursed!

Nicol seemed determined that if he was not to be the most feted actor in town, he would be the most notorious. By 22 June 1991, the final night, people were laughing at *I Hate Hamlet* for all the wrong reasons. Tara Hugo was in the audience for the last performance:

I was curious to see the closing night. Nicol didn't know I was there. The show wasn't the same, nor was Nicol. At the curtain call, with all the actors standing in a line, including a very uncomfortable Celeste Holm, Nicol lectured the audience about critics, Tony Award nominations, the *New York Times* and led them in a sing-song of *Happy Days Are Here Again*. They finally brought the curtain down, but he crawled from underneath it back on to the apron of the stage and continued the lecture! A theatrical event never to be forgotten.[10]

Rudnick said that the atmosphere backstage on the final night was toxic:

I had no intention of talking to Nicol. I was still too angry. As I was heading upstairs, to bid farewell to the more lucid actors, the door to Nicol's dressing room swung open. He stood there, a soused, lunatic, 52-year-old Hamlet. We stared at each other. Nicol finally spoke, and his tone was both kind and accusing. He said, 'You knew this was going to happen.' And then he smiled and shut the door.

Rudnick said that on closing night he 'briefly considered lacing Nicol's blood pressure medicine with rat poison' but settled instead for shooting his nemesis an icy stare.

The portrait of Nicol that emerged from *I Hate Hamlet* was of a temperamental, impetuous boozed-up bore, at war with cast and critics, determined to be centre stage, and peeved if not. It wasn't the real Nicol but it chimed with the public's jaundiced view of him. Perhaps Nicol, sensing that other actors had a preconceived view of him as a rake, had decided to live up to his black sheep image. He must have known how weird he seemed, especially crawling under the curtain to continue haranguing the critics.

Yet again, Nicol's behaviour hid the fact that parts of his performance were stupendous. Anthony Page remembers Nicol, as Barrymore, doing an excerpt from *Richard III*. He found it 'electrifying' ... 'This, I remember thinking, is what Shakespeare should be like'.

Nicol felt everything deeply but, perhaps paradoxically, never cared much about what others thought of him. Leslie Megahey seemed to have as good a handle on Nicol's temperament as anybody:

There usually seemed to me to be a good reason for the irritation or frustration, even if the speed of escalation was startling at times. His temperament was a major part of him as an artist – a key to his power as an actor as well as something of a danger to his reputation ... As a person he never sought to be liked, never expressed any regret about his behaviour, and (this may sound odd in the light of his reputation) he could have a row or argument and get over it by the next day, as long as he felt you were basically a friend and on his side. He didn't seem to me to hold grudges unless someone really and truly crossed him or double-crossed him. There were people he took against pretty much on first meeting, but I thought his judgment was usually spot-on – he could sense bull-shitters and time-servers. Generally he responded not to flattery but to what he sensed was genuine respect and warmth. Then you could say almost anything sensible and he'd listen and take heed.

Luke describes the kind of approach that worked best with his dad. 'He required an innocence in the people he was talking to. If people were overbearing or pushy then it would very often go the other way.'

Kenneth Tynan had put it rather differently, but concluded similarly, in his classic portrait of Nicol. 'Nicol demands utter fealty, and hates flatterers – a behavioural cliché now as ever – which is another way of saying that the flattery mustn't seem like flattery.'

Luke also noted that Nicol didn't hold a grudge. 'Dad had an infuriating way of never wanting to clear the air over past argument. You might have a fierce argument and then want to smooth it over the next day, but for him it was like it never happened. It was just never mentioned again.

As for Evan Handler … well, he continued to feel aggrieved about the incident. And the press, as Nicol must have known they would, milked his (Nicol's) behaviour in *I Hate Hamlet* for all it was worth.

Significantly, apart from a few performances of *King Lear* in 2001, *I Hate Hamlet* was the last occasion Nicol shared a stage with other actors. Nicol's life seemed to be growing more solitary. In 1993, his father died. 'Dad had me and his dad. We were the two that were in his corner. And when Papa died, he lost that tremendous bank of advice,' recalled Luke who describes his grandfather as 'a funny, warm person, a real gentleman whom everyone loved'. Jill also remembers Hugh fondly: 'If Nicol had had too much to drink, he'd tell him off. "Not now, Nicol, not great." Always short and sharp.'

Nicol believed Hugh had never really recovered from Mary's early death. Hugh had ended his days humbly:

> He had a plant of his own where he manufactured aluminium sticks for the British Steel Corporation. When Margaret Thatcher killed off the British Steel Corporation he went to the wall for his workers. He could have been well off but he plunged his life savings into keeping them on the payroll, hoping the BSC would reopen. It never did.

With Hugh gone, Luke, then 20, became Nicol's close confidant and best friend and, according to Luke, 'the best father ever'. Nicol had lost out on some of Luke's growing up after the divorce from Jill and was now trying to compensate. 'He definitely missed me and we had missed each other. He wasn't given a lot of time with me, but he made sure I knew he loved me, and he tried to make every minute we did spend together special.'

Jill too believes that, over time, Nicol became a good father to Luke. 'I used to say to Luke when he was little, your dad doesn't know how to be around little kids. The older Luke got, the more they could relate and share.'

With offers drying up Nicol was concluding that he'd better 'create' some work of his own. 'I wasn't doing roles I should be doing. And I can still play the big ones, so I decided to write it and do it, and other actors will only be able to watch.'

The decision would lead to Nicol taking one of the biggest gambles of his life, banking his reputation on a one-man show in which he would again play one of Hollywood's most brilliant but self-destructive stars. Nicol knew that such a portrayal could easily lurch into self-parody and set tongues wagging that he could only work with … himself.

FROM PIG TO JACK

'A good actor is like a good stripper – you have to lay everything bare arsed naked.'

Nicol Williamson as Jack Barrymore in *Jack*

By 1993 Nicol was no longer a household name. *The Independent* published a profile of Nicol, noting his growing elusiveness and fifteen-year absence – since the revival of *Inadmissible Evidence* – from the London stage. The portrait was mostly fair and accurate. To the public, Nicol did indeed seem to have disappeared. The writer of the article, Robert Butler, noted he had visited his local video shop (remember them?) only to be met with a blank stare when he cited Nicol's name. And, naturally, as if to cap Nicol's growing obscurity, even Butler got Nicol's birthdate wrong, citing 1938, a mistake repeated in many articles after his death.[1]

When the National Theatre launched an (interminably long) revival of *Inadmissible Evidence* in 1993, critics seemed to spend more time bemoaning Nicol's absence than reviewing the play. Patricia Denison noted the vacuum that no young pretender, certainly not Trevor Eve,[2] could fill. She summarised critics' responses to the play without Nicol:

Perhaps the most widely stated criticism of this production, though, was its lack of a Nicol Williamson. Most of the reviewers had seen Nicol Williamson as Maitland, and the extent to which that portrayal had ingrained itself as synonymous with Osborne's character was widely evident. Reviewers yearned for his 'electrifying performance' (Neil Smith in *What's On*) his 'demonic energy' (John Gross – *The Sunday Telegraph*) his 'poisonous misery' (John Peter in the *Sunday Times*) his 'crumpled despair' (Steve Grant in *Time Out*) and his 'whiff of spreading yeasty rot' (Paul Taylor in *The Independent*). Neil Smith felt that 'bereft of his (Williamson's) magnetism the play's weaknesses become chasms'. Sheridan Morley in *The Spectator*: 'Without such voltage, *Inadmissible Evidence* doesn't really work at all: a desperately overlong, sloppily conceived and rambling legal nightmare; it was hauled off the page and driven into lifelike drama by Nicol Williamson's blazingly electric and mesmeric talent to abuse – about that production I can remember nothing but him.'[3]

Butler's *Independent* piece also quoted Leslie Megahey who had recently directed him in *The Hour of the Pig*. Megahey refuted the view that Nicol was a 'difficult' actor following their collaboration on what was certainly one of the strangest films of the period.

Megahey recounted how *The Hour of the Pig* had evolved:

A friend who knew I was drawn to the more bizarre of historical and social oddities gave me the long out of print book on which it was based – *The Criminal Prosecution and Capital Punishment of Animals* by E.P. Evans. I researched the medieval period with a special view to discovering how 'modern' some individual (and necessarily private) views were amidst all the religious superstition, and found that many intellectuals (lawyers, priests) were privately sceptical about all that witchcraft stuff, and also that some apparently secret societies (e.g. the Seigneur's brotherhood) were, in practice, ways of keeping economic control of their fiefdoms. Though it seems to be a total farce, a lot of the events, moral and religious opinion and key speeches were based on real sources, and sometimes turned into dialogue almost verbatim, especially in the case of Ian Holm's priest Albertus and Colin Firth's lawyer Courtois.

Max von Sydow was due to play Seigneur Jehan d'Auferre but dropped out when he was offered a higher sum for a horror film. The search then began for a top-rate actor to play the heavy. Megahey continues:

The 'usual suspects' were all busy – Richard Harris, Peter O'Toole, Oliver Reed; and then somebody said 'whatever happened to Nicol Williamson?' I had never met him before and he was already a half-vanished legend from the past. Nobody knew where he was or where he even lived. We tracked him down (he had no agent at the time and he used to work through a New York-based accountant) and we sent Nicol the script, and he accepted. His reputation was already such that everyone felt a touch uneasy, but I had rung Jack Gold who directed *The Reckoning* and *The Bofors Gun* and he told me: 'Don't believe the myths about him. Nic is as professional an actor as you'll ever work with. He's there when you want him, he does his bit, and he goes back to his dressing room until you need him again. I guarantee you'll have no trouble from him on set.'

Megahey succeeded in gathering quite a cast, not only Nicol but also Donald Pleasance and Ian Holm, both of whom Nicol had acted with before. Megahey remembers Nicol telling the costume designer that he wanted his tunic cut 'up to the balls', perhaps to flaunt his legs and (for his age) athletic build.

If the proceedings seemed risible and perhaps, to the amateur eye, almost over-farcical, everyone observed the golden role of taking it seriously, treating it exactly for what it was, a drama based on historical events. 'No good actor will play comedy or farce with anything other than complete seriousness – that's what makes it funny. Nic did add a few facial reactions of his own which were entirely in character, and I kept them in. I found them very funny,' recalled Megahey.

With Holm there was bad blood and the older actor, in his autobiography, noted that he spent much of the filming avoiding Nicol. Megahey claims he knew nothing of Nicol's 'history' with Holm until Nicol had been cast. 'After the formal introductions they totally steered clear of each other, made easier because they only had one scene together and that was a big courtroom set-up, so there was never any close contact. Both actors behaved impeccably throughout.'

Holm was one of those unsung heroes of British theatre and cinema, an enduring and ultra-reliable leading man and, more often, in movies at least, supporting player; he was self-effacingly brilliant, a diminutive powerhouse. Holm's autobiography has a few acerbic comments about Nicol's behaviour and boozing. 'Too many drops of the hard stuff can actually spoil an actor. Nicol Williamson had a great talent which was adversely affected, I think, by a self-conscious desire to dazzle.'[4,5]

The Hour of the Pig turned out well, a bawdy romp complete with medieval superstitions. John Walker said, 'It doesn't work as well as it might but at least it tries something a little different from the endless reworking of over-familiar material.'

If Nicol had hoped that *The Hour of the Pig* would usher in some great screen offers, he was to be disappointed. He *was* given the part of Gregor Dunnigan in *Return to Lonesome Dove*, a popular miniseries of the time. Nicol arrived in Montana but soon exited. Producer Dyson Lovell said he had personally spoken to Nicol who had accepted the part, to be filmed in Butte – 'not the most glorious place on earth' according to Lovell. The story goes that Nicol arrived at Butte's small airport and waited to be collected. Who knows what was on his mind that day? The driver arrived. He must have seen Nicol in films and would have had a rough idea of his appearance.

'Are you Nicol Williamson?'

Nicol looked at him.

'No,' he replied.

The driver later told Lovell that Nicol then went and sat on a bench and watched him asking other people if they were Nicol Williamson.

Eventually, it would appear, the driver managed to establish Nicol's real identity and take him to his hotel. Lovell continues:

> I called him up at the hotel and asked him how he was. He said, 'horrible'. I said, 'But it's the best hotel in Butte'. He said, 'It's still horrible'. I said, 'Well, would you like some dinner?' 'Yes,' he said. 'I'm starving'. I called Rick Schroder and he'd done *Little Lord Fauntleroy*[6] [sic] with him and he said he'd like to see Nicol. So Rick came and Nicol wasn't eating – he just drank a lot and wanted to go on a pub crawl. I said, 'We can't – it's the first day of shooting tomorrow and we can't go on a pub crawl. I went to the set the next morning where Jon Voight decided to have a prayer vigil for the Native American Indians to bless the production and so the prayer meeting was underway when the phone goes and it's Nicol. And he said, 'I need you at the hotel immediately' ... Nicol was in the bar with the script and wanted to go through the script and make some changes. So I said 'fine'. So we sit there for the entire day and he goes through the script and the changes are brilliant. He acts it for me brilliantly. So I said I'd get them to the production office and get them done. So I go to the set next day ... and there's another phone call, 'I need you at the hotel', 'where are the pages?' and he gets them, he likes them and he acts it all for me ... The next day I'm at the set and I'm summoned back to the hotel and he says, 'Well, it's over, I've played the part.' I said, 'You're on tomorrow, we have 200 extras' ... I said, 'You can't do this', and he said, 'Yes, I can, I won't be there' and he left that night.[7]

Leslie Megahey, a close confidant of the time, recalls a phone conversation in which Nicol offered his own version of events:

> Nic rang me after walking out of the filming and flying home. We just chatted for ten minutes or so about this and that and then I got a bit puzzled and asked if he was still in Montana and he said 'no', he had walked. I seem to remember he said it was something to do with the way he felt he'd been treated. I think he said from the moment he arrived nobody took any notice of him, nobody in authority greeted him, he was left to sit around on his own for days, etc. No idea how true that was or if it was partly or wholly Nic's misapprehension. I didn't ask him for more details, and I think – unusually – it caused him some anxiety about walking out on this one.

I suppose it's possible that people over there were scared of his reputation and didn't want to bother him too much, I don't know. Like most talented people, he quite liked the old-fashioned courtesies (though not sycophancy). When he did *The Hour of the Pig* I made a point of going into the make-up room to say hello on his first day, and how glad I was that he was in it, etc., and he seemed pleased.

I seem to remember him also saying that he wondered if, when he arrived in Montana, they had quickly decided he was wrong for the part and started already looking for a substitute actor, and that's why he was kept waiting around. He said he had heard that Oliver Reed arrived incredibly speedily after he left, almost as if their planes had crossed mid-Atlantic.

Luke thinks Nicol might have had an argument on set:

I've heard different stories. He told me that there were [sic] some jiggery-pokery going on and rewrites that he wasn't fond of. He and Jon Voight had a disagreement over something but you must bear in mind it was TV and so he was probably loath to take it in the first place.

Nicol clearly disliked the original script. The rest seems an elaborate 'game' as if Nicol was teasing Lovell with the real cause of his unease left unspoken. Perhaps, simply, Nicol was tiring of the whole enchilada – the sense of being a mannequin in a mass, sprawling cattle farm production where he counted for little.

Nicol had a bigger project on the backburner. After *The Hour of the Pig* he approached Megahey at Ealing Studios with a script. He wanted Megahey to direct it and hone it for the stage. It was about Jack Barrymore, the idol Nicol had impersonated in *I Hate Hamlet*. Nicol had developed a genuine fascination with the rakish figure whose character resembled his own. It would be a one-man show, one that would further illuminate Barrymore's character and allow Nicol to parade his own versatility. There would be room for Shakespeare, funny theatrical anecdotes about Broadway and Hollywood and … he could even flaunt his musical talents with a rendition of *Nessun Dorma*. He knew that after *I Hate Hamlet* the press would be waiting to pounce. He could anticipate the jokes … 'Who's he gonna hit now? Himself?' So Nicol decided to weave some of his own story into Barrymore's. 'He [Barrymore] would do outrageous things sometimes on stage,' said Nicol:

If people were coughing in the audience during *Hamlet*, as they were carrying him out dead, he would sit up, turn to the audience – and he did this a couple of times – and say, 'alright, you can cough all you damn well want. I'm damn well fucking dead.' And then they'd take him off. They never even reported this in the papers. They just glided over it and always referred to his greatness as an actor.

Nicol implied that the press should have taken the same attitude with him, just weathered his on-stage idiosyncrasies. He expanded on Barrymore's appeal:

He did what no other actor, living or dead, has ever done. He was a vaudeville man, a light comedian, a matinee idol, and a silent star who then became a talking picture star. And in the middle of all this he became the greatest classical actor in America and the Hamlet of his generation. Not bad, nobody else has ever done that. Olivier didn't come near it … I wanted to give myself the ultimate test of putting forward everything that this man was. What is in this is vaudeville, light opera, grand opera, about 24 characters, material from the movies, and also Hamlet, Romeo, Lear and Richard … what I loved about Barrymore was that he was not a wanker, he wasn't maudlin at all. Even when things were hardest for him, he would break the mood with a very wry or ironic joke.

Nicol and Leslie Megahey became close collaborators over the next few months. Megahey recalls:

He gave it to me, hand-written. I read it at home and thought it had real promise, just needed a bit more structure and shaping and some extra scenes that rather emphasised some of the similarities between attitudes to Barrymore and Nic's own career and temperament. Barrymore also had this deep love of this craft that wasn't matched later in his life by the quality of the parts he was offered (though, of course, Barrymore did some wonderful leading film roles, unlike Nicol). So we did the final version together. I thought it an interesting proposition to have a one-man show that could be so personal, i.e. where the actor performing it was famous or notorious for similar traits to the character he was playing. And, of course, this meant that the actor had to be pretty famous, almost as famous as the person he was portraying which, at the time, Nicol just about still was (at least to our generation). Nic responded to this and we put in several extra scenes and jokes that exploited the connection and also Nic felt so strongly that Barrymore was such a truly great actor that even if the connections weren't clear to a younger audience, they would still make for good drama and comedy, and final tragedy – though Barrymore, like Nicol, was never self-pitying.

We worked on the script and rehearsed the lines to see what worked and what didn't in both Nicol's house and mine, working in the kitchen, the living room, the pub, etc. It was a happy collaboration and I got to like his work ethic, which seemed to me very strong in spite of his recent inactivity. It seemed to me that he really opened up and was happy when he worked. Also it was great chatting about other things – a lot about Shakespeare, and when we shared thoughts about the big Shakespearean roles Nicol would suddenly demonstrate what he was saying by breaking into one of the great speeches from *Hamlet* or *Macbeth*.

It took a year or so to get a production financed and a venue, the Criterion Theatre, with the help of Sally Greene the owner. All the time Nic would say to me with some glee – 'just wait till I hit that stage'…! I wasn't sure what he meant until we did the first rehearsal on stage with the stage manager and the designer and me as his audience. He pulled out all the stops. By now he knew the lines, and he absolutely blew us away with his power and energy – I've never seen such a sustained and energetic performance. *Jack* was an incredibly athletic exercise, with Nic on stage the whole time and for a lot of that time he was at full throttle. Also he had to do physical feats like running throughout the theatre while speaking the To Be Or Not To Be speech, and singing *Nessun Dorma* at the top of his voice (that was his idea – he loved singing and had a good voice, but *Nessun Dorma* is quite a challenge!) … I thought often that this was just too much for a man hitting 60, but he loved it and got fitter and fitter as the days went by. He was a huge man – a big frame and very strong – and was in great physical shape by the time we opened.

Some of the funniest parts of *Jack* noted the collusion between Barrymore and Nicol. Luke feels that *Jack* was an autobiography with a different name on it. 'I think he felt a tremendous kinship with some of the things that happened to Jack Barrymore. He put a lot of his own personality into it along the way.'

When Nicol – as Barrymore – stated that 'I've never punched out an actor in my life', it's clear that the audience, mindful of Nicol's history, would pick up on the similarity. Fortunately, Nicol, with an endearingly self-deprecating touch, decided to milk it, citing an incident in which an actor he accosted 'couldn't take it and left the show' – an obvious reference to Handler. In this respect it resembled *Jeffrey Bernard is Unwell* in which notorious rake Peter O'Toole played Bernard, a journalist with a history of drink and debauchery.

Sally Greene knew little of Nicol's reputation beforehand other than he was 'a hellraiser'. Greene, who had found Nicol a little flat in nearby German Street, was alarmed to see that a gin bottle was never far from Nicol – although it's possible that was, of course, a stage prop in keeping with the character of Barrymore. Megahey, however, recalls:

I never saw Nic drinking gin, nor being into spirits much at all. Beer and wine mostly, and a glass of cognac and dark chocolate late at night. I had a bottle of Madeira in my fridge which we referred to from time to time while working on the script. He occasionally got a touch merry when 'off duty', but not drunk.

'He used to flirt with me a lot,' Greene recalls. 'He had very big hands and he'd put his hand on mine and say – "we're gonna get on really well"'. She also recalls the strange paradox of Nicol – the hard-drinking hypochondriac, forever talking of his fear of imminent death while seemingly doing as much as he could to precipitate it. 'I really shouldn't drink so much', he would tell her. She was surprised to hear that Nicol was only 57 at the time, believing he was closer to 65 or thereabouts.[8]

The play opened at the Criterion Theatre on 18 May 1994. Critics and fans had waited sixteen years for an appearance by Nicol on the West End stage. Nicol invited his first-night audience to stay behind for champagne and an impromptu jazz concert.

On the second night, however, fans were left disappointed. Nicol walked off the stage after just six minutes. Nicol, in character as Barrymore, made a comment to the audience about a spotlight missing him. The audience thought it was part of the play. Then he turned to the audience and said, 'I don't want to do this any more. I'm sorry this has cost you money'. He then left.

Megahey thinks Nicol's walk-off was genuinely down to exhaustion:

He worked very hard and used up so much energy. His behaviour was never consciously eccentric. He wasn't trading on his image as publicity, he'd have despised that, and if he identified with Barrymore – well, in some ways he did resemble Barrymore. The close parallels in the script of *Jack* were often down to my encouraging him to insert elements of himself that I thought close to the character of Jack. I thought it made an interesting hybrid to include in his performance as Barrymore a kind of self-portrait.

After his walkout Luke remembers that he went for a long stroll with his father all around London, until 3 a.m., talking about everything under the stars, until Nicol regained his composure.

Nicol recovered and for the rest of the run was generally impressive, sometimes brilliant. Nicol liked to dismiss critics as unimportant – or, perhaps more accurately, liked to pretend he ignored them. He did, however, keep a review by Bernard Levin because he felt it captured the essence of what he was trying to convey. Levin, in

his column in *The Times*, had ranked Nicol's performance as one of the greatest
he had ever seen.

Levin had written that he had witnessed 'acting not just on the grand scale but
acting that broke the scale to pieces'. He saluted Nicol for committing more than
20,000 words to memory and went on to say that 'as Williamson blends more
and more into Barrymore, and Barrymore into Williamson, we gradually realise
that there are two greatnesses on that stage'. He also praised Nicol's remarkable mimicry:

> Barrymore met Winston Churchill. They got on well. There is a little cameo
> passage in which Williamson impersonates Churchill; well, we are all familiar with
> the Churchillian tones, but no, we have been tricked all this time. Williamson's
> Churchill is so dazzlingly exact that we realise that his, and no one else's, is the
> real impersonated Churchill.

Levin wrote that – as a seasoned theatregoer who had seen more than 2,400
productions – *Jack* had given him an evening 'that goes immediately into the top
dozen theatrical experiences of my life'. The critic, lamenting Nicol's long absence
from the London stage, concluded that he 'was an actor of genius'.[9]

Small wonder that Nicol prized Levin's contribution. Truth was, he was more
nervous about critical reaction on *Jack* than he cared to admit. He knew that
this time, more than with any other production, he only had himself to blame if
it bombed.

After Nicol died, theatregoer Antony Attard wrote to the *Daily Telegraph* with
his recollection of the opening night. His account shows that, contrary to Nicol's
devil-may-care facade, he was all too aware of the critics' power:

> I attended the first night of Nicol Williamson in *Jack* and witnessed the actor
> giving a mesmerising, electrifying performance as Barrymore. After the interval,
> Williamson strode in through a side door in the auditorium and, in character,
> headed towards the stage. Suddenly he checked, then hurried up on to the stage
> and continued his astounding performance. After taking his bows, Williamson
> invited the audience to join him in the bar for a drink. There he revealed that, as
> he reentered the auditorium, he had spotted Clement Freud, the theatre critic,
> sitting in an aisle seat, and was worried about the review. Published in your
> newspaper, Freud's review stated that Williamson's performance ranked among
> the greatest he had seen. I met Williamson in Jermyn Street that afternoon. He
> was in a state of shock at Freud's review. It was tragic to see a truly great actor
> reveal so much insecurity.

Other critics were less complimentary. Some noted that Nicol had milked a lot of laughs but not revealed Barrymore's core. Peter Hepple in *The Stage* thought that the show 'was not really the stuff of theatre, showing up the weakness of the one-man format as well as of Barrymore himself'.

Jack, however, had its ardent fans. Beryl Bainbridge, for one:

> The general opinion seemed to be that in failing to uncover the dark forces which drove Barrymore to drunken ruin, the audience had been cheated of an insight into the nature of Nicol Williamson's own particular genius. I couldn't disagree more. At the matinee at the Criterion on Saturday it was quite clear why Nicol Williamson has such power. For one, he's tall, has superb balance, and a pleasing, if sad face. Also, he has a superb voice and delivery.[10]

Roland Jaquarello thought the show marked a splendid return to form for Nicol:

> Contrary to all the tabloid rantings, after he didn't complete a performance, it was good to see that Nicol hadn't lost any of his ability. He sustained this one-man show brilliantly, although I'm not sure that he was perfect casting for Barrymore, despite having certain things in common with the grand old American thespian. Still, he certainly imbued his spirit with energy, wit and his own unique humour. In any case, it was great to see him back in London. As we had a mutual acquaintance, after the show I briefly met him backstage, where he was most affable and did a funny impersonation of director Anthony Page!

Other star visitors, like actress Saskia Wickham, remembered the production as 'magical' and thinks that Nicol was 'mesmerising and just sublime … a genius … he just had that indescribable quality to him'.[11]

Luke, who observed Nicol closely throughout, thought that *Jack* ranked amongst his finest work. The show was recorded for posterity but Luke believes just listening to it does not do the show justice. 'He did the audio recording in a booth. It's still good but it doesn't have the physical quality of him doing it on stage. He really wanted to challenge himself and it was definitely beyond the ability of anyone else to do what he did.'

The recording can still make one laugh out loud as Nicol, playing Barrymore, prepares for his own Hamlet and sends up the exaggerated, mannered enunciation of the old school. He describes the old-fashioned approach as 'outrageous horseshit' and makes a case for an altogether more robust prince. 'This Hamlet,' declared Nicol as Barrymore, 'had to be so male that from the moment I hit the stage they could hear my balls clank.'

Leslie Megahey makes a point worth repeating, 'Maybe that's why his Hamlet seemed so powerful and truthful, as opposed to actors who are self-consciously speaking and savouring the words of the immortal bard, etc.' (Megahey won't give names of the 'offenders' – those whom Nicol repeatedly criticised – because he still bumps into some of them in the course of his work!)

Nicol still liked to give his audiences a little pep talk, perhaps even more so on this occasion because he was effectively talking to himself during the actual performance. One theatregoer, Laura Cella, seeing *Jack* in June, later wrote of the show and the follow-up drinks. She recalls that the theatre was perhaps only half-full at best:[12]

Nicol Williamson bounded on to the stage in a roaring Barrymorian vocal flurry, like a pot verbally boiling over in fury and shame at being fired from the film *A Star is Born*. He stalked the stage, trench coat tossed elegantly over his shoulders, then stopped suddenly upstage left and poured himself a drink. Crystal glass in hand, he prowled downstage to tell us, the audience, of his travails on Broadway, in Hollywood, while married. In all of these scenes, Williamson's acting was pitch perfect, embodying Barrymore's admirable and less admirable qualities with a wry and witty tone. The time flew by. When the curtain came down I clapped as wildly as everyone else in the theatre. After taking his curtain call, Mr Williamson motioned for the applause to die down, for everyone to sit, and then, breaking character, he began to talk about the play. He talked about his lifelong affection and admiration for Barrymore, both personally and professionally. He mentioned what it is like to be considered a difficult actor to work with, something he knew from personal experience, he confided to audience laughter. He talked about how this performance was a risk for him, an experiment, but one near to his heart. He thanked all of us for coming and then, suddenly, he invited every person sitting there to join him for a drink as a way of thanking us for believing in him and his dream. He said that he would meet us in the bar of the Criterion restaurant next door within thirty minutes. Then he swept from the stage.

… Within forty minutes or so, Nicol Williamson entered and the real party began. I don't know whether he was drunk or just having a good time now that his night's performance was over, but he was funny and charming, much as I imagined John Barrymore must have been. He asked me where I got my accent and how long I would be in London. When I said that I was on my way to study at Oxford, he began to recite lines from *Hamlet* with such passion and power that I developed goosebumps.

Then, almost in a puff of smoke, he stopped, stood, and was on his way to work the room, to sit at the next table, to thank those people for coming.

Nicol was giving some great performances as Barrymore. Yet some seemed determined to whine. A sad story from one theatregoer has it that 'John Osborne was further down my row. Not very long into the (very good) performance he stood up and clearly drunk, loudly exclaimed "This man used to have talent – then he went to America!" and stormed out. Williamson, to his credit, didn't bat an eyelid'.

The friendship with Osborne – to judge from a vitriolic piece published by Helen Osborne in *The Spectator* over a year after the writer's death – had not survived. She described *Jack* as 'lamentable' and added that 'it was galling to think that the prissy managements who had shunned Williamson in the intervening years as "too difficult" were perhaps right and that he was on self-destruct'.

Jack continued until early July. By then Sally Greene, in view of dwindling audiences, had made the difficult decision to take *Jack* off even though, personally, she claims she loved the show. Jack Hughes, writing in *The Independent*,[13] attending on the final night, noted that 'the play ... is uneven, but the acting is sensational, every mood, rage and stupor in the book'. Nicol took his final bows before, again, thanking the audience for coming and, in particular, Bernard Levin for his flattering review.

If there was a slight spoiler it was Nicol drawing attention to Sally Greene from the stage as being responsible for 'pulling the plug' on him. She remembers him mentioning her from the stage – perhaps in jest – as 'the bitch took me off', hence it would be his final performance. Greene, who was in the audience, waved and replied, 'The bitch is in the room.' She recalls a kind of tennis match as the audience kept turning between them to see the interplay. Greene, whose first big production this was, reflects that she was 'very green' at the time and rather intimidated by Nicol. She does recall, however, that he was 'great' as Barrymore.

Megahey, also present for the final evening, offers a different take:

I don't at all recall Nicol calling Sally 'a bitch' from the stage. I doubt that happened. He was too canny about sensibilities (the audience's, I mean). I recall him doing his final curtain speech, thanking the crew and me, and then saying 'is Sally Greene here?' And she held her hand up and said 'yes' – (in fact she was a couple of rows in front of me, and I was thinking oh God, here we go ...) and then he let rip at her for pulling the show. I always thought she'd done it too soon although at the time she wasn't to know there would be such a fantastic review from Bernard Levin which apparently came too late for her to change her mind. I wasn't altogether surprised she'd done it, as she was, I think, quite new to theatre management and had been very shocked by Nic's walk-off. (The rest of us were maybe more prepared for something to happen, based on Nic's history.) So he had a real go at her from the stage for, as he saw it, her weakness in not sticking with it, and made a point of saying how good the audiences had become since the Levin piece. I even felt sorry for her at the time, although she probably realised he was hardly likely to keep schtumm about it all … the actor on stage automatically gets the audience's sympathy and applause for speaking out, especially when it's against management, so what could she say? I don't remember her saying anything back to him from the audience and I certainly don't recall the word 'bitch' coming from either of them. I am sure Nic was far too canny to use that word publicly to someone's face and thus lose the sympathy of the audience.

Nicol was proud of *Jack* and Luke says that Nicol particularly relished singing *Nessun Dorma*. 'Music was his first love; he really loved singing. Watching his rendition made me realise that he could have been an opera singer. There were so many things he could have excelled at.'

And although Nicol may have been difficult at times, he still had a gift for cultivating friendships and spreading a little sunshine. Cheryl Bunton, who worked with him briefly on *Jack*, wrote to Luke on Nicol's passing with a 'notepad' of happy memories:

> The trips to the recording studio to record not only some sound for the show but also for his own jazz collection (I still have the tape). The best First Night party (unpretentious) when we never left the theatre and he sang and entertained us all. The beautiful bouquet of yellow roses he left at the stage door for me on my birthday. The honour he gave me by coming to a summer party I was having and captaining the winning cricket team on Kew Green! Also his wicked sense of humour, when after returning home from the party he rang, posing as a neighbour, demanding that the noise be kept down! A year later I called in to see him when he played at the Pizza on the Park. That evening I was ushered to a table right at the front where he proceeded to sing to me with that mischievous twinkle in his eye.[14]

Box office receipts from *Jack* were still encouraging enough for Nicol to take the production to America eighteen months later – first to L.A. to the Geffen Theatre, Westwood, where it ran for several weeks, and then to Broadway. It received good reviews but not the out and out raves to guarantee such an unorthodox show's success.

The *Los Angeles Times*, which gave it a warm welcome, albeit with reservations, commented, '*Jack* is a worthwhile evening, not as a great play but as an opportunity to see two famous personalities merge in a hodgepodge of bravura acting and self-destruction.'

The L.A. run was in a friendly and welcoming environment. Leslie Megahey remembers Christopher Walken shyly introducing himself after the show and asking for a quick audience with Nicol because he thought it was the greatest acting he had ever seen on stage. They chatted for over an hour.

Nicol always remained *hugely* respected in the business. We remember the extravagant tributes paid by other gifted performers like George Segal and Brian Cox. There was still an audience for Nicol despite the shenanigans on *I Hate Hamlet*, as Megahey makes clear:

> He was more respected by his peers than he ever knew. I never heard an actor say anything negative about Nic's acting skills – they were usually in awe of them – he was a legend among those who remembered his stage work in particular. I had a few problems casting the heavy in *The Hour of the Pig*, the Seigneur that Nicol eventually played. At one stage I thought I'd written him a bit like the Sheriff of Nottingham, so I offered the part to the much younger Alan Rickman, who turned it down for exactly that reason – it was a bit too reminiscent of his part in Robin Hood. When I met Alan at a party a few years later I reminded him of this and he asked who I had eventually got, and I told him Nicol. He widened his eyes and said, 'wow, you really fell on your feet there.' I got a similar reaction from every major actor I met – if I mentioned Nicol they were agog, and full of questions about how it was to work with him.

In New York the play ran into what Leslie Megahey describes as a few glitches:

> He'd been great during the previews, but I suspect he must have stayed up late the previous night with some friends, one of whom he had known in South America. I reminded him to go to bed early – some hope! – and he assured me he would. The next night he did a terrible first act and the producer was very angry and threatening to stop the show. In the interval I went to have a confrontation with him in his dressing room and he said he knew it was crap, and I said he'd better pull something out of the hat for the second act or we were finished in New York. Somehow he got himself back into form – the second act was far better. So were the subsequent nights. Nevertheless the run was cut shorter than we had hoped, even though audiences were hugely enthusiastic (more curtain speeches from Nic) and the theatre not packed but pretty full. Throughout the London, L.A. and New York runs, I was constantly amazed at his energy and power. He seldom flagged and this was one of the most physical parts for any actor – even a young one.

New York Magazine commented that Nicol bore little resemblance to the real Barrymore, neither did he sound much like him. It then praised the show for its entertainment value and Nicol's deft footwork. 'The way he rattles through stories, segues from unfinished sentence to erupting next one, cavalierly tosses off lines, mugs and mutters, slinks and sashays – his entire verbal quick change artistry – makes him raffishly, buoyantly good company.'

Yet the New York production of *Jack* only ran for twelve performances from 24 April to 5 May 1996. The *New York Times*'s Ben Brantley wrote that 'Mr Williamson can, of course, be a brilliant actor. There are some moments of heart-clutching pathos in *Jack*, especially in its second act ... And certainly it is heartening to see this actor in such good shape on a New York stage again' but then added that 'too often, the shifts between stories feel abrupt, as if one were leafing through a book called *Amusing Barrymore Anecdotes*'.

Leslie Megahey explains:

> We got pulled from the Belasco for the usual Broadway reason. Although we had some good reviews, the *New York Times* was the only one managements, and theatregoers allegedly, were interested in, and the power of the paper was such that a show stood or fell by what it said. We weren't slagged off by them, but it wasn't hailed as a huge palpable hit; that's what was regarded as the yardstick, and still is as far as I know.

Overall, *Jack* had been a modest success. Staging a one-man show is just about the biggest test out there for an actor and to do so at the age of 60 took nerve, especially when the press have flayed you in the past. The only possible downside was that *Jack* perhaps proved what many had long since suspected about Nicol, that he was *not* a team player.[15] A one-man show is inherently difficult to make dramatic. Again, one can look to a play like *Jeffrey Bernard is Unwell* to see how a story laden with stream of consciousness anecdotes and reminiscences (Bernard is locked in a pub for the proceedings) can be enlivened by introducing some minor characters to 'bounce off'.

Apart from a smallish role in *The Wind in the Willows*, Nicol's career was now winding down. John Goldstone, producer of the film that was based on Kenneth Grahame's children's classic, thinks it was casting director Irene Lamb who suggested Nicol play Badger – 'a rather grumpy character with whom Nicol could identify'. He describes the film as 'a very pleasant experience' overall, shot at Shepperton Studios and on location in Suffolk during the summer of 1995. Goldstone recalls that Nicol respected the director Terry Jones 'who whipped everyone into a state of enthusiasm' and that he took the work seriously. Sadly, the film, which made for agreeable entertainment, did not do well. 'It never knew to whom it was appealing,' says Goldstone who told me he was trying to get the film re-released.[16]

Patrick Phillips, QC, the theatregoer so entranced by Nicol's performances in the sixties, agreed to loan his house as the location for Toad Hall:

> I revealed my youthful enthusiasm for his playing and we became fast friends. The same electricity that had imbued his playing inhabited his social self. In two weeks of close company I (and all those about him for the film) never knew when he would erupt. Yet his explosions did not bother me, rude and difficult though he would suddenly become without significant cause. It was the outward sign of the intensity which had always informed his playing.
>
> He was an accomplished mimic and a great raconteur, and on the last night of filming we gave a party for the crew which saw him drunk, yes, but at his entertaining best. Someone tried to drag him away before the dam broke but he kept on performing for us, playing the piano and singing between his stories. It was a memorable, immensely enjoyable evening heightened by the tension which most of those present felt.
>
> No one would ever persuade me that there was ever a more powerful actor than he. Some people are at their best at the height of their youth and reach that apogee because of the people they are. Change one jot of their personality and there may be lost the very quality that astounds.[17]

Luke tells a funny story from around this time that testifies to his dad's guile. Stars were entitled to per diem expenses. Some demanded buckets of roses, others limitless bowls of sweets. Around this time, Nicol, aware that Luke was now free and able to travel on his own, usually chose open return air tickets:

> One time he called me up when he was filming and asked me over, first to London and then to Amsterdam. This was just before everything was computerised. Everything was filled out in red ink. I think they were due to expire in 1995 and so he had taken a red biro and amended the year to 1996. On one of the last legs of the journey we were accused by an inspector of tampering with the tickets. Nicol pretended to be aghast and the man let me through.

Nicol could be forgiven for milking the system for all he could get. The truth was, pickings were getting thin on the ground. Nicol's film career ended not with a traditional bang but rather with a dull thud in *Spawn*, a movie he quickly renamed *Prawn* on account of its ineptitude. Luke takes the 'blame' for his dad's film career ending so sourly:

He was in L.A. doing *Jack*, and I saw all these comic books in his hotel room and I asked what that was about and he told me he had been offered this role and he was going to turn it down and I explained to him that Todd McFarlane[18] had a huge cult following and that it might prove to be a very popular movie. I explained it was the first African–American superhero who wasn't a sidekick and so he took that on board and eventually agreed to do it.

Luke was hired as Nicol's personal assistant and driver after a disagreement between his dad and the producers over a wig and beard the props department wanted Nicol to wear. In the end Nicol simply refused to wear either. 'When I visited the set a few days later, I tried to explain to a producer that everything was in the way you presented things,' said Luke. 'If you made something an order, or demand, it was going to backfire. If you made everything collaborative it would likely work out. I think they thought it was just easier to hire me to present things smoothly.'

Despite Luke's involvement and Nicol's genuine commitment it became clear that amateurs were in charge. 'Within a few days it was obvious things were not going well,' says Luke:

> We knew it was going to suck about three weeks into shooting. I could tell the special effects guys knew their stuff, but the director was just awful and the guy who played Spawn just sulked though the whole thing; he was hating every minute. I remember standing with Dad and cinematographer Guillermo Navarro and we were waiting forever for the next shot and Dad saying 'what are we waiting for?' and Guillermo saying 'they do not know what the fuck they are doing'. Some of the actors were so poor with their delivery. I remember one scene in particular. The actor said his line and it was awful and I figured we're going to have to go through this like twenty times until he gets that sounding good. And the director just called it a wrap.

On *Spawn* Nicol got on best with Navarro, according to Luke, 'He liked him and wanted him to work on one of his projects.'

Nicol never stopped wanting to act; it was in his soul but the offers were derisory and music was something he could do any time. Around this time he did a series of twice-nightly gigs at London's Pizza on the Park where he sang some of his favourite numbers, including *I Can't Give You Anything But Love*, *Baby Face* and *My Blue Heaven*. David Benedict, writing in *The Independent*, thought the evening was marred by Nicol's unfunny jokes and 'anodyne' singing – 'you keep waiting for wit or passion or something' – but acknowledged Nicol's 'fine deep baritone that recalls the fifties crooner Michael Holliday'.

Lisa Martland in *The Stage* opened her review of Nicol's show by saying, 'Nicol Williamson is still not a familiar name to theatregoers under the age of 40' [implying somehow that he never was] before acknowledging that 'his deep baritone voice could be strangely affecting. His chat in between songs was also entertaining, as was a slightly different interpretation of *Pennies From Heaven*.'

Nicol once told a journalist that he was much happier in a recording studio, surrounded by musicians, than he was on stage or in front of a camera. And Leslie Megahey believes that, in the end, music was Nicol's first love:

> He certainly gave the impression he'd rather have been a singer all along. But he loved acting so much I think he would have needed to be both a great actor and a great singer. Yet in terms of acting assignments he drew the line at taking anything unless there was some really urgent financial need as with *The Exorcist III*.

By now, Nicol totally accepted that his moment in the sun had passed. The love of good food and wine remained but he had swapped lunch at L'Etoile (where he and Kenneth Tynan used to dine) for a modest slap-up dinner in his local curry house. Leslie Megahey recalls evenings out with Nicol in London and Amsterdam:

> We went to bars and restaurants where Nicol was known to the owners/waiters and where he had his favourite dishes, wines, etc. He often asked for a bottle of Gewürztraminer which seemed to be his favoured white wine. Late at night he liked a cognac and dark chocolate. He liked Italian food, and was always up for an Indian meal. He used to like a local curry place near my house in London. He didn't like more exotic stuff like Sushi. I once took him to a favourite Japanese place in London, and he didn't last more than five minutes before he said very politely did I mind if he went off somewhere else, and I said not at all, and off he went.

By the mid-nineties, Nicol, who was turning 60, had certainly mellowed. He was still drinking but generally the roustabout behaviour of the past had ceased. Long-time fan Louise Penn got to know Nicol during this period and recalls him fondly:

> I found him a sweet man, a funny man, a man with a kind heart, a man of astounding intellect and perception, a cultured man. I was lucky enough to hear some of his *Hobbit* word-play and I treasure the recording he made of it many years ago. In that recording he is truly 'alive'. I can see why some called him difficult, but I never saw it first-hand, although I heard stories of chairs being

smashed during arguments. I knew he drank, and I know sometimes he was weak, as those afflicted often are.

Nicol's acting career was effectively finished after *Spawn*. He was open to a great offer, a great part, but he had turned down so many in the past, and then spectacular offers didn't come. But there remained one final stab at glory.

THE LAST HURRAH

'Like Eric Morecambe playing the piano, he knew all the notes, but not necessarily in the right order.'

Michael Coveney reviewing Nicol Williamson's King Lear

There always seemed to be two Nicols; one the carousing raconteur and singer, taking to the piano with a boozy rendition of *Nessun Dorma*, a great, magnetic showman of energy and charisma; the other, the rather befuddled loner. Now that he had effectively retired from acting, and had not remarried, people were seeing rather more of the latter.

Nicol's main base was still Amsterdam. Sometimes he would leave his house on the Singel to drink alone in one of the nearby bars. A couple recount their encounter with Nicol:

My husband discretely pointed out that Merlin was drinking alone at the next table. The bar was small enough and quiet enough to engage him in conversation, and when the bar closed, he invited us back to his house. We were new in town, we didn't know many people, and this turned out to be the first of several epic drinking sessions over the following few months.

Nick was larger than life, immensely entertaining, and we greatly appreciated the kindness and generosity he showed to us. I used to think of him as Old Nick, because a night's drinking with him was as exciting and as punishing as a night's drinking with the Devil himself. And he had the best tunes, whether it was *Sing, Sing, Sing* at maximum volume on the old stereo, or a ribald song in a robust tenor banged out on the piano. In his cups he could give the impression that his intensity and immense talent were about to consume him and all about him. I sometimes suspected that at heart this must have made him quite lonely.

He had made *Spawn* a year or two before, and while we made some consoling and complimentary noises, it was clear that he was disenchanted with how his film career had ended up. But the man we knew showed no loss of vitality, nor of talent, and he clearly still had much to offer.[1]

Nicol also enjoyed frequent trips to London. He no longer owned a home in Britain but liked to stay at various bed and breakfast-type pubs.

An encounter in a London pub – taken from the internet – from this period seems to capture Nicol's self-imposed isolation:

I was in one of my local pubs, the Cock and Bottle in Notting Hill. The saloon bar was empty except for me and the actor Nicol Williamson. We sat with our pints at separate tables and I could not resist breaking the silence. 'May I say hello?' I said. 'Hello,' he said in his deep and distinctive Midlands voice with echoes of his Scottish birth. I said, 'I saw you in *Rex* at the Lunt-Fontanne Theatre on Broadway in 1976.' Williamson sighed and gave a wan smile. 'Ah, yes,' he said. 'Not the maestro's best.'

The actor did not appear to be well and he clearly wished to be alone, but I said, 'I enjoyed it.'

He raised his glass to me and I said: 'How are you?'

Williamson thought for a moment and looked me in the eye. He said: 'Breaking even.'

Nicholas Meyer, who wrote *The Seven-Per-Cent Solution*, remembers seeing Nicol in L.A. at around the same period:

Years after the film, I was driving west on Sunset Blvd and crossing Horn Avenue, and I beheld Nicol standing on the island in the middle of the Sunset, waiting for the light to change. Presumably he was headed for Tower Records, which then occupied the northwest corner of Sunset and Horn, but that is merely a guess.[2] The light was in my favour and I was therefore going too fast to stop and hail him, but I've never forgotten what a forlorn figure he cut. For all I know he was perfectly happy at the time, but that was not the impression he made as I watched him standing there … He seemed always to be alone. Anhedonic is the other word that comes to me as I remember Nicol.

Yet Luke is adamant we shouldn't take the isolation too far. And, of course, Meyer's impression was just that – a fleeting intuition. 'Dad was just living his life. He wasn't really that interested in acting unless it was something special. He travelled, spent time with friends and me. I don't think he was isolated as much as private. But there were definitely people he had no time for.'

Luke also recalls another pertinent comment from Nicol on the subject of solitude. 'Dad often mentioned how Greta Garbo was misquoted as saying she 'wanted to be alone' when what she was clearly saying was she wanted to be *left* alone. And that 'alone' and 'lonely' are two different things.'

Nicol also spent a lot of time reading poetry, prose and philosophy, but he also had a great love for Tolkien, and even books on Buddhism. Luke agrees that Nicol ultimately preferred the company of musicians to actors, believing that he found their sense of shared accomplishment refreshing.

Spurning the company of other actors is by no means unusual in a profession where insecurities, bruised egos, addictions and vanity are widespread. Acting, like other artistic professions, is a lottery in terms of employment, reward and recognition. Actors may greet each other effusively but it can be difficult to make friends. The employed actor dreads meeting the 'resting' actor for fear of sounding complacent. Likewise the resting actor dreads meeting those more successful lest it triggers a bout of 'what went wrong?' soul-searching.

Many actors – and star performers at that – shared Nicol's aversion to mixing too much with other actors. Marlon Brando remembers that an actor 'is a guy who if you ain't talking about him, ain't interested'. Anthony Hopkins maintained he had few friends among actors, noting their tendency to talk about themselves. Oliver Reed preferred the company of artisans, telling Michael Aspel – with arch luvvie Richard Attenborough looking heartbroken by his side – that he simply disliked his fellow actors as a breed. Richard Harris once told some other actors not to phone him after their collaboration on a film had ended. They might have had fun during shooting but that's where it stopped.

Nicol's long spell in Amsterdam and periods of unemployment meant that he was losing touch with old friends. A strange, strictly speaking, (non)-encounter was with John Thaw, Nicol's oldest buddy in the business. In her book *The Two of Us*, Thaw's widow, actress Sheila Hancock, relates how, circa the late nineties, John was walking along Harley Street in London when he saw Nicol nearby. Sheila reported that John was certain that Nicol had seen him. So, according to Sheila, Nicol either hadn't noticed Thaw or seemed to deliberately avoid him. Sadly, there was little time to rekindle their friendship because Thaw died of cancer in January 2002. The truth, as revealed by Leslie Megahey with whom Nicol was staying at the time, was that Nicol *did* indeed ignore John. It seems incredible – Nicol walking through the West End and seeing John nearby but saying nothing. But … 'to thine own self be true' and Nicol subsequently told Megahey that he simply hadn't been in a mood to talk.

Jill believes there was another factor that explained the, not exactly broken but certainly lapsed, friendship:

> Nicol loved John's humour. We had such a great time together … but I believe John had a measure of control over himself which Nicol never had. I don't know when they stopped being great friends. When John stopped drinking, I think that was, for Nicol, the feeling that he had lost a great drinking buddy. I don't believe he was ever angry with John … it was his success and stopping alcohol and then he felt thrown away again.

Megahey suggested they should arrange a get-together with John and Sheila because they lived so close but it never happened. 'I don't think there was some awful dislike there,' says Megahey, 'I think he just didn't want to revisit that part of his past, chinwag about old times, etc. He was entirely unsentimental about that sort of thing, though I am sure it was hurtful to others.'

John Thaw and Nicol had been good friends for a long time, but somewhere along the line they fell out of touch and, according to Luke, Nicol didn't seem too interested in rekindling it. No wonder Sheila Hancock simply wondered in her autobiography 'whatever happened to Nicol Williamson?'[3]

Other friendships petered out too. Trevor Nunn recalls that:

> I met up with him sometimes in New York. On two occasions, we went to bars where a jazz combo was playing. Nicol knew them, they welcomed him on to their platform and he sang a set of numbers – superbly, and entirely as if his only career was as a jazz singer.

But:

> Time, distance, new directions in life … we gradually lost each other. Nicol was toughing it out in America. I was moving the RSC from the Aldwych to the Barbican, and opening our new theatre in Stratford called The Swan. I so wish the fates had thrown us together again, to work again, or talk and laugh again …

Leslie Megahey also, ultimately, lost touch with Nicol:

> After *Jack* we kept in touch and worked on a few more ideas for plays and films, with Nic coming every so often to stay with us in London. We'd had plans to do a documentary on his life, but I couldn't sell it at that time to the arts department of the BBC, which was its natural home. He was disappointed at that, and when

he was disappointed he didn't wait for you to have another go; he kind of counted something out, crossed it off the list. Things went quiet between us for a couple of years and I regret greatly that the next I heard of him was when Luke announced his death – the usual feelings of sadness at having lost someone whose company I had enjoyed and admired and guilt at not having got in touch with him. It isn't a question of whose 'turn' it was to get in touch, it's just that neither of us did. He would have said resignedly as it didn't happen there was no point in feeling bad about it (never apologise, never explain was his view) but to me it mattered, and still does.

Tara Hugo felt the same way. Nicol simply drifted off the radar. In the years post–*Macbeth* she had received a Laurence Olivier nomination, and become a singer as well as an actor:

I'd see Nicol in New York and London. I went to his dive in midtown Manhattan[4] ... I read an adaptation he did of Gogol's *Diary of a Madman*. He knew all the waiters at the best London restaurants. I never drank with him and he seemed to like my non-alcoholic status. I met some of his friends; was around when he did *Jack* at the Criterion. He saw me perform at Pizza on the Park in 1995 (and then he had a gig there in 1996), I went to Amsterdam on business and stayed in a guest room in his incredible house. He sang and played recordings of himself all night long, including a command performance at the Nixon White House in 1970. In 2000 he came to see me do a play at the White Bear Pub Theatre in London. I think the last time I saw Nicol, we met for lunch at a restaurant in West London. He gave me a first draft of a CD he'd made of his jazz songs. I was in New York full time and lost touch with him. I tried to phone a number I had, but it didn't work. I thought I'd see him again ... and then he was dead.

Few acting offers were coming Nicol's way. Nicol's financial situation was not, as later reported, all that desperate and he could afford to decline roles. He still had some projects on the backburner as Luke recalls:

He was more interested in possible stage roles, I remember him talking about a specific role, Marullas, he wanted to play in *Julius Caesar* so he could give his character's tremendous speech and be home and in bed before the rest of the cast got to Phillipi! ... He had several other projects he tried to get made. One was called *The Alphaman*, about Russian kids being turned into special forces and what they went through.

(Recalls co-writer Alex Pym: 'We were working on a film script, *The Alphaman*, which was sadly never made. Nicol was going to star in and direct it. I have fond memories of us writing together in Amsterdam. He was always charming, witty and incredibly amusing and I was always aware that I was very fortunate to be working with such a great artist.'[5])

Luke recalls other projects:

> There was another movie he tried to get made about a guy who meets and tries
> to escape death/the grim reaper that was very funny. I'm not entirely certain if he
> wrote the original screenplays or just rewrote them. I know he certainly rewrote
> them as I worked on it with him and typed it all out. There were always offers,
> but he wasn't very interested. It would have had to be something really special
> or one of his projects. He had his own adaptation of Gogol's *Diary of a Madman*
> that he very much wanted to do about ten years before he died but it was always
> hard for him to get a backer.

Around this time Nicol decided to leave Holland. 'He was tired of Amsterdam. The Dutch are lovely but can be a bit insular,' recalls Luke. Nicol moved to Rhodes. He had been visiting the island since the late sixties or early seventies for holidays. His new home would be in Lindos, several minutes' walk from the town centre. It was an old captain's stone house, previously owned by Willard Manus, from the late 1700s – no pool, jacuzzi, tennis court or, indeed, ostentatious luxury. According to Luke, there was little theatrical memorabilia, bar photos of Nicol with Nixon in 1970 and with Prime Minister Margaret Thatcher, taken in Downing Street in 1984 when he was playing Mountbatten.

If one 'special' role was out there for an actor of his age, it was, of course, Lear. Director Terry Hands had been trying to interest Nicol in Lear for some time, even approaching him back in 1994 when Nicol was in *Jack* at the Criterion. Eventually Nicol agreed. Another example of Nicol's rather detached attitude to friends was that Leslie Megahey knew nothing of Nicol's plans to play Lear until John Thaw told him in their local newsagents. Thaw joked with Leslie that they should take a charabanc of friends to Wales to see Nicol.

In 2001, Hands visited Rhodes to discuss the forthcoming production with Nicol. He found Nicol approaching the part in his usual eccentric manner.

> Academic analysis didn't interest him. Instead he simply was Lear throughout the
> day. Whether in bars, shops, during interminable lunches, or on walks, he blustered,
> confronted, dominated, insulted, ate, drank, and showed extraordinary, if wayward,
> generosity. By the end of the week we both knew the direction his Lear would take.[6]

During rehearsals in Clwyd, Wales, Hands found that Nicol always took risks:

> Some were well judged, others weren't. He could reduce the company to tears
> in rehearsal, and the audience in performance. On his night he equalled Paul
> Scofield. He was a big, powerful, unconventional, aggressive actor, slightly mad,
> a dominant figure in any situation, with a superb voice … Nicol contributed to
> all aspects of the work.

He and Nicol decided to emphasise Lear's kingly, patriarchal qualities:

> We talked about Edward I. Might he have been Shakespeare's inspiration? The
> great warrior-king who had united the kingdom, now residing over its division?
> … Lear is an orchestra piece, in which all the instruments are given their full
> value. The company responded as an ensemble, inspired by Nicol's performance.

Luke did not see his father's final stage performance and, indeed, final acting role:

> I was not invited to see Lear, which to me meant either he wasn't sure it was
> going to be good enough for me to see him do, or that he just couldn't spare any
> concentration. Or a bit of both … He was behind on knowing his stuff. He felt
> guilty because he was supposed to be carrying the load. He wasn't on top of his
> game and he felt that his acting had become rusty.

Charles Spencer penned a lacerating, even cruel, review in *The Daily Telegraph*.
After (rather unnecessarily) ridiculing Nicol's appearance, Spencer went for
the jugular:

> More damagingly, he is vocally underpowered with an accent that veers bizarrely
> between English actor laddie plumminess, New York, and his native Scotland. He
> also has a far from confident grasp on his lines and a cloth ear when it comes to
> the rhythm of Shakespeare's poetry. There would be time to boil an egg during
> the absurdly long pauses he inflicts on the single line 'I am a man more sinned
> against than sinning' and again and again great speeches are gabbled, stammered
> or ruined by false emphases. He can't even be bothered to get the number of
> howls right in the last act. None of this would matter so much if you felt that
> Nicol Williamson was digging deep into the role and into himself. But this is
> a depressingly superficial reading in which the king's fear of madness, his wild
> rage and his painful growth into full humanity seem to have been applied from
> without rather than torn from within.[7]

Michael Coveney, writing in the *Guardian*, was kinder:

> Many of the speeches were misplaced. Like Eric Morecambe playing the piano,
> he knew all the notes, but not necessarily in the right order ... he spat and
> crackled like an unruly fire, whining and drawling through the play with all the
> magnificent temperament he brought to his greatest modern role, the solicitor
> Bill Maitland in Osborne's *Inadmissible Evidence*.

Michael Kelligan thought it more impressive, 'Nicol Williamson's powerful Lear
finds his greatest degree of sensitive playing in the second part of the play. His
forgiveness and reconciliation with Cordelia and his tenderness over her dying
body demonstrate Nicol Williamson's greatest ability to engage with his audience.'

Leslie Megahey remembers that he never saw Nicol's Lear but that he met Terry
Hands at a memorial service for another actor in London and he spoke warmly
of working with Nicol.

Nicol was still only 64 at the time of his Lear. Ahead of him was a decade under
the Aegean sun and a battle he had always dreaded but somehow expected.

19

SEAMUS THE SQUAMOUS

'It makes me extremely sad that he was so troubled.'

Jill Townsend-Sorel on Nicol Williamson

All his life, according to Luke, Nicol feared two things – cancer and death. His mother's death had given him a dread of the disease, not just for himself but for others. The thought of children stricken with cancer appalled him. Somehow Nicol was always convinced that 'it' was coming for him.

Presentiments of early mortality are hardly unusual. Perhaps in Nicol's case a lifetime of heavy drinking and smoking – although by now he had long since forsaken the ciggies – made him all the more certain. Maybe in some way he reckoned it would be payback for a rumbustious life.

Nicol's retreat to Rhodes in the early noughties ushered in a quieter time. He was getting seriously into his music. At a time when many of his contemporaries – the likes of Finney, Hopkins, O'Toole, McKellen and Jacobi – were still going strong, he had effectively retired. Luke remembers his dad's reaction when another hellraising contemporary, Richard Harris, whom Nicol had little time for, died in 2002 from cancer, aged 72:

> I was having lunch with Dad when somebody brought the newspaper with news that Richard had passed. They were sort of gloating a bit, I think, because they thought that Dad would be happy since he didn't get on well with him. Dad was horrified on both levels; he was very sad to hear that he had died and horrified that people could take any joy in it.

Harris's death triggered an offer that typifies everything Nicol came to despise about the movie business. The late 'Irish firebrand' – as Harris was always described

– had played Dumbledore in two Harry Potter movies. The producers were now urgently seeking a replacement. They even sent Nicol a script. Yet, a couple of weeks later, the casting directors contacted Nicol to tell him that he was not wanted because 'he had an American accent'. Given Nicol's impeccable, even flawless mimicry (let alone the obvious fact that Nicol was *not* American) the producers' reasoning was ludicrous. 'Dad dined out on that for two weeks,' says Luke with a laugh:

> It was absolutely hilarious because – obviously – he could do any accent that was required. We had a lot of fun with that. That ridiculous kind of excuse … it was that kind of thing he really disrespected, the inability to give an honest answer. It was so obvious that that was not the real reason. But I'm not sure Dad would have enjoyed playing Dumbledore anyway.[1]

If an autumnal resurgence had passed Nicol by, Luke believes his dad had little cause for regret. 'I know there were things he would have liked to have done, but I don't think he regretted anything. And when you look at it, he played Hamlet, Macbeth and Lear and was acclaimed for those roles. Not many actors get to do that.'

In Rhodes, Nicol swam and drank a lot, and generally cultivated an air of an irascible eccentric around town. It was a secluded place, even more so outside the tourist season. 'After Dad died I lived out there for about eighteen months. It can be very quiet, especially in the off season. Ideally, Dad probably needed something more,' says Luke. 'Lindos is too small. You cannot possibly be anonymous there. It's sort of like a Greek Peyton Place. Everyone knows everyone else's business, or thinks they do, and the gossip is out of hand.'

At this point in his life – all acting ambitions fulfilled – Nicol spent a lot of time travelling or composing music. Tara Hugo recalls:

> Shortly before his death he had made (and self-financed) a CD of his favourite songs with an ad hoc band of musicians he'd got to know. He gave me a copy, but it was never distributed commercially. I went out to see him where they were recording and the musicians and technical people clearly loved collaborating with him and going to the pub with him. He seemed far happier in the presence of musicians than of other actors, I'd say. And, of course, when he made these tracks, he was totally in control – no producers, financiers, moguls to infuriate him.

Nicol seemed to be retreating into himself. Luke said:

He was extremely private, more so in later years. He really just wanted to be left alone. He was always gracious to families, kids etc. but he had a limit for being accosted during meals. I remember one Greek magazine guy came up to him during a meal and wouldn't take the hint, and Dad was gracious and this guy took it that they were now buddies and he saw him again and tried to sit down with him. Dad told him to 'fuck off' and then this guy wrote this big article saying 'don't approach this man'. Dad found it quite funny.[2]

Lionel Larner recalls hearing a story, uncorroborated, that Nicol threw a brick at a building contractor while he was on Rhodes. In another account by actor Stephen Lyons – almost certainly hearsay about the same incident – a young Greek was up a ladder in the street whitewashing a wall (whose house it was is unclear) when Nicol rushed out and attacked the man with a hammer.[3] Luke has never heard of such an incident and figures the press and the rumour factory always exaggerated his dad's penchant for a punch-up:

He was a big guy and he was in the Paras so he had some training but I never saw him fight anybody. I've seen him tell people to get on their bikes. And they usually did. There was one time when somebody's husband picked up a beer bottle at Dad's house. I stepped between the two of them. He picked me up with one hand [!] and held me against the wall while he told that man what he could do with the bottle. But I never saw him fight anyone.

Notwithstanding the odd press rumour, these were gentler times. Luke recalls his dad's prowess in the kitchen, his love of spicy food – especially a good curry. For Nicol, dining, whether outside or at home, merited close attention. A perfectionist in the kitchen as well as on the stage, so it seems.

Yet, Luke believes, there were periods when Nicol was certainly at a loose end:

I think he was bored and he probably felt unchallenged. But he wasn't really that interested in doing any acting. He didn't have an agent for probably the last ten years. When I was packing up after he died [in the house in Lindos] I found many scripts unopened. It was always very important the way things were pitched to him. And I think in Hollywood they're used to everyone wanting to jump on to the coattails of someone else's success. So if they put a note attached to a script, saying something like 'an Al Pacino vehicle', then 99 per cent of actors would want to board that gravy train. But what would have appealed to Dad was simply the story – a good story.

Nicol remained receptive to meeting and befriending new people, depending on his mood. One such 'friend', who wrote to Luke after Nicol died, was Susan Younge:

> We were unexpectedly taken to your father's beautiful house in Lindos by a mutual friend and he made us very welcome. He had me in awe with his songs and fantastic presence which rendered me speechless. He asked me:'Why are you wearing that ridiculous hat?'The hat was a joke but I was too in awe to string two sentences together. That says what an impressive orator he was and it was a pleasure to have known him and hear his tales. My partner met him a couple more times and my biggest regret is that we never made time to go back and have that drink with him in his favourite bar.

Luke remembers his dad went into the sea for the last time in around 2006. But he would accompany Luke to the beach, sheltered under a big parasol. Nicol was spending more time alone. He liked to read poetry but also composed songs and verse himself. A piece like *These Latter Days* stressed the inevitability of degeneration and death:

> Failing knees and weakened hands.
> So slow to obey commands,
> Fast, erratic drumbeat roll,
> Arrhythmia beyond control,
> Disorientations in the dark,
> When balance flies wide of its mark,
> And brings that sudden catch of death,
> Harbinger of the ego death,
> My foot jams on the brake of fear,
> To put me in slow motion phase,
> But it can't halt the slow motion gear,
> That speeds me through these latter days.

Another, *Grow Old with Grace*, was more defiant, in line with Nicol's bid to kid interviewers that he was several years younger than his age:

> I never judge my image in the glass,
> It springs unaltered into view each day,
> Let others fear the ravage of times past,
> My late October bursts with buds of May,

> To my true age I'll ever play the liar,
> And I'll bet the hand I'll deal myself,
> The mirror shows me that which *I* desire
> Sod all the geriatrics on the shelf.

Another, *Retro Rocket*, perhaps written by Nicol as a kind of self-reproach, urging him to live in the present:

> Shut fast that door ...
> Don't board the train
> That bears the name plate memory lane
> The past that demon driver mocks
> With proffer of Pandora's Box.

Nicol's rendition of a popular song *Autumn Leaves* – also from around this period – reveals a rich and varied voice, somewhere between Frank Sinatra and Matt Monro. Ultimately, singing gave Nicol most pleasure. To that end, in the summer of 2009, Nicol performed a fundraising concert in Rhodes for a child injured in a motorcycle accident. 'During the first of two performances, his throat had locked up and he felt awful. He did the second performance and then started to feel better,' said Luke.

Nicol was encouraged by the reaction to the concert, 'It really made him happy to use his music to help improve the quality of someone's life. The positive feedback he received spurred him on to keep creating.'

But all wasn't well. 'A few months later he had a terrible sore throat, but he wouldn't go to the doctor until he couldn't swallow. He hated doctors, so it was hard to make him go,' recalled Luke.

Nicol eventually went for an examination at the end of 2009. The verdict was advanced throat cancer. Nicol was given just a few weeks to live but, Luke believes, by sheer obstinacy and willpower, he turned it into two years. Luke, in an act of extreme devotion that testifies to their closeness, took care of Nicol throughout this period.

He was impressed by his father's courage:

He was odd, he was a bit of a hypochondriac when he was healthy, but as soon as he got sick, he was fine ... he wouldn't stay in bed, he would make himself carry on as usual, whether it was flu or a broken bone or indeed cancer ... he was determined to beat it and he almost did, pretty much on willpower alone.

Nicol even invented a name for his illness. He called it 'Seamus the Squamous' – in a bid to belittle it. Luke says he never complained and fought all the way.

When Nicol received his cancer diagnosis he just stopped drinking on his oncologist's orders. He never touched another drop for the last two years of his life.

Luke, who had been convinced that his father *did* indeed have a problem with booze, was surprised how easily he quit:

> I thought, there's no way ... but he stopped drinking on day one. No withdrawals or DTs. He didn't sit around gasping for drink. He never even mentioned it. I just concluded that he'd been self-medicating all along. He would occasionally order a glass of rosé and just let it sit on the table. I was really grateful for that. He was very clear and we had many great and long conversations over that time. He also did his best to be an easy patient, knowing that it wasn't easy for me, having to negotiate my way through the vagaries, the minefield, the veritable maze of foreign medical institutions and requirements, hotels and transportation systems.

Nicol swore his son to secrecy over his diagnosis. He hated the thought of people pitying him and his 'weakness' being exposed. He was especially keen to keep his illness out of the British press. 'He said to me a few times it felt like "what will Bigfoot do now?" and whatever he did, it would be framed a certain way. He had no love for the paparazzi, that's for sure.'

Nearly all the two-year period during which Luke cared for Nicol was spent in the UK or Holland. Because Luke was an American citizen, however, the immigration people kept trying to bar him from entering Britain. This was a problem since Nicol was set on undergoing treatment in London where he had a doctor he liked.

In between medical treatments Nicol liked to stay in a bed and breakfast in Chislehurst in Kent, and another in Devon. Yet Luke had to watch his dad closely. Nicol would be exhausted for at least a week after each gruelling bout of chemotherapy.

On one occasion, in April 2011, Luke drove him back to Rhodes, an exhausting five-day trip involving a ferry ride. But it was difficult for Nicol to be in Lindos because of the lack of transport. It was also very hilly, so Nicol tired easily. In addition, the medical care in Rhodes was, according to Luke, abysmal. On the ferry over to Lindos, Nicol became very ill and Luke panicked that he'd have to be permanently hospitalised in Rhodes, a situation best avoided.

Luke was now Nicol's constant companion. They agreed that, as long as Nicol was able to get out for one meal a day, Luke would look after him. 'Eventually the time came when Dad couldn't take further treatment and was struggling to get out of bed,' said Luke, 'and I had to get a wheelchair for him. After about two weeks of that he just couldn't do it anymore. I didn't like the doctor and the poor treatment I thought he was getting.'

Towards the end of 2011 Nicol's health worsened. Luke suggested a hospice in Hoorn, in the Netherlands, near his closest Dutch friend, Kees. Nicol agreed. Luke drove his dad back to the country which had been home to him for more than twenty years. Luke tried to have a last day out with his father, exploring old haunts, but he was simply too frail and exhausted. So he checked into the hospice – *still*, according to Luke, *not* giving up – but grateful just to rest.

A female counsellor monitored the patients, on stand-by in case they wanted a heart to heart. Right up to the end, however, according to Luke, Nicol refused to 'dismantle the watch':

> The counsellor and I talked one day and, after that, whenever she would check on Dad he would act as if she was there for me. And if I wasn't there, he'd tell me later, 'that girl came by for you again'. He was absolutely uninterested. He would share with people he carefully selected and no one else. He picked people he really adored and trusted to speak about these things, if it wasn't 'Papa' as everyone called his father, or me, it would usually be a woman that he felt an emotional attachment to but was not involved with.

Nicol died ten days later on the stroke of midnight, on 15 December 2011. His last words were, appropriately, to Luke, who was with him when he took his last breath. 'I love you,' he told him. Luke reflects:

> Dad loved me more than the world. I loved him too. He was a very generous, loving, empathetic sweet guy if he trusted you enough to show it. It's funny, he wasn't big on saying 'I love you', but he didn't really need to.

Jill recalls that, even though she knew Nicol had been very ill, she felt 'devastated'. Today, six years after his death, she reflects:

> I'm very, very grateful that Nicol was in my life. I always tell Luke that I will never stop loving him. It makes me extremely sad that he was so troubled for so much of his life. I'm convinced it was something that happened in his childhood. I've always said to Nicol, 'whatever else happens in the whole world, honey, look at what we created together, a wonderful boy'.

She believes that, ultimately, nobody measured up to his flesh and blood. 'In his life, Nicol's first love was always his mother and father – Mama and Papa. At the end of his life, his love was for Luke.'

Luke withheld the news from the press until after his father's funeral. He knew Nicol would have hated the thought of colleagues chiming in with their comments. Or journalists, who had never met him, copying and pasting rehashed information from old articles:

> He knew it'd all be sensationalism and salacious detail. He gave me strict instructions to say fuck all to them after he died. He didn't care for them at all. He used to point out how people who got in the papers would suddenly realise that a bunch of shit had been written about them and then, in the next breath, believe the next story in the same paper.

The press, desperate as ever for an 'angle', maintained that Nicol had died in penury. Luke denied this. His dad wasn't rich but neither was he poor.

Only six people attended Nicol's funeral. Luke says one reason was Nicol's determination to keep his illness a secret:

> You have to understand that Dad didn't want anyone to come to see him. Even when he was in the hospice he was still making plans to survive. He didn't want visits … he didn't want anyone's last memory of him to be in that state. He was under 50kg. He was a shadow of his former self. He had very good friends in Holland but he simply didn't want to see them. And I was forbidden to discuss his illness with anyone.

The only mourners, apart from Luke, were Nicol's close confidant, Kees, two other local Dutch friends, Meta and Sandy, and another British friend, sound engineer Nick Taylor and his wife, Margaret. Luke also found a Scottish bagpiper who lived nearby to come and play.

Nicol was cremated. 'We all have a hereditary claustrophobia in our family about being in a box,' says Luke.

The news eventually surfaced in Britain several weeks after he died. Even though Luke tried to convince them otherwise, many papers quoted the wrong birth year, citing 1938. In fact, Nicol was 75 when he died. Predictably, the press headlined his bad boy antics. His electric performances on stage were buried under a pile of mud.

THE STENCH OF DEATH

'Who can tell the mysteries of the human heart?'

Leslie Megahey

The word 'underrated' is so often applied to an actor that it has become a cliché. Yet, in order to gauge Nicol's true greatness, we should consider that the reverse also applies – that we can overpraise certain performances. Marlon Brando once noted in his autobiography that often when people see a star in a great role they say, 'what a performance!', when the truth is that with a powerful script most decent actors can't lose. Doubtless, Nicol would have agreed. Hence, he thought actors such as Michael Caine, Sean Connery, even Anthony Hopkins and Jack Nicholson, were overrated. Yet Nicol also thought some of Olivier's performances were hammy.

Although Nicol was a leading man who played classical roles on stage to great acclaim, took the lead in several Osborne plays and, yes, made a memorable Merlin, it's also true he was sorely underrated. The reasons are complex. Nicol's failure to abide by the rules surely played a part. Luke sums up his father's independent spirit. 'In order to be the big star, and maintain that, you have to kiss a lot of arses and do all the right things to the right people. He was completely incapable of that. He was absolutely a loose cannon and he refused to be controlled.'

This doesn't quite explain why Nicol drew so few major roles in his later years. For example, the usual suspects – Reed, Harris or Hopkins, his natural contemporaries – behaved just as badly. Think of Oliver Reed's serial disruptions on chat shows. Or Richard Harris's constant sniping against the likes of Michael Caine, Charlton Heston, Tom Cruise, Bruce Willis and Ian McKellen. Harris, in 1987, once even told chat show host Gloria Hunniford that many big stars were 'very boring people'. And 'hellraising' need not be a drawback.

Journalist Terence Blacker correctly noted that the British public had a soft spot for self-destructive drunks, citing the 'popularity' of Oliver Reed, footballer George Best and Soho scribe Jeffrey Bernard. Yet Blacker also noted the strange 'primness' of Nicol's obituaries. They failed to do him justice. Blacker concluded that Nicol 'refused to play the game required of celebrities'.

Yes, Nicol did misbehave at times but so did many other actors who continued to be sought after. So we must look for other reasons.

Nicol simply refused to compromise. Although Nicol was often unemployed from the age of 50 onwards, he refused to lower his sights. He seldom accepted villainous roles. Luke explains:

> He didn't like to be framed as a bad guy. He found these parts tedious. There were definitely parts he was offered with the promise that they would make a lot of money. But he used to ask – what has the role done for the actor in it? He wouldn't take a role with a character he couldn't connect to. He was concerned that he would be pigeonholed as the bad guy. And you should bear in mind that he was really one of the most sensitive, loving people. He constantly felt he was being portrayed in an unfavourable way. He wanted to be seen as the good guy.

Luke is almost certain that Nicol was offered the part of Longshanks in *Braveheart*, eventually accepted by Patrick McGoohan. 'I remember saying he should have had that role and he said "who said I wasn't offered it?" But what did it do for McGoohan? And I guess he was right and Longshanks was not a sympathetic character.'

But perhaps some great roles passed Nicol by. For example, Nicol would have made a great Bond bad-guy. Witness his sly power in a movie like *Passion Flower*. Yet it's likely – given what we know – that Nicol would have passed on the chance, probably viewing it as the big screen equivalent of his villain in *Columbo* … to be accepted only if the wolf was at the door!

Nicol was exceptionally discriminating unless financial necessity demanded otherwise. It partly stemmed from the 100 per cent commitment he gave to every part. For Nicol, acting was not a trick or an illusion but a total devotion of heart and soul:

> I've talked to actors who have played the same parts I have, and when I tell them 'I'm tired' or 'I'm shattered' or 'I'll go nuts if I do this any longer', they say 'oh, but I played it for x number of performances and I didn't find it tiring at all'. The simple answer to this is 'no, because you don't work the way I do.'

Also, although the likes of Hopkins, O'Toole, Harris and Hurt were all capable of recalcitrance, they all appeared on the London stage regularly and made it clear they were 'in the game'. Most kept a British base and were easily contactable. Yet Nicol, in disappearing off to Amsterdam, then spending so much time in New York, seemed to remove himself from the radar.

Ultimately, perhaps Nicol simply didn't want film stardom badly enough – or at least not the kind of 'character actor stardom' that Hollywood offered. He once told Kenneth Tynan that he was no longer interested in being 'the greatest actor in the world and all that jazz'. (Well, as Tynan observed, he *was* interested in the jazz, so it turned out!) So it was, in cinema at least, Nicol didn't get the roles or the credit he was due. Perhaps, ultimately, Nicol was too dismissive of film as an art form. Journalist David Taylor once noted, 'He [Nicol] claims to know at the moment of shooting whether or not a scene is working, has no inclination to agonise over the rushes, indeed seldom bothers to go and see the finished picture.'[1]

Nicol, who never received an Oscar nomination, was even omitted from the In Memoriam section at the 2012 Oscars – honouring performers and personalities in the industry who had died the previous year. (Just in case their excuse was that the delayed announcement of Nicol's passing led some to think he had died in 2012, he was also excluded the following year.)

Nicol made many stage appearances but nothing rivals film or TV for reaching a huge audience. Luke reflects, 'He didn't make blockbuster movies every year. He wasn't the standard leading man, and people were nervous about working with him. In America he's now almost unknown. People have short memories.'

Jill believes that although Nicol played most of the bravura stage roles, he was still untapped. 'I think there was so much more for him to give, for us to appreciate, than he gave us. The film industry – given that he had a great voice, great looks and could have played more leading roles beautifully – was short-sighted not to see that.'

Curiously, Nicol maintained few friendships with other actors. To that extent, Nicol seemed to engineer a kind of self-imposed isolation. Richard Harris once penned a lacerating character assassination of Michael Caine in the *Sunday Times* in 1995. In the article he condemned Caine's decision to transplant himself to L.A. and compared his behaviour to the likes of himself, Burton, O'Toole, Finney, Courtenay and Stamp. But there was no mention of Nicol anywhere in the piece. By then Nicol had simply disappeared.

Ironically, Nicol was better than all his main rivals. His theatrical roles, sadly, cannot be revisited. Yet, if you see the film of *Inadmissible Evidence*, it still triggers goose pimples. The few clips that remain of Nicol's stage performance as Maitland reveal a mesmerising presence. Yes, 'paddling for his life' as Elaine Bromka had it or, as Oscar James said, almost knocking you down with the force of his words. Even when, in the film version, the script demands a look of forlorn defeat, he still does so with thunder.

Nicol was, I think, at his best on the boards and this partly explains why his name doesn't resonate today with the general public. Magnificent stage performances, seldom recorded for posterity, are just a memory. As Trevor Nunn says:

> The achievements of those who work in the theatre are no more than 'writing on the sand'. There may well be a vivid and important message for all to see, for a while, but by and by the tide comes in, and when it next goes out, that writing has disappeared. Whatever the message was then exists only in the memory, the most treacherous of our human capabilities and not really to be trusted.

While Nicol's name is still greeted with awe among those fortunate enough to have seen him on stage, Trevor Nunn feels 'distress' that later generations of theatregoers have never heard of him:

> Nicol was capable of greatness. Exceptional talent is bound to derive from exceptional intelligence, and very probably an unusual highly strung psychological make-up that has a different metabolic rate from the rest of us, and produces a form of nervous tension that makes that individual startling, special, different. Nicol was all of those things. I want him to be remembered for everything positive that he brought to his art form.

Roland Jaquarello believed that Nicol's passion and intensity were underappreciated, perhaps not even understood, by Britain's theatrical establishment:

> You always felt that he was searching for something more alive, daring and emotionally revealing than the average actor. I admired and learnt from his bravery and daring. He was always looking to make a performance fresh and spontaneous, which is, of course, the essence of live theatre. He took us into raw emotion in a way too often missing in today's productions and dared to go where others often fear to tread. He never was afraid of showing the dark side of human nature in an unsentimental way. He didn't go out of his way to be loved by an audience, which is the bane of some performers. Instead, he looked to be rigorous towards the truth, not in a humourless way, but with a vigorous passion. To those like myself, who were fortunate enough to see him in his prime, Nicol was a beacon of light to encourage daring, risk and, yes, fun!

Many people I interviewed spoke of his acting with awe. Saskia Wickham: 'mesmerising, sublime, unique, magical … he was a genius.' Carolyn Seymour: 'I loved his darkness and his massiveness. He could go so deep.' Jill's abiding memory of Nicol's acting is his charisma: 'He always took my breath away. He had so much physical power that it just exploded on stage.'

Nicol once said that he had 'the stench of death' in his nostrils. Perhaps this scared directors. They may have thought he was simply *too* powerful. *Not* because, as Pauline Kael alleged, he was trying to reach out and strong-arm you, but simply because of his enormous presence. Rather like Burton, even when he was still and saying nothing, he still commanded attention.

John Calder recalled Nicol's unique way with a line, his ability to convey emotion with a flick of a wrist, or as in *Waiting for Godot*, with a piercing cry. 'Whoever saw his Vladimir and heard that despairing scream, embodying the whole anguish of the human condition, which is then followed by a resumption of the human need to regain a vestige of dignity, will never forget it. Metaphorically it also encompassed his life.'

Several observers thought Nicol was peerless. Michael Coveney wrote that 'he was the most exciting actor I ever saw'.[2] Tara Hugo agreed:

He was perhaps the greatest actor of our time and I am a student of the theatre. He compelled me and we had a friendship. He was a phenomenon who was compelled to show *all*, he had no boundaries, wrote his own rules and abused himself and others in the process. His raw honesty and risk-taking took no prisoners.

She adds, 'I had time for him despite his wickedness, and his alcoholism. But I kept a distance and was careful not to get too close.'

Nicol brought tremendous passion to live performance. Danger was inherent in him at all times. Robert Gore Langton wrote that today's actors seem tame by contrast, 'He [Nicol] was a thrilling actor fuelled by a hatred for his audience and a fabulous blow-torch talent. If there's a problem with acting today, it's a lack of actors who can make the hairs on the back of your neck stand up.'[3]

Roger Lewis agreed that today's stars all seemed anodyne, 'Actors of the past had a sense of danger, now it's all sparkling water and pilates.'[4]

Glenda Jackson believes that, in spite of his brilliance, Nicol's demons destroyed him. 'He was a remarkable actor who always seemed to undermine himself when it was time for the next step … he could have done greater things. Some actors like Marlon Brando break the mould of all actors. Nicol could have taken it to that level.'

Edward Fox, although acknowledging some of Nicol's 'truly great' performances, feels his friend's career was a bit of anticlimax. 'It nonetheless saddens me even now to recall how his truly enormous powers and God-given talent underwent a decline. If fortune had, I feel, been more benevolent, Nicol would have become in later years a world renowned actor and rightly thought of as a truly great actor.'

Theatrical agent Ro Diamond, who knew Nicol at the time of his Nixon engagement, admits to feeling 'anger' at how he sometimes behaved, 'The reputation you start with stays with you throughout your whole career. What's the point of being a bad boy?' She thinks that Nicol's 'misbehaviour' undermined his brilliance.

Perhaps jealousy played a part in the press and critics – and possibly even fellow actors – throwing barbs at Nicol. Sarah Nolte, who worked as his assistant on *Jack*, certainly thinks so. 'People were often critical of him, but these people were either jealous of his unreachable talent or they were too small to understand what that meant.'[5]

Nicol did not believe that acting was an art form. He rather defined it as 'a testing craft'. It was his duty to convey the writer's intentions. Tara Hugo recalls Nicol's Macbeth, and his injunction to the witches to 'Show! Show! Show!' Reflecting on the actor she believed to be the finest of his generation, she says simply, 'He showed.'

In his David Frost interview, Nicol had expressed his fear that a premature death would fell him before he could display his talent. Fortunately, Nicol *did* have time to show off his greatness even though, at least on film, he never really reached his potential.

As for Nicol the private man it's clear that despite his roustabout behaviour he was a depressive at heart. Apart from family and the occasional love interest, Nicol seemed wary of intimacy. He could also shun friends if he thought they had let him down. All agree that Nicol adored Luke – and Luke's loving memories testify to that:

> I'm tremendously proud of him and I will love and miss him every day for the rest of my life. He absolutely could drive me crazy, but he was also the most amazing person. He was always honest regardless of other people's feelings. But, if he loved you, then you really felt loved.

Today, six years on from his father's death, Luke still feels Nicol's presence strongly when he stays at his house in Lindos. When Luke feels depressed, the memories of their uproarious times together carry him through:

It's hard to convey someone else's humour. I could tell you something he said but it just wouldn't be the same. He was the most devastatingly funny person to be around. He just had the most incredible timing. I can't tell you the number of times he got me, or someone else, to spill our drinks through our noses.

For Luke, his father's standout quality was his uncompromising integrity:

He is one of the few people I know, if not the only person, who lived his life according to his principles and his feelings, regardless of the personal outcome. It's a very human thing to present an affable personality to the world in order to be liked but Dad didn't do that. You always knew where you stood with him. He really appreciated people who were authentic. And you didn't have to be loud and outgoing. There were definitely people he appreciated who weren't like that.

In his total unwillingness to dissemble, Nicol resembled the central protagonist, Meursault, of Albert Camus's great novel *L'Etranger* (*The Outsider*) about whom the author wrote, 'He refuses to lie. Lying is not only saying what isn't true. It is also, in fact especially, saying more than is true and, in the case of the human heart, saying more than one feels.' Camus could easily have been writing of Nicol.

Perhaps, also, Nicol's brittleness was inseparable from his greatness. Louise Penn noted Nicol's solitariness, the sense that few penetrated his inner core:

After the nineties he was gone as a presence, off to his island, his music, and his loneliness. When he died it was sad to know he'd not been missed, that we hadn't known his real age, or his real name. He'd walked away from fame, and he'd always held some of himself back and I think somehow that's just what he wanted.

Nicol's willingness to stand alone – his intransigent integrity – most impressed Leslie Megahey:

He was, in the *Reader's Digest* phrase, the most unforgettable character I ever met because he was so much true to himself. And that trueness necessarily meant he let others down from time to time, and it seemed, unrepentantly. He inspired, but also sometimes offended and hurt others. Yet there was something magnificent about someone so true to their lights. The rest is to do with whatever private dreams he had that went unfulfilled, and whatever private demons he might have had. Who can tell the mysteries of the human heart, etc? And the

demons were, to my mind then and now, genuinely private ones and entirely
his own business.

Megahey, who knew Nicol better than most colleagues in show business – and so
perhaps is entitled to the last word – believed there was something unreachable,
even profoundly solitary about Nicol. Not just in the physical sense but in his
refusal to compromise:

> I draw your attention to Ken Tynan's essay about him. Tynan says that Nicol
> is living proof against John Donne's belief that 'no man is an island, entire of
> itself'. Well, wrote Tynan, and I finally agree with him, Nic was his own island.

NOTES

Chapter 1

1 'My family is Norwegian Scots', Nicol once told an interviewer. 'There's no English blood. We're like the old Vikings, all born with the silver fair hair which darkens and darkens and darkens.' Interview with Mervyn Rothstein, *New York Times*, 15 April 1991.

2 President Woodrow Wilson (1856–1924).

3 Ruth Etting, American singing star and actress (1897–1978).

4 *Not* 1938 as so many obituaries had it.

5 *The Day the Music Died* by Tony Garnett.

6 Curtain to Rise On Lighter Side of Nicol Williamson, *Los Angeles Times*, 19 August 1986.

7 Sir Rodney Marshall Sabine Pasley, 4th Bt (1899–1982).

8 Entry on Birmingham History Forum.

9 Author's interviews with Tony Croft, May 2017.

10 Poem sent courtesy of Nicol's friend Tony Croft.

11 Kenneth Tynan, English theatre critic and writer (1927–1980).

12 Edward Fox once said of this period, 'I feel desperately sorry for the young actors of today without repertory theatres to train in. They have no option but to try to get into television straightaway. All you could do in my day was go into repertory. It was so wonderful – no state subsidies, no Arts Council support. You had to learn to entertain the audience, to get them to sit there. One was probably terrible most of the time, but the company feeling was tremendous. You learnt that the audience expect to see a persona on a stage. They need to be magnetised.'

13 Letter from Edward Fox to the author, 7 August 2017.

14   The company was housed in Foresters' Hall (6 Nicoll Street to 3 Rattray Street).
15   Gawn Grainger, actor, born 1937.
16   Author's interviews with Brian Cox, 19 January 2017 and 27 May 2017. Some of these comments were also published on Luke Williamson's tribute website to his father.
17   Author's interview with Kate Binchy, 23 May 2017.
18   The part of Frank Machin in *This Sporting Life* went to Richard Harris (1930–2002).
19   Author's interview with Peter Gill, 25 May 2017.

Chapter 2

1   Al Bowlly (1898–1941), South African/British singer, songwriter, composer and band leader.
2   Author's interview with Sally Alexander, 8 May 2017.
3   *The Two of Us* by Sheila Hancock.
4   Author's interview with Trevor Nunn, 21 June 2017.
5   The director was David Scase (1919–2003).
6   *Serves Me Right* by Sarah Miles.
7   *Arthur Lowe* by Graham Lord.
8   Letter to *The Times* from Patrick Phillips QC, 2 February 2012, after Nicol's death.
9   Author's interview with Brian Blessed, 3 March 2017.
10   Arthur Askey (1900–1982), diminutive British comedian and actor.
11   *Tales I Never Told!* by film director Michael Winner (1935–2013).

Chapter 3

1   Letter to the *Guardian* from William Gaskill, 29 January 2012. William Gaskill (1930–2016).
2   John Osborne (1929–1994): *Looking Back: Never Explain, Never Apologise*.
3   Author's interview with Peter Gill, 22 March 2017.
4   Beuselinck (1919–1997) was a business and media lawyer who was also Nicol's lawyer for a time. He was described as 'a randy, abusive, brilliant

tyrant who made most people laugh and some cry' – at least in the perception of strangers – in his obituary in the *Guardian*, 30 July 1997. Beuselinck once paid tribute to Nicol's powers of mimicry. 'Even today I cannot think of Tony Richardson or John Osborne without recalling Nicol's rendering of their voices. The impersonation has usurped the original.' He attended Nicol's wedding to Jill in 1971.

5   Stephen Frears recalls, 'One day Peter Gill said there was a girl in the *Daily Mirror* who'd just made her first record and would be very good as Nicol Williamson's daughter in *Inadmissible Evidence*. The girl auditioned (for the non-speaking part), got the job, came to the read-through; her name was Marianne Faithfull. That week her record went up seven places in the charts. We went down to the ABC Café in Kingsway (next to the Thames Television studio where she was recording *Ready Steady Go*) and Andrew Loog Oldham, her manager, explained the facts of life. Money was never any help at the Court. Leading actors got 30 pounds a week. Olivier got 50 pounds for Archie Rice.'

   Sheila Hancock was another actress who declined a part in *Inadmissible Evidence*, according to her autobiography.

6   Alan Brien (1925–2008).
7   Author's interview with Roland Jaquarello, 10 April 2017.
8   From Paul Sidey's blog.
9   Letter from John Osborne to Richard Eyre when Eyre was mounting a revival of *Inadmissible Evidence* in 1993.
10 Author's interview with Natasha Pyne, 6 April 2017.
11 Eleanor Fazan quoted in *The Scotsman*, 27 January 2012.
12 *The Grand Surprise: The Journals of Leo Lerman*, diary entry dated 4 October 1964.
13 *Looking Back* by John Osborne.
14 George Devine (1910–1966).
15 *The Royal Court Theatre and the Modern Stage* by Philip Roberts.
16 *Untold Stories* by Alan Bennett.
17 Patrick Magee (1924–1982), one of Beckett's favoured interpreters and most famous for *Krapp's Last Tape*.
18 Lindsay Anderson's Diaries.
19 Author's interview with Glenda Jackson, 20 April 2017.
20 *The Day of Ragnarok* (BBC2, 2 January 1965) together with Exit 19 (BBC2, 8 August 1966) were screened in a double bill as part of the *Forgotten Dramas* season at BFI Southbank on 22 February 2017.

21 In Philadelphia Nicol liked to frequent Frankie Bradley's restaurant. One patron, writing in 2012, recalled, 'On the way out of the restaurant, we ran into Nicol Williamson with an attractive lady on his arm. He was dressed all in white – pants, jacket, shirt, shoes. I can see him as vividly now as I did 47 years ago. We told him how much we enjoyed his performance. It was truly a tour de force. He graciously thanked us, signed our programmes, and went into Frankie Bradley's restaurant.' From Selma's *Views*.

22 *Fading into the Limelight: The Autobiography* by Peter Sallis (1921–2017).

23 *Looking Back: Never Explain, Never Apologise* by John Osborne (1929–1994).

24 David Merrick (1911–2000), nicknamed 'the abominable showman' had famously, in 1980, withheld news of the death of Gower Champion, the director of musical *42nd Street*, until curtain call on opening night. According to Merrick's obituary in the *New York Times*, 'the show's notoriety and success were assured, but an ugly aftertaste lingered'.

25 As recounted to Kenneth Tynan. But it seems that Nicol did, in fact, forgive Page because they worked together on a revival of *Inadmissible Evidence* in New York in 1981.

26 The story goes that someone once remarked of Labour cabinet minister Herbert Morrison that he was his own worst enemy, and Bevin immediately butted in to say, 'Not while I'm alive, he ain't'. One suspects that this could have applied to Nicol Williamson.

27 Interview with Lionel Larner, 13 April 2017.

28 Frank Tours (1877–1963).

29 Donald Sumpter, actor, born 1943.

30 Author's extensive interviews with Jill Townsend-Sorel, April–June 2017.

31 *The Stage*, 16 February 1967.

32 Retrieved from an account by Vivienne Griffiths in University of Sussex bulletin, 1992.

33 Identity unknown, but certainly *not* Jill Townsend.

34 Author's interview with Vivienne Griffiths, 18 May 2017.

35 *Illustrated London News*.

36 Probably *The Offence*, later made with Sean Connery in the lead, a traumatic psychological study of a policeman's breakdown, directed by Sidney Lumet.

37 Author's interview with Ted Kotcheff, 6 January 2017.

38 Author's interview with George Segal, 18 January 2017.

39 Letter to Luke Williamson, published on his tribute to Nicol.

Chapter 4

1 Jack Gold (1930–2015). In addition to their five screen collaborations, *The Bofors Gun*, *The Reckoning*, *The Resistible Rise of Arturo Ui*, *Macbeth*, and *Sakharov*, Gold also wanted Nicol to play the part of Morlar in *The Medusa Touch*, the film eventually made with Richard Burton in 1977. Burton was deemed more 'bankable' at the time.

2 John McGrath (1935–2002). The play, written in 1966, was based on his own experiences in National Service.

3 *Shut It – The Inside Story of The Sweeney* by Pat Gilbert.

4 *Once a Villain* – a memoir by Peter Vaughan (1923–2016).

5 Letter to the *Guardian* from Jack Gold after Nicol's death, 26 January 2012.

6 Interview taken from David Warner's website.

7 Letter to the *Guardian* from Richard Norton-Taylor and Simon Hattenstone, following Barry Jackson's death, 10 December 2013.

8 *Acting My Life* by Ian Holm.

9 Quoted from Nicol's conversations with Kenneth Tynan, as recorded in the critic's *New Yorker* profile of Nicol.

10 Interview with Ingrid Boulting, 12 October 2016.

11 *Frost on Saturday*. This episode aired on 30 November 1968. David Frost (1939–2013).

12 *Rewrites* by Neil Simon.

Chapter 5

1 Peter Bowles offers his account of what had happened in his autobiography, *Ask Me If I'm Happy*, as related to him by Richardson. 'He (Richardson) told me with great sadness in his voice that when he was alone with Burton, he had asked him to apologise, not to him, not at all to him, about anything, but to his fellow cast members he had kept waiting for three hours. (The scene had included Sian Phillips, and other actors besides myself.) Burton had pointedly refused. "Fuck off" I think Tony told me he'd replied and Tony therefore felt he had to tell Burton he was no longer on the picture – otherwise his position would have been totally undermined. However, Tony told me he had gone to see Burton that evening on the boat to patch things up and felt he had succeeded. Then Burton changed his mind and that was that.'

2   *The Richard Burton Diaries*, edited by Chris Williams. 'The fact that I was
    right about *Laughter* and he was shown to be catastrophically wrong should
    have made him even more shy in approaching me for anything else ever
    again as my attitude to him in any future co-labour would be savagely
    contemptuous … everyone is convinced that his good films have been
    accidents and that his bad ones are just a reflection of his abysmal talent.'
        Footage of Burton's first few days' filming on *Laughter in the Dark* was
    eventually retrieved and first shown at the Bradford Film Festival in 2002.
3   *Ask Me if I'm Happy* by Peter Bowles.
4   In other words, the re-shooting of the same scene that had featured
    Richard Burton.
5   Interviews with Philippa Urquhart, 15 September 2016 and 21 March
    2017. Urquhart adds: 'Many years later I was in a play in the West End of
    London with Richardson's daughter Joely. I talked with her about my
    involvement with *Laughter in the Dark*, and she said, rather gravely, that
    sacking Burton had finished her father's career as a film director.'
6   Glen Kenny's interview with Anna Karina in the *New York Times*, 4 May
    2016.
7   Author's interview with Tom Kempinski, 1 March 2017.
8   *English Bull* by Pauline Kael (1919–2001) – *The New Yorker*, 17 January
    1970.
9   Penelope Gilliatt (1932–1993).

Chapter 6

1   Shelia Hancock wrote in her autobiography, *The Two of Us*, that 'Nicol
    Williamson and Richard Burton, between the two of them, virtually
    patented a whole new aggressive style for approaching Shakespeare's
    language, hitherto hostage to the elocution of genteel versifiers.' Yet, to
    judge from excerpts of Burton's performance, his interpretation was still far
    more 'poetic' than Nicol's.
2   From the audio recording of *Jack* – Nicol Williamson's one-man show from
    1996.
3   Professor Nigel Krauth, head of the writing programme at Griffith
    University, wrote that he believed Nicol had succeeded in illuminating the
    text. 'I didn't understand Shakespeare until I saw Nicol Williamson play
    Hamlet. My Australian education insisted I read Hamlet's "What a piece

of work is man" speech as if delivered by Sir Laurence Olivier – nobly, admiringly, a celebration. But a celebration of what? British colonialism? British class structure? British limited perception? … Shakespeare shows here how unimpressed he was with humanity. He also delivers a great lesson about not reading the sentence to its end. He meant the sentence that begins "What a piece of work is man" to be delivered with the spitting, defeated, abhorrent, fuck-the-lot-of-you-and-thanks-for-nothing attitude that Williamson wonderfully gave it.'

4   *A Story Lately Told: Coming of Age in London, Ireland and New York* by Anjelica Huston.

5   *Faithfull* by Marianne Faithfull and David Dalton.

6   Kevin Brownlow quoted in the book *The Cinema of Tony Richardson: Essay and Interviews*.

7   Richardson quoted in *There's Nothing Like A Dane* – edited by Clive Francis.

8   Speaking in 1994, Nicol expressed his admiration for Annis. 'I think Francesca Annis knocks Helen Mirren into a cocked hat. Francesca is the best lady around. She is good. I tell you, she is good.' Cited in *The Herald*, 18 June 1994.

9   Nicol's habit of walking off, or talking to the audience, was also noted by Ian Holm in his autobiography. 'Nicol had a method all of his own for dealing with nerves, rarely allowing them to get the better of him, and sometimes just saying to the audience. "I'm sorry, ladies and gentlemen, I'm not very good tonight."'

10 Letter to *The Times*, 2 February 2012. Patrick Wymark (1926–1970).

11 Letter from W. Cunliffe to *The Stage*, 26 June 1969.

12 Letter from Lesley Denny to *The Stage*, 3 July 1969.

13 Ted Kalem (1920–1985).

14 Walter Kerr (1913–1996).

15 *Up in the Cheap Seats* by Ron Fassler.

16 Taken from Luke Williamson's tribute site on his father.

17 Luke, however, recalls that Nicol was a great fan of Guinness, praising his performances in the movie *The Ladykillers* and also *Murder by Death*.

Chapter 7

1   Eric Porter was cast as Enobarbus instead.

2   Author's interview with Ro Diamond, 1 May 2017.

3   Nicol later commented that a bejewelled socialite at the White House had told him that he had played Willy Loman, the tragic protagonist of *Death of a Salesman*, 'very well – for a limey'. Nicol just said he replied '"thank you very much" because, after all, I couldn't equal the bang with which she let herself down'.

4   Bob Haggart (1914–1998), Dixieland double bass jazz player who co-led The World's Greatest Jazz Band, an all-star jazz ensemble active from 1968 to 1978.

5   *The Best Gig in Town: Jazz Artists at the White House, 1969–1974* by Edward Allan Faine.

6   *You Don't Look Like a Musician* by Bud Freeman (1906–1991).

7   'Vamping with Nora' by Dick Cavett in the *New York Times*, 29 June 2012. Nicol's agent Lionel Larner remembers Nicol's previous appearance on the Dick Cavett Show in which he discussed the possibility of having a daughter. Nicol, somewhat inebriated, said that 'she'd probably look just like her mother and then I'd be the first to slip it in'. If Cavett is to be believed, he had had several run-ins with Nicol, including a dangerous late-night swimming escapade. His wife came to Nicol's rescue. 'He was bombed one night and decided to go swimming in a dangerous cove and she went in and pulled him out. I held the light. We'd all been to several waterfront bars and someone thought it would be cute to go swimming in the pitch dark, which is a stupid thing to do in the ocean. You can lose a cherished part of your anatomy, either to a rock or to an irritated sea-dwelling creature. Suddenly, there was Broadway's current Hamlet, who swims like a lead piano, foundering in the briny. I grabbed a flashlight and ordered my wife into the water – she swims and dives like a porpoise – assuring her I'd run for help if she got in trouble. She hauled him out and earned the unwitting gratitude of many a theatregoer. I ran to the house and made hot tea for myself, having caught a chill from the cold flashlight.'

8   Troy Kennedy Martin (1932–2009) had originally wanted Nicol to play the part of Mr Bridger in *The Italian Job* but the director, Peter Collinson, offered the part to Noël Coward instead, resulting in a very different character.

9   *John Flynn: Out For Action* by Harvey F. Chartrand.

10   Author's interview with Jill Townsend-Sorel, 12 March 2012. This was an interview for my biography of Ian Hendry.

11   Author's interview with Daria Halprin, 8 March 2017.

12   When the club opened in 1967, a double-page spread in the *Evening Standard* asked, 'Are you one of the beautiful people? Simple test: Can

you get in to the dell'Aretusa?' The establishment attracted diners such as Princess Margaret, Sammy Davis Jr, David Bailey and Twiggy.

13   Buñuel hoped to cast either Omar Sharif or Alain Delon as Ambrosio, while Jeanne Moreau was set to play Matilda and Michel Piccoli was signed up to play the Grand Inquisitor. But disagreement between the film's two producers led to the collapse of the project. In 1972 Buñuel and friend and fellow surrealist Ado Kyrou were able to finance a film starring Nero, Delon, and Nicol, which screenwriter Jean-Claude Carrière observed 'was very different and not very successful'.

14   According to Garnett, 'I thought it a long shot, but to my surprise he (Sellers) accepted, inviting Jack and me to see him in Ireland, where he lived for tax reasons. We were hospitably received, given lunch and then he talked interestingly about the play, which he had clearly thought about. He acted some of it to us, brilliantly. We weren't surprised by his accurate American accent but the focus, the rage he brought to the Hitler character impressed us. This was our warning, but neither of us realised it. We shook hands and left in high spirits.

Soon after I realised it was slipping away. He couldn't be reached. His agent told me that he had changed his mind. It occurred to me that the minuscule BBC fee might have put both him and his agent off the idea. But the fact was he had done it. He had acted the part out to us and we had loved it and praised it. He had already played Arturo, in his mind. Why go through weeks of it for little pay? Move on. Perhaps a film start date had suddenly become more concrete.'

Another possibility was Leonard Rossiter (1926–1984) who had created the part in the West End to great acclaim.

15   Author's interview with Tony Garnett, 16 February 2017.

16   *Snapshots: Encounters With Twentieth-Century Legends* by Herbert Kretzmer.

Chapter 8

1   During the run of *Plaza Suite* actress Maureen Stapleton had confided to director Mike Nichols that she was frightened of George C. Scott. Nichols's reply became one of the most famous quotes about any actor, 'Darling, the whole world is terrified of George!'

2 'Vanya Stars Tie Success to Nichols' by Mel Gussow in the *New York Times*, 18 June 1973.

3 *Rage and Glory: The Volatile Life of George C. Scott* by David Sheward.

4 Richard Burton's daughter, Kate, who became an actress, recalls this production as especially memorable. 'I think I was about 15 years old when I saw Nicol Williamson and George C. Scott do *Uncle Vanya* at Circle in the Square, and I thought it was incredible.' Quoted in *Theatre Mania*, 7 January 2007.

5 *Watch Me: A Memoir* by Anjelica Huston.

6 Author's interview with Tony Walton, 26 April 2017.

7 *New York Times*, 18 June 1973.

8 *Julie Christie* by Tim Ewbank and Stafford Hildred.

9 Author's interview with Tony Osoba, 10 November 2016.

10 Oscar James quoted in *The Independent*, 5 June 1993.

11 Author's interview with Tony Rowlands, 4 June 2017. (Janet Suzman, cited here by Tony Rowlands, was married to Trevor Nunn between 1969 and 1986.)

12 Author's interview with Sir Trevor Nunn, 21 June 2017.

13 'Actors prolong this moment for as long as they can manage, gauging its length each night by audience response. The longest seems to have been Nicol Williamson (RSC, 1973), who paused for 60 seconds before he stretched out his hand, then was able to hold the silence for an incredible 90 seconds more before he finally sobbed out "Oh mother, *mother* … what … have … you … DONE?" giving each word "like a pint of blood", according to Alan Brien.' Quoted in *The Tragedy of Coriolanus*, edited by R.B. Parker.

14 *Middle-earth Envisioned: The Hobbit and The Lord of the Rings: On Screen, On Stage, and Beyond* by Paul Simpson and Brian J. Robb.

15 Luke Williamson's tribute website to his father.

16 Author's interview with Peter Gill, 15 March 2017.

17 Ian Holm was another actor who mentioned these two in the same breath. 'And although I consider myself to be a reasonably brave actor, I have to do it from a secure position, unlike people such as Nicol Williamson and Victor Henry.'

18 *In the Frame: My Life in Words and Pictures* by Helen Mirren.

19 *The Two of Us* by Sheila Hancock.

20 Buzz Goodbody, stage director and the RSC's first female director, (1946–1975). Goodbody committed suicide four days into the run of Ben Kingsley's acclaimed *Hamlet*. These articles chart her rise and fall:

www.telegraph.co.uk/theatre/what-to-see/how-a-decrepit-tin-hut
transformed-the-rsc-buzz-goodbody-and-the/ www.theguardian.com/
stage/2014/jun/11/buzz-goodbody-other-place-royal-
shakespearecompany

21   *Something Sensational to Read in the Train: The Diary of a Lifetime* by Gyles
      Brandreth (born 1948) writer, broadcaster and former Member of
      Parliament.

22   From article by Phil Ball in *When Saturday Comes.*
      Another (uncorroborated) story from Nicol's run as Macbeth at Stratford
      related how a theatregoer was following Nicol's performance, reading
      with a penlight from his own collected works of Shakespeare. When Nicol
      seemed to forget a line the theatregoer started ostentatiously clapping.
      Nicol stopped the scene and addressed the man: 'Alright, dammit, give me
      the line, you ass …'

23   Interview with Jack Gold in *The Stage*, 31 December 1975.

24   Denis Healey's description of Nixon in his autobiography *The Time of My Life.*

25   Author's interview with Shane Rimmer, 7 February 2017.

Chapter 9

1   Nicol's name was once invoked during an interview with Jay Bernstein
     about stardom. 'A star is someone that people care about. For example, is
     Elizabeth Taylor married? Is Tom Cruise married? These people are stars
     that we care about as people and people want to know about them. Is John
     Travolta married? You have an idea but if I asked if Robert Loggia, or Roy
     Scheider, or Nicol Williamson was married, you wouldn't know. That's the
     difference between a star and a fine actor. There are many fine actors, but
     only a few stars.'
        Perhaps Bernstein meant that 'stars' had a certain sex appeal, or more
     simply, projected a certain screen personality that created an intimacy with
     their audiences.
        Cited in *Creating Television: Conversations with the People Behind 50 Years of
     American TV* by Robert Kubey.

2   *Sir Michael Caine* by William Hall.

3   Nicol sometimes did newspaper interviews but it seems that he was
     increasingly drawn to a sing-song. Journalist Conrad Wilson recalls,
     'Then there was the edgy Nicol Williamson, a great, raucous actor, much

encouraged by Kenneth Tynan, whom I had seen several times and greatly admired. Again we met in a pub – he was a hearty drinker – and he came home for something to eat and further conversation.

   In later years, in America, he would build a big reputation. But he had spent his prentice period with the Dundee Rep and had plenty to say – and, it transpired, to sing. Spotting my grand piano, he sat down at the keyboard and spent the rest of the evening performing pop songs and music hall ditties. It was all very merry and I got my article.' From Conrad Wilson's blog.

4   *The Authorised Biography of Ronnie Barker* by Bob McCabe.
5   John Osborne's diaries noted Nicol's reaction to Shaw's passing, aged just 51, in 1978. 'I broke the news to Nicol Williamson, who was staying in my house, as I took him his breakfast. He paled. He had an envious respect for Shaw's commercial stardom and his athletic drunken ambition. He proceeded to execute a persuasive mime of the manner of his death.'
6   *Audrey Hepburn* by Barry Parris.
7   *The Private Life of Sherlock Holmes* starred Robert Stephens and Colin Blakely.
8   The part of Guthrie eventually went to Robert Carradine in the film directed by Hal Ashby.
9   Interview with Nicholas Meyer, 24 January 2017.
10   *Sherlock Holmes and Conan Doyle: Multi-Media Afterlives* edited by Sabine Vanacker, Catherine Wynne.
11   This was an interview Jill Townsend gave to the *Guardian*, 3 February 2015.
12   *People, Who's Afraid of Nicol Williamson? Everyone but His Spouse*, Jill Townsend, 5 April 1976.
13   *The Richard Rodgers Reader* by Geoffrey Block.
14   *Snapshots: Encounters with Twentieth-Century Legends* by Herbert Kretzmer.
15   *Somewhere for Me: A Biography of Richard Rodgers* by Meryle Secrest.
16   Penny Fuller quoted in *Show and Tell: The New Book of Broadway Anecdotes* by Ken Bloom.
17   Penny Fuller interview with Rabbi Sol Solomon, 20 February 2016.
18   *McQueen: The Biography* by Christopher Sandford.
19   Author's interviews with Carolyn Seymour, 25 October 2016, 16 March 2017. Seymour, I should hasten to add, has since stopped drinking.
20   From Luke Williamson's tribute site to his father.
21   *This Way to Paradise: Dancing on the Tables* by Willard Manus.

Chapter 10

1   Quoted in the *New York Times* on 10 May 1981 in an article by Michael Billington – 'The Theatre That Sparked a Revolution'.

2   *The Royal Court Theatre and the Modern Stage* by Philip Roberts.

3   Quoted in a review of *Ming's Kingdom*, published in *The Spectator*, 23 March 1996.

4   Quote from a passage in an unpublished autobiography by Clive Swift, granted to the author.

5   Author's interview with Julie Peasgood, 8 January 2017.

6   Ironically, someone (by the name of Keith Norman) had written in to *The Stage* to complain that the court ruling would steer Nicol towards the dreaded 'box'. Norman wrote, 'I fear that Nicol Williamson may not be able to exercise his enormous talents in serious drama on the stage. He will probably be reduced to appearing in a TV series to earn some money.' This proved to be true. Letter dated 9 November 1978.

7   *Finding Peter: A True Story of the Hand of Providence and Evidence of Life After Death* by William Peter Blatty.

8   Anthony Hopkins quoted in *Review* magazine, August 1986.

9   *Punch* magazine. *Just Williamson*, 18 July 1979.

10 *The World and its Double: The Life and Work of Otto Preminger* by Chris Fujiwara.

11 *As Luck Would Have It* by Derek Jacobi.

12 *Vicar to Dad's Army: The Frank Williams Story* by Frank Williams and Chris Gidney.

13 *Travels in Greeneland: The Complete Guide to the Cinema of Graham Greene* by Quentin Falk.

14 *Otto Preminger: Still Making Movies the Hard Way* by Bart Mills in *The Washington Post*, 3 February 1980.

15 *Otto Preminger: The Man Who Would Be King* by Foster Hirsch.

16 *Travels in Greeneland: The Complete Guide to the Cinema of Graham Greene* by Quentin Falk.

17 Bruce Forsyth (1928–2017) – happy-go-lucky British TV presenter, most famous, back in the seventies, as a game show host.

Chapter 11

1   *In the Frame: My Life in Words and Pictures* by Helen Mirren.
2   An interview with Paul Geoffrey – *The Neon Rewind*.
3   From Alex Epstein's blog.
4   John Thaw's *This is Your Life*, broadcast 18 March 1981.
5   Author's interview with Anthony Heald, 28 November 2016.
6   Richard Harris apparently felt the same way about McKellen, describing him – and Kenneth Branagh and Derek Jacobi – as 'technically brilliant but passionless'.
7   Author's interview with Elaine Bromka, 6 October 2016.
8   *Behind the Curtain: The Job of Acting* by Peter Bowles.
9   As McEnroe admitted in his autobiography, *Serious*, in what read like an attempt to explain his bad behaviour.
10 *The Kokomo Tribune*, 6 July 1969.
11 Quote by John Calder from Nicol's obituary in *The Independent*, 26 January 2012.
12 Author's interview with Jeanne Ruskin, 12 October 2016.
13 Nicol Williamson interview in the *New York Times*, 20 March 1981.
14 Frank Rich's review appeared in the *New York Times* on 24 February 1981.
15 Actor Sam Dastor, on the set of *Mountbatten – The Last Viceroy*, recalls Nicol asking him out of the blue whether he had ever worked with Klaus Kinski. Dastor shook his head. Nicol replied, 'He's a cunt.'
16 *Bolt from the Blue* by Sarah Miles.

Chapter 12

1   Author's interview with Rand Bridges, 22 March 2017.
2   Author's interview with Ray Dooley, 14 October 2016.
3   In 1986, Weaver, in an interview, added, 'I consider myself quite lucky I was fired because I would probably have stayed until the bitter end.'
4   Author's interview with Tara Hugo, 17 November 2016.
5   Frank Rich, the chief drama critic of the *New York Times* between 1980 and 1994, became known for his alleged undue influence over the fate of certain Broadway productions. His reputation grew to such an extent that by 1989, for example, when Paul Libin was producing director at the Circle in the Square, Libin made an impassioned plea after a performance

of Joshua Sobol's controversial play *Ghetto* to the effect that 'Frank Rich's negative review would have the effect of a death knell for the play'. In his review Rich had written that '*Ghetto* is almost perverse in its ability to make the true nightmare of our century ring completely false'.

So Libin said that 'if they liked the play, they should call six friends (that night) to come and see it. One man does not have the right to close down a play.' Libin's plea didn't work and the play closed after one month.

Yet, according to some writers who monitored his reviews, 'A read through of Frank Rich's reviews … reveals him as the highly intelligent, discerning and knowledgeable writer a demanding editor like Arthur Gelb would have required for the person succeeding Walter Kerr … the quality of his writing could lead one to suspect that readers of his reviews came to trust his judgements and hence his influence grew – to the detriment of shows he didn't assess very highly. He did not become influential because he was unreasonable, outrageous or grandstanding.' From *Observing Theatre: Spirituality and Subjectivity in the Arts*.

6 Author's interview with Andrea (Dreya) Weber, 5 December 2016. This was the only comment that she was prepared to give about their relationship.
7 Interview with Louise Penn, 24 April 2017.
8 Author's interview with David Rabe, 26 October 2016.

Chapter 13

1 Author's interview with Keith Reddin, 4 November 2016.
2 Joseph H. Shoctor (1922–2001).
3 Rand Bridges was apparently Nicol's first choice but he had to decline because of a prior commitment. 'He called me up and said: "Bridges, would you like to come with me to Edmonton?" I was dying to but I had already signed up to another play.'
4 Author's interview with Luciano Iogna, 18 November 2016.
5 Retrieved from a letter written to Luke Williamson's tribute website to his father.
6 Interview with Walter Murch on *Film Freak Central*.

Chapter 14

1   Author's interviews with Janet Suzman, 15 October 2016 and 7 February
    2017.
2   Author's interview with Sam Dastor, 11 October 2016.
3   Nicol Williamson interview in the *Sunday Times*, 30 December 1984.
4   Author's interview with Lady Pamela Hicks, Lord Mountbatten's daughter,
    14 October 2016.
5   Quoted in *Alistair Cooke: A Biography* by Nick Clarke.
6   Author's interview with Laila Robins, 4 October 2016.
7   Entry on Mobius Home Video Forum by Anne Bobby's friend Ian
    McDowell.
8   Author's interview with Bruce Boxleitner, 7 February 2017.
9   Interview with Debra Winger, the *New York Times*, 6 July 1986.
10 Author's interview with Bob Rafelson, 25 January 2017.
11 This little masterstroke of invention, in line with Nicol's injunction about
    acting to 'show, show, show', reminds us of something Nicol once said
    to Kenneth Tynan, 'Some people can remember rational processes of
    argument. I can't. What I do remember, after ten or fifteen years, is exactly
    how a man fiddled with a matchbox while he was talking.'

Chapter 15

1   *I Hit Hamlet* by Paul Rudnick, published in *The New Yorker*, December
    2007.
2   Author's interview with Marianne Velmans, 31 October 2016.
3   From the late Paul Sidey's blog and website.
4   Review published 23 March 1996.
5   Fanny Blake in *The Independent* reviewed the book thus, 'In his first
    novel actor Nicol Williamson ably demonstrates that making the switch
    to another medium is not always easy. His hero Rick, a successful actor,
    marries a woman who defines many a male fantasy – beautiful face,
    stunning body, great in the sack and an apparent brain by-pass. So devoted
    is she to the temple that is her body she breaks off her wedding lunch to
    go for a "twat-splitting" workout. The sex is hot and graphically described:
    "The thermodynamic and his heat-seeking missile locked in their
    timebomb quickstep by death." And even when she pees, "Jesus, what an

awesome little turbine". But Adrienne is increasingly absent from her new husband and surrounds herself with her grotesque family and friends. Why doesn't Rick cotton on sooner to the fact they're using him? It's hard to feel anything for so many characters who need a good shake.'

6   Ricardo Franco directed this tale of love in a wintry Berlin. Nicol was to have played the part of Professor Huessler. His part was inherited by Keith Baxter.

7   Author's interview with Robert Bierman, 23 January 2017.

Chapter 16

1   *I Hit Hamlet*, Paul Rudnick's article in *The New Yorker*, 24 December 2007.

2   Author's interview with Tara Hugo, 17 November 2016.

3   Adam Arkin interview with Bonnie Churchill on CNN, 3 October 1997.

4   Nicol Williamson's interview with Mervyn Rothstein, 'What Its Star Dislikes About I Hate Hamlet,' *New York Times*, 15 April 1991.

5   Nicol also told Rothstein, 'Who cares, anyway? Someone once tried to find out how old Cary Grant was and sent him a wire that read, "How old Cary Grant?" And Grant sent back a message saying, "Old Cary Grant fine; how you?" So I think you should say: "How old Nicol Williamson? Old Nicol Williamson fine. How you?"'

6   Author's interview with Tony Osoba, 11 October 2016.

7   Interview with Elaine Stritch, 'The World According to Elaine Stritch', *New York Times*, 11 April 1993.

8   From article in the *New York Times*, 4 May 1991.

9   Interview with Jane Adams in *Theater Week Magazine*, June 1994.

10 Craig Wolff, in a *New York Times* article of 22 June 1991, wrote of the final night, 'Mr Williamson stopped the applause and said, "Ladies and gentleman, you know we're closing tomorrow. Shows don't usually end like that. Usually you go out with a smattering of people. You don't go out jam-packed." As his co-star, Celeste Holm, and the other cast members looked on a bit awkwardly, Mr Williamson chided the nominating procedure for Tonys that he felt had slighted the play. He then gave a dramatic reading of an article from yesterday's *New York Times* about changes in the nominating procedure. He had bitter words, also, for the emphasis on the business side of the profession, and used the Irving Berlin song *There's No Business Like Show Business* to make his point.'

Chapter 17

1   Gone to Ground – Article on Nicol Williamson in The Independent, 5 June 1993, by Robert Butler.

2   Of this revival, Michael Billington wrote, 'Nicol Williamson, great actor that he is, always had the lineaments of an extraordinary human being. Mr Eve is more like your next door neighbour falling apart before your very eyes.'

3   *John Osborne: A Casebook* by Patricia D. Denison.

4   *Acting My Life* by Ian Holm.

5   Comments Luke, 'Nicol didn't want to dazzle. He wanted to immolate.'

6   Lovell is incorrect. Nicol had acted with Schroder in *Apt Pupil*, the film that was aborted due to financial problems. It's possible that this revived bad memories for Nicol.

7   Comments by actor and producer Dyson Lovell in an interview in November 2012 with John Alan Simon.

8   Author's interview with Sally Greene, 10 May 2017.

9   Bernard Levin's article for *The Times* was called 'A Man For All Mankind' – June 1994. Bernard Levin (1928–2004).

10   Beryl Bainbridge quoted in *Front Row: Evenings at the Theatre*.

11   Author's interview with Saskia Wickham, 23 January 2017.

12   Author's interview with Laura Cella, 18 April 2017. Excerpt taken from her blog. https://laurastalesfromtwocities.com/

13   'Arts, Cries and Whispers', *The Independent,* 9 July 1994.

14   From Luke Williamson's tribute website to his father.

15   Playwrights hadn't finished with the Barrymore legend. The following year Christopher Plummer starred in a play called *Barrymore*, written by William Luce, which depicted Barrymore a few months before his death. Nicol apparently told a fellow drinker (Sharlene Springer who had been a neighbour of his in the city's Chelsea Apartments) that he thought the production was 'tame' when they met in a New York bar.

16   Author's interview with John Goldstone, 14 March 2017.

17   Letter to *The Times*, 2 February 2012.

18   Todd McFarlane, born 1961, Canadian cartoonist and entrepreneur.

Chapter 18

1   From Luke Williamson's tribute site to his father.
2   Luke thinks that Nicol was probably heading to a restaurant called Mirabelle.
3   Sheila Hancock also wrote in *The Two of Us*, 'Nicol was in London when John died' – January 2002 – 'and it was in all the papers. He had lunch with one of their mutual friends but never mentioned John's death'.
4   Nicol once told reporter Mervyn Rothstein that, while in New York, he spent most of his time on the West Side of Manhattan. 'I won't go to the East Side. I love the jungle.'
5   From Luke Williamson's website tribute to his father.
6   From *Performing King Lear: Gielgud to Russell Beale* by Jonathan Croall.
7   Charles Spencer review in *The Daily Telegraph*, 22 February 2001.

Chapter 19

1   Richard Harris's family lobbied to have his close friend Peter O'Toole take over the role of Dumbledore but the part went to Michael Gambon.
2   Stephen Lyons, who kept a website about Lindos, wrote in 2009, 'Should you recognise former actor Nicol Williamson in the village I advise you not to approach him as you are likely to get a rude response. He clearly wants to be left well alone so, please, keep clear of him.' Lyons, a fellow actor, recalls approaching Nicol in Sinatra's Bar and Restaurant in Lindos and getting short shrift. This could be the same incident to which Luke referred.
3   Author's interview with Stephen Lyons, 18 May 2017.

Chapter 20

1   *Punch* profile, 18 July 1979.
2   Michael Coveney in *What's On Stage*, 26 January 2012.
3   *The Daily Express*, 7 March 2012.
4   *The Daily Telegraph*, 26 January 2012.
5   From Luke Williamson's website tribute to his father.

BIBLIOGRAPHY

Bainbridge, Beryl, *Front Row: Evenings at the Theatre* (Continuum; New edition, 2006)

Bennett, Alan, *Untold Stories* (Faber & Faber; Main edition, 2006)

Blatty, William Peter, *Finding Peter: A True Story of the Hand of Providence and Evidence of Life After Death* (Regnery Publishing Inc., 2015)

Block, Geoffrey, *The Richard Rodgers Reader* (Scolars Press, 2002)

Bloom, Ken, *Show and Tell: The New Book of Broadway Anecdotes* (Oxford University Press, 2016)

Bowles, Peter, *Ask Me If I'm Happy* (Simon & Schuster UK, 2010)

Bowles, Peter, *The Job of Acting* (Oberon Books, 2012)

Brandreth, Gyles, *Something Sensational to Read in the Train: The Diary of a Lifetime* (Hodder Paperbacks, 2012)

Clarke, Nick, *Alistair Cooke: A Biography* (Weidenfeld and Nicolson; 3rd Impression edition, 1999)

Croall, Jonathan, *Performing King Lear: Gielgud to Russell Beale* (Arden Shakespeare, 2015)

Denison, Patricia, *John Osborne: A Casebook* (Routledge, 2015)

Ewbank, Tim and Hildred, Stafford, *Julie Christie* (Andre Deutsch Ltd, 2008)

Faine, Edward Allan, *The Best Gig in Town: Jazz Artists at the White House, 1969–1974* (IM Press, 2015)

Faithfull, Marianne, *Faithfull* (Penguin Books, 1995)

Falk, Quentin, *Travels in Greeneland: The Complete Guide to the Cinema of Graham Greene* (University of Georgia Press; 4th edition, 2014)

Fassler, Ron, *Up in the Cheap Seats* (Griffith Moon Publishing, 2017)

Francis, Clive, *There's Nothing Like a Dane!* (Nick Hern Books, 1998)

Freeman, Bud, *You Don't Look Like a Musician* (Balamp Publishing, 2012)

Fujiwara, Chris, *The World and its Double: The Life and Work of Otto Preminger* (Faber & Faber, 2009)

Garnett, Tony, *The Day the Music Died* (Constable, 2016)

Gilbert, Pat, *Shut It! – The Inside Story of The Sweeney* (Aurum Press Ltd, 2010)

Hall, William, *Sir Michael Caine* (Blake Publishing, 2000)

Hancock, Sheila, *The Two of Us* (Bloomsbury Publishing, 2005)

Hirsch, Foster, *Otto Preminger: The Man Who Would Be King* (Knopf Publishing Group, 2007)

Holm, Ian, *Acting My Life* (Corgi, 2015)

Huston, Anjelica, *A Story Lately Told: Coming of Age in London, Ireland and New York* (Simon & Schuster UK, 2014)

Huston, Anjelica, *Watch Me: A Memoir* (Simon & Schuster UK, 2015)

Jacobi, Derek, *As Luck Would Have It* (HarperCollins, 2013)

Kretzmer, Herbert, *Snapshots: Encounters with Twentieth-Century Legends* (The Robson Press, 2014)

Lerman, Leo, *The Grand Surprise: The Journals of Leo Lerman* (Knopf Publishing Group, 2007)

Lord, Graham, *Arthur Lowe* (Orion, 2003)

Manus, Willard, *This Way to Paradise: Dancing on the Tables* (Lycabettus Press, 1999)

McCabe, Rob, *The Authorised Biography of Ronnie Barker* (BBC Books, 2005)

Meyer-Dinkgrafe, Daniel, *Observing Theatre: Spirituality and Subjectivity in the Arts* (Rodopi, 2013)

Miles, Sarah, *Bolt from the Blue* (Phoenix, 1997)

Miles, Sarah, *Serves Me Right* (Macmillan, 1994)

Mirren, Helen, *In the Frame: My Life in Words and Pictures* (Atria Books, 2008)

Osborne, John, *Looking Back: Never Explain, Never Apologise* (Faber & Faber, 2004)

Parris, Barry, *Audrey Hepburn* (Orion, 1998)

Robb, Brian J. and Simpson, Paul, *Middle-earth Envisioned: The Hobbit and The Lord of the Rings: On Screen, On Stage, and Beyond* (Race Point Publishing, 2013)

Roberts, Philip, *The Royal Court Theatre and the Modern Stage* (Cambridge University Press, 1999)

Sallis, Peter, *Fading Into the Limelight* (Orion, 2007)

Sandford, Christopher, *McQueen: The Biography* (Taylor Trade Publishing, 2003)

Secrest, Mervyle, *Somewhere for Me: A Biography of Richard Rodgers* (Bloomsbury Publishing, 2002)

Sheward, David, *The Volatile Life of George C. Scott* (Applause Theatre Book Publishers, 2008)

Simon, Neil, *Rewrites* (Pocket Books, 1997)

Tibbetts, John and Welsh, James, *The Cinema of Tony Richardson: Essays and Interviews* (State University of New York Press, 1999)

Vanacker, Sabine and Wynn, Catherine, *Sherlock Holmes and Conan Doyle: Multi-Media Afterlives* (Palgrave Macmillan, 2012)

Vaughan, Peter, *Once a Villain* (Fantom Films Ltd, 2016)

Williams, Frank and Gidney, Chris, *Vicar to Dad's Army: The Frank Williams Story* (Canterbury Press, 2003)

Winner, Michael, *Tales I Never Told!* (Biteback, 2011)

INDEX